DATE

POLITICAL INSTITUTIONALIZATION
AND
THE INTEGRATION OF ELITES

Volume 21, Sage Library of Social Research

SAGE LIBRARY OF SOCIAL RESEARCH

Political Institutionalization and the Integration of Elites

ROBERT S. ROBINS

Foreword by RALPH BRAIBANTI

Volume 21
SAGE LIBRARY OF
SOCIAL RESEARCH

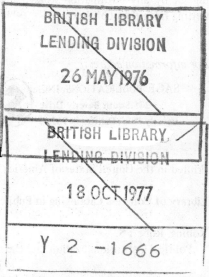

SAGE PUBLICATIONS   Beverly Hills   London

Copyright © 1976 by Sage Publications, Inc.

For information address:

SAGE PUBLICATIONS, INC.
275 South Beverly Drive
Beverly Hills, California 90212

SAGE PUBLICATIONS LTD
St George's House / 44 Hatton Garden
London EC1N 8ER

Printed in the United States of America

Library of Congress Cataloging in Publication Data

Robins, Robert S.
  Political institutionalization and the integration of elites.

  (Sage library of social research ; v. 21)
  Includes bibliographical references.
    1. Political sociology.   2. Elite (Social sciences)
3. Social institutions.   I.   Title.
JA76.R6   301.5'92   75-11134
ISBN 0-8039-0497-5
ISBN 0-803900498-3 pbk.

FIRST PRINTING

To my mother, Katherine Sidwar Robins

TABLE OF CONTENTS

FOREWORD
THE CONCEPT OF INSTITUTIONALITY

Contemporary Relevance

Rarely if ever in the past century has the systematic appraisal of institutions in both comparative and unique dimensions been more crucial than at the present. Several reasons for this may be noted.

First, the idiom of discontent of the 1960s, however muted in the 1970s, seeks renovation or abolition of institutions (the semantic equivalent in radical ideology is "establishment") to cope with rapidly changing demands. Renovation constantly occurs in nonepisodic ways, but the issue here is the rapidity and radicality of change which accentuate the need for systematic appraisal. Closely allied with this is the prognosis of tension, crisis, disintegration and the prescription of therapeutic measures to forestall such conditions.[1]

The strains placed on political institutions in our time result partially from the congruence of escalating, perhaps insatiable, mass demands with new perceptions of representational, participatory, and confrontational behavior in organizational contexts. The idiom of "immediacy-involvement" which appeared as an anomic response to the frustrations of alien rule in systems struggling for independence had earlier been diverted or sedated by a quiescent "immersion involvement" in nature. This was sustained both by sacral text and by instrumental fatalism—a thin veil of psychic protection against the cold of economic reality.[2] In Western systems long independent, there was no restraint by resignation to the embrace of nature. In our time immediacy, identification, involvement, and confrontation are accentuated by subliminal effects of communications media signaled by McLuhan's popularization of the affective reciprocity of the "medium [as] the message."[3]

The contemporary revolt against the dehumanizing consequences of computerology has sustained a rising disenchantment with "logic" and "rationality." This condition, elevating feeling and intuition as modes of understanding, is remarkably similar to the "new technique of thinking" described by Lasswell nearly half a century ago: the blending of "free-fantasy" with "logic."[4] The contemporary equivalent of the "free-fantasy" technique is the radical, New Left attention to "feeling" and "essence" with its supporting occultism and implicit Oriental aestheticism. If it continues as an influential idiom, institutions which have been admittedly created to sieve out, deny, deflect, or sublimate "free-fantasy" must be reconstructed so that "free-fantasy" and "rationality" exist in a constructive dialectic. Indeed, this reconstruction has already started. The massive participatory and representational behaviors resulting in such practices as open city council meetings, access to records, repudiation of confidentiality and loyalty as bureaucratic norms, and communal (ethnic, etc.) representation in the bureaucracy have loosened an ordered process, diminished what had appeared to be "logic" and admitted what amounts to a folk variation of Freudian "free-fantasy."

The contemporary idiom of increased sensitivity to institutional restraints on personality development is not new. The relationship between man and institutions was described by Ortega, Wittfogel, Von Hayek, Von Mises, and Burnham, among many, typically in terms of the erosion of personal freedom by complex bureaucratic institutions. Lasswell's term, "hominocentric politics," raised the issue in a context deploring the foci in political studies of power and wealth to the exclusion of "human consequences of power."[5] Psychoanalytic theory has refined our perceptions and sensitized us to inner personality needs formerly unobserved or ignored.

Second, the maturation of cross-national comparisons requires systematic appraisal of institutions of various political systems. Only when variant institutional manifestations of action are identified and associated with factors in the total social context can associational or causal inferences be drawn. Such association can then be related to transmutation of action among and within institutions and with value-diffusion. This intriguing prospect depends on terminological standardization and indices for appraising institutionality.

A third reason relates to the instrumental use of an appraisal construct in prescribing for new political systems strategies based on institutional growth. The absence of such a construct is glaringly revealed by the new demands of Title IX of the Foreign Assistance Act of 1966 as amended in 1967.[6] It is doubtful if the institution-building implications of this provision can be effectively carried out without a standard for evaluation. Decisions to support some institutions and ignore others must be based on some rationale which considers the peculiar role and present condition of each institution in the total context and the issue of symmetry or balance in the performance of all relevant institutions. Such a measurement construct can be used to evaluate all political systems. As transnational development efforts of Australia, Britain, Canada, Japan, and the United Nations Development Programme are added to and perhaps displace those of the United States, its application to new systems by many older systems operating independently will be all the more useful.

Fourth, disenchantment with American political institutions and a vanishing American imperial posture have given rise globally to vigorously renewed demands for institutions authentically indigenous or at least thought to have sprung from roots in native soil. Such disenchantment occurs at the same time that U.S. policy, manifest in the Nixon Doctrine enunciated at Guam, withdraws from the interventionist posture premised on an ethnocentric national hubris.[7] Thus, Fanon pleads for institutions inspired from Africa,[8] and Illich even more incisively calls for indigenization in Latin America.[9] Despite these pleas, imitation by caricature will continue to be the consequence of increased transnational flows of technology unless a construct for institutional appraisal emancipated from ethnocentric ties can be used.

Fifth, strident demands of the New Left for a participatory democracy which seeks to extend active citizenship to all institutions raises serious issues with respect to organization and the quantum, locus, and quality of participation which may be desirable.[10] These demands are a contemporary expression of an early romantic utopianism epitomized by Whitman who, in *Democratic Vistas*,[11] would have us believe that democracy cannot be mature unless every institution within it duplicates a democratic structure of power and shares regnant democratic values. This implication that every component of the social order must be a miniaturization of the system as a whole may appear naive, but organizational changes premised on this notion are becoming a reality in many systems. Patterns of participation must be correlated with the renovation in the context of personality development alluded to earlier. This suggests the appraisal of institutionality as a prior requisite. The theme of Hirschman's intriguing *Exit, Voice and Loyalty*[12] is the "optimal mix" of change by removal of personnel (exit), participation (voice), and the identity of person with institution (loyalty).

The Reemergence of Institutionality as a Focus of Analysis

In the past half-decade, some concern for institutional analysis has been evident. The political sociologist Eisenstadt reminded us that the major problem facing developing societies "is the necessity to develop an institutional structure which is capable of continuously 'absorbing' the various social changes which are inherent in the processes of modernization."[13] In political science, it was de Jouvenel who redirected attention first to the crucial relationship of policy to institutions, then to the responsibility of the political scientist as a designer of institutions and as a prognostic specialist in foretelling their maladjustments.[14] Stressing institutions, Huntington, whose formulation is used as the paradigm of Robins' analysis in this volume, reminded us of de Tocqueville's caveat that the "art of associating together must grow and improve in the same ratio as the equality of conditions is increased."[15] Subsequently, Pennock deftly stated the case:

> Whether political and governmental structures are formal or informal, incorporated in the legal structure or not, it is of greatest importance that they should be institutionalized; and the process of institutionalization is as surely part of development as are specialization of function and differentiation of structure. It is when certain forms and procedures become the accepted ways of doing things that they become effective instruments of stability and of legitimation.[16]

A similar view of institutionalization as a primary prerequisite for a "stable democratic future" is shared by Nordlinger.[17] An analyst commonly associated with the misnamed "behavioral school," writing in a leading journal of that persuasion, asserted that the

> institutional structure of the policy is of particular importance because it shapes the public policy-making process, determining which issues and problems are accorded what order of priority, and is itself in part the actual outcome of policy. . . . This being the case the institutional structure of a system is of paramount importance in political life.[18]

Riggs[19] and LaPalombara[20] have shown similar concern recently for institutional factors. Indeed, the study edited by LaPalombara and Weiner suggests that institutionalization should precede power-diffusion if an "overload" on institutions is to be avoided.[21] Nordlinger has advanced promising hypotheses emerging from the sequence or timing of institution-building and other characteristics of political development. His hypotheses point to the need for a rapid rate of institutionalization preceding mass suffrage and the formation of political parties.[22] An additional indicator of a "return" to the study of institutions is the organization of a round table at the Salzburg meeting of the International Political Science Association in September 1968 on political institutionalization under the aegis of Carl J. Friedrich, the association's president, whose influential work, *Constitutional Government and Democracy*[23] has long given emphasis to institutionalization as a process consequent to constitutionalism.[24] The remarkable emergence of the policy sciences[25] two decades after the concept was first advanced by Lasswell must ultimately focus attention on systematic institutional appraisal. This redirected attention will be the consequence of the conjoining of concern for value diffusion and process within the institutional matrix.[26] This concern can be satisfied only by analysis of the interrelations of process and institutional components. Finally, the seventh and final volume of *Studies in Political Development,* begun in 1963 by the Committee on Comparative Politics of the Social Science Research Council, emphasizes institutionalization as a focus for determining the sequence and the mode of handling crises in a system.[27] This return to institutions is in contrast with the earlier emphasis of the committee on input—i.e., participatory and behavioral phenomena. It signals the full turn of the wheel.

It would be wrong to view these indicators as suggestive of merely a return to institution-building as conceived in development operations. What we require is the use of institutionality as a construct for a new mode of determining the interrelationship of policy process, value-diffusion, and perennial institutional reconstruction.

Definitions

Efforts to arrive at consistency in terms and definitions relating to institutionality must be encouraged. Such consistency is essential to the use of a construct especially if such use is extended to comparison of different political systems. Efforts to achieve such consistency are neither new nor limited to political science.[28] The range of variation in use of the term "institution" extends from the simplicity of the characterization by the director of the U.S. Army Military Assistance School where "institution-building" is a central doctrine to the complexity of Parsonian and other sociological analyses. As to the former, Major General Edward M. Flanagan said, "We must develop institutions. Not the great ones like universities, but small ones like dams, roads, culverts, schoolhouses, dispensaries, and so forth."[29] The grouping of culverts and universities together in the same definition may be an act of the wisdom of innocence perhaps more meaningful than scholars would like to admit. However that may be, we allude to it here as an example of a not uncommon elasticity in use of the concept of institution.

Titus, nearly half a century ago, in an effort to define union, group, and society presented a definition, "$O_{[Titus]} = U$," a narrative rendition of which came close to later definitions of "institution."[30] It is an unsurprising curiosity in the sociology of knowledge that there was almost total discontinuity between Titus' rather prescient cryptographic efforts and later attention to institutions.[31] Elaboration of the concept of institution in political science derives not from Titus but from Friedrich and Lasswell, influenced by Parsons. In this instance, the collateral descent from sociology was economical and beneficial since the relevance, refinement, and equivalence of the Parsonian analysis were of a high order. Parsons in 1951 defined an institution as a "complex of institutionalized role integrates [status relationships]

which is of strategic structural significance in the social system in question."[32]
Attachment to common sentiments or "value-attitudes" and integration of
these values with constituent personality needs is a central aspect of this
definition as he expanded upon it. Friedrich's definition, which he compares
with Parsons' 1951 definition and which he implies is consistent with that
definition, refers to a political institution as "any stably organized syndrome
of political acts or actions having a function and/or purpose in the political
system, or to put it another way, a relatively stable collection of roles."[33]
Lasswell and Kaplan embrace in their definition Parsons' emphasis on interaction but they give additional emphasis to values. They regard institution as
"a pattern composed of culture traits specialized to the shaping and distribution of a particular value (or set of values)."[34] For them, a culture trait is an
act characteristic of a group that is recurring under comparable circumstances.
Berger and Luckmann emphasize that this habitualization precedes institutionalization which "occurs whenever there is reciprocal typification of
habitualized actions by types of actors."[35] Objectivation, historicity, and
control are additional characteristics emphasized by Berger and Luckmann.
The value-laden nature of institutions is central to our definition given below.
Other analysts, including those mentioned here, regard value as the characteristic which distinguishes institution from other organizations.[36] Values are
absorbed, accumulated, reformulated and diffused by institutions. In our
view, the explicitness of value absorption, accumulation, reformulation, and
diffusion is a fundamental difference between *institution* and *structure*. The
former is defined below; the latter is defined elsewhere.

A definition which will facilitate an appraisal of institutionality must be
broad enough to encompass both rapidly oscillating institutional roles in all
systems and the fact that virtually all institutions play some part in the use of
public power. In the definition of institution here set forth, Parsons' 1951
definition is accepted as a base. To this we add an emphasis suggested by
Lasswell and Kaplan modified to suit the needs of new systems. To those
parts of Parsons' as well as Friedrich's definitions which emphasize the relatively stable and syndromic qualities of a collection of roles, we add a quality
of permeative dynamism which has both intra- and interinstitutional influence. With respect to such influence, the "shaping and distributive" qualities
in the definition of Lasswell and Kaplan are approximated. Use of their term
"distributive" is less than satisfying since it has a connotation of passivity or
quiescence. There is need to imply in our definition an effervescent dynamic
manifest in the forced recirculation of norms and values within the institution
and the propelled rediffusion of norms from one institution to others. These
dynamic (shaping), circulating, rediffusing actions are directly related to the
phenomenon of spiralling contextuality analyzed earlier and of "institutional
permeability," discussed elsewhere. The latter, in turn, is directly related to

functional transformation. The suggestion that the effervescence of this shaping-diffusing action is important especially in new systems is based on the presupposition that ascribed and perceived roles and actions processed may be less stable in institutions of new systems. This instability may increase the incidence of transformational actions, hence accentuating the dynamism of the process. Our definition, which follows, also directs attention explicitly to the effect of institutions on the behavior of actors within them, thus reflecting both an emphasis on Parsons[37] and additional psychoanalytic insights regarding personality formation. This is implicit in Lasswell and Kaplan's concept of value distribution, but we feel it is not specific enough with respect to imposition of norms and values in personality development. Considering, then, the foregoing exposition of genesis, we propose the following definition of institutions. *Institutions are patterns of recurring acts structured in a manner conditioning the behavior of members within the institutions, shaping a particular value or set of values and projecting value(s) in the social system in terms of attitudes or acts.* Institutions which are relevant to political systems are those which share in any measure in the formation or use of public power. Institutions acquire such characteristics by dealing with events. Since events merge and react with one another, it is impossible to distinguish between political and nonpolitical events; rather, there are gradations or proportions in the political content of events.[38] Institutions necessarily partake of the same characteristics as events, hence they too must be conceived of in terms of gradations of political content of events which they act on. Thus it is likely that the range of institutions subject to analysis in the political system may be coterminous with those found in the total social system.

The Present Study

Three analytical systems for analyzing institutionality have thus far appeared in political science. The most ambitious undertaking is that of the consortium financed by the Agency for International Development.[39] The second is my own formulation identified by the acronym RABCIRR by which I seek to appraise characteristics identified as Receptivity, Autonomy, Balance, Congruence, Internality, Reformulation, and Roles. This analysis was first presented at a conference at the Villa Serbelloni in 1967 and published two years later.[40] Subsequently, the formulation was refined and linked to the problem of value diffusion in the administrative process.[41] The third and earliest formulation is that of Huntington, first published in 1965.[42] Robins uses the Huntington formulation exclusively in the present volume.

This study by Professor Robins is distinctive and important in several respects. First, it is the first major analysis of institutional appraisal applied in depth and in a comparative context. Second, it analyzes an ecclesiastical entity, certainly a legitimate and valuable, though almost universally ignored, unit for political analysis. Third, it analyzes selected institutions of a major new state—India—and this has also never been elsewhere essayed in this manner. Last, the study seeks to make tentative comparisons of a European, Christian, ecclesiastical entity with a contemporary, Asian, predominantly Hindu, non-Christian entity. In these four respects, Professor Robins' study is pioneering, important, and suggestive of further research directions which might be advantageously pursued.

Ralph Braibanti

NOTES

1. The growth of the futurist movement on a global basis is worth noting. The "Futuribles" movement in France, future societies in Korea and Japan, the World Future Society and its first general assembly in 1971, are merely a few of the evidences of systematic concern for considering alternative futures and therapeutic measures to avert crises. See issues of *The Futurist,* especially Vol. V, April 1971. Of particular relevance here is Kurt Baier and Nicholas Rescher, *Values and the Future: The Impact of Technological Change on American Values* (Glencoe, Ill., Free Press, 1969).

2. The most extreme social manifestation of fatalism is the notion of psychic inferiority induced by colonialism. See the perceptive but overdrawn analysis in Frantz Fanon, *The Wretched of the Earth* (New York, Grove, 1963). See also, Peter Geismar, *Fanon* (New York, Dial, 1971), David Caute, *Frantz Fanon* (New York, Viking Press, 1971), and Irene L. Gendzier, *Frantz Fanon* (New York, Pantheon, 1973). Cf. Satish K. Arora and Harold D. Lasswell, *Political Communication: The Public Language of Political Elites in India and the United States* (New York, Holt, Rinehart & Winston, 1969), pp. 107-117.

3. Marshall McLuhan, *Understanding Media: The Extensions of Man* (New York, McGraw-Hill, 1964).

4. Harold D. Lasswell, *Psychopathology and Politics* (Chicago, University of Chicago Press, 1930), (new edition, New York, Viking Press, 1960), p. 37.

5. Harold D. Lasswell and Abraham Kaplan, *Power and Society: A Framework for Political Inquiry* (New Haven, Yale University Press, 1950), p. xxiv.

6. *Foreign Assistance Act of 1967,* Part I, chap. 1, sec. 102. Prior to enactment of Title IX, there was a substantial inter-university research effort headed by Milton Esman at the University of Pittsburgh on "institution-building." For a review of this effort, see Ralph Braibanti, "External Inducement of Political-Administrative Development: An Institutional Strategy," in R. Braibanti et al., *Political and Administrative Development* (Durham, Duke University Press, 1969), pp. 52-53, esp. n. 128. See also Joseph W. Eaton, ed., *Institution Building and Development: From Concepts to Application* (Beverly Hills, Sage Publications, 1972). Cf. Martin Landau, "Linkage, Coding, and Intermediacy: A Strategy for Institution-Building," *Journal of Comparative Administration* 2 (1971), 401-429, which does little to clarify terminological inconsistencies.

7. For general analysis, see Henry Brandon, *The Retreat of American Power* (New York, Doubleday, 1973).

8. Fanon, *The Wretched of the Earth,* p. 315.

9. Ivan D. Illich, *Celebration of Awareness: A Call for Institutional Revolution* (New York, Doubleday, 1970).

10. Richard Flacks, "On the Uses of Participatory Democracy," *Dissent* 13 (1966), 701-709; Tom Kahn, "On Participatory Democracy," *Dissent* (1967), 247-255; Dennis H. Wrong, "Economic Development and Democracy," *Dissent* 14 (1967), 723-741.

11. Walt Whitman, *Democratic Vistas and Other Papers* (1871), (New York, Scholarly, 1949), p. 30.

12. Albert O. Hirschman, *Exit, Voice, and Loyalty* (Cambridge, Mass., Harvard University Press, 1970).

13. S. N. Eisenstadt, *Modernization, Protest and Change* (Englewood Cliffs, N.J., Prentice-Hall, 1966), p. vi.

14. Bertrand de Jouvenel, "Political Science and Prevision," *American Political Science Review* 59 (1965), 29-39, esp. 38. See also Daniel Katz and Basil S. Georgopoulos, "Organization in a Changing World," *Journal of Applied Behavioral Science* 7 (1971), 342-370, for an emphasis on reformulation of values through institutional change.

15. Samuel P. Huntington, "Political Development and Political Decay," *World Politics* 17 (1965), 386-430, quotation at 386.

16. J. Roland Pennock, "Political Development, Political Systems, and Political Goods," *World Politics* 18 (1966), 415-434, quotation at 418.

17. Eric A. Nordlinger, "Representation, Stability, and Decisional Effectiveness," in J. Roland Pennock and John W. Chapman, eds., NOMOS IX, *Representation* (New York, Lieber-Atherton, 1968), p. 115.

18. William C. Mitchell, "The Shape of Political Theory to Come: From Political Sociology to Political Economy," *American Behavioral Scientist* 11 (1967), 8-20, 37, quotation at 17.

19. Fred W. Riggs, "The Dialectics of Developmental Conflict," *Comparative Political Studies* 1 (1968), 197-226.

20. Joseph LaPalombara, "Parsimony and Empiricism in Comparative Politics: An Anti-Scholastic View," in Robert T. Holt and John Turner, eds., *The Methodology of Comparative Research* (Glencoe, Ill., Free Press, 1968), pp. 123-150.

21. Joseph LaPalombara and Myron Weiner, eds., *Political Parties and Political Development* (Princeton, N.J., Princeton University Press, 1966), pp. 428-429.

22. Eric A. Nordlinger, "Political Development: Time Sequences and Rates of Change," *World Politics* 20 (1968), 494-520. The optimality of this sequential relationship is expressed also by Giovanni Sartori in his "Political Development and Political Engineering," in John D. Montgomery and Albert O. Hirschman, eds., *Public Policy* 17 (1968), 261-299.

23. The latest revised (fourth) edition (New York, Blaisdell) appeared in 1968.

24. More detailed references can be found throughout R. Braibanti, ed., *Political and Administrative Development,* esp. pp. 52-53. See also, Fred W. Riggs, ed., *Frontiers of Development Administration* (Durham, N.C., Duke University Press, 1971).

25. For a survey of the growth of the policy sciences in universities, see the special issue in two parts of *Policy Sciences* 1 (1970), 401-483, and 2 (1971), 1-85.

26. See Harold D. Lasswell, "Foreword," in Ronald D. Brunner and Garry D. Brewer, *Organized Complexity* (New York, Free Press, 1971), x-xii, in which the interplay of "structure," "function," and social process is explicated.

27. Leonard Binder et al., *Crises and Sequences in Political Development* (Princeton, N.J., Princeton University Press, 1971), esp. pp. 300-316.

28. See, for example, efforts in sociology: Harold E. Smith, "Toward a Clarification of the Concept of Social Institution," *Sociology and Social Research* 48 (1963-64),

197-205; Paul Meadows, "The Rhetoric of Institutional Theory," *Sociological Quarterly* 8 (1967), 207-214.

29. Ward Just, "Soldiers," Part II, *The Atlantic* (November 1970), 74.

30. Charles H. Titus, "A Nomenclature in Political Science," *American Political Science Review* 25 (1931) 45-60, 615-627. Titus' definition $(0_{[Titus]} = U)$ of an entity which he did not otherwise label includes the concept of "human organisms [who] feel the pressure of similarity and express through their activities the spirit of unity," idem. This approximates our definition of institution.

31. Titus was only fleetingly mentioned by Merriam in 1939 and thereafter vanishes from political science literature. See above, n. 30.

32. Talcott Parsons, *The Social System* (New York, Free Press, 1951), p. 39. Cf. his somewhat different definitions in his *Structure and Process in Modern Societies* (Glencoe, Ill., Free Press, 1960), p. 177. See also his "The Principal Structures of Community: A Sociological View," in Carl J. Friedrich, ed., *NOMOS* II, *Community* (New York, Lieber-Atherton, 1959), pp. 152-159.

33. Carl J. Friedrich, *Man and His Government* (New York, McGraw-Hill, 1963), p. 71.

34. Lasswell and Kaplan, *Power and Society,* p. 47.

35. Peter L. Berger and Thomas Luckmann, *The Social Construction of Reality* (New York, Doubleday, 1967), p. 54.

36. See, for example, Philip Selznick, *Leadership in Administration: A Sociological Interpretation* (Evanston, Ill., Northwestern University Press, 1957), p. 40.

37. Parsons, *The Social System,* cited above in n. 32, esp. pp. 58-87.

38. This is derived from and follows the Lasswell and Kaplan "principle of temporality" operating on power as a processual flow of events. See their *Power and Society,* p. xvi.

39. See above note 6 for references.

40. Idem.

41. Ralph Braibanti "A Theory of Political Reconstruction," in Harold Lasswell, Daniel Lerner, and John D. Montgomery, eds., *Values and Development: The Asian Experience* (Cambridge, Mass., Harvard University Press, 1974).

42. See above, n. 15 for reference.

PREFACE

In the following six chapters, I attempt to relate, in a systematic fashion, a theory of elites to one of political institutionalization. Both theories are what are generally called middle range. The context in which they are described is a broad one in terms of time and geography.

This book is written under the assumption that there are affecting political behavior general principles that operate consistently over time and in various places. Obviously, these principles are modified in their effect by their context, but the context only affects the precise form that the relation takes, it does not change the essential relationship. I have consequently chosen my cases and illustrations from a wide variety of countries and periods, the better to note the uniformities.

Second, I have assumed that there are several methodological paths to truth. Some of the analyses are based on highly analytic arguments, as developed, for example, by Braibanti and Riggs; others are more straightforward historical analyses, such as in the writings of Southern; others are more quantitive, such as those by Frey. Generalizations are more secure where they are supported by a variety of approaches than if they rely on only one.

Finally, and following necessarily on the two previous points, this work draws on a large number of scholarly works, as well as upon my own research. In the 1950s and 1960s, a very large number of particularistic studies were published. I attempt here to interrelate some of them and identify their uniformities as they apply to the aspects of the elite and developmental theory with which I am concerned.

These assumptions have led to a work that intensively deals with a middle-range theory in a broad methodological, historical, and geographical context. I hope it will be at least a small contribution to what has already been written.

St. Antony's College
Oxford
1973

ACKNOWLEDGEMENTS

Because this is a monograph on institutions and elites, it is appropriate that my acknowledgements also fall into these two categories. Concerning the institutions that have aided me, first mention should be given to Duke University and the Fulbright Foundation, which assisted me in carrying out field research in India. The Ford Foundation and the National Science Foundation both contributed substantially to my support at various times, and the American Philosophical Society assisted with essential travel. St. Antony's College, Oxford University, and the Institute of Commonwealth Studies, University of London, both extended their facilities and gave me an official status, which greatly aided this work.

My principal thanks for institutional support must, however, go to Tulane University, which has helped me not only with financial support but in a great many other ways as well.

Individual assistance is more difficult to acknowledge, because so many have helped in various ways. Ralph Braibanti of Duke University, John Courtney of the University of Saskatchewan, Samuel Huntington of Harvard University, Richard Southern of St. John's College, Oxford, and Donald Eugene Smith of the University of Pennsylvania all discussed with me either the concept of the study or the manuscript itself and made worthwhile comments. My wife, Marjorie McGann Robins, read, commented upon, and helped edit much of the manuscript before its submission. Whatever clarity comes out of what had to be a difficult and sometimes awkward presentation should be credited to her.

Of course, these institutions and individuals are not responsible for any shortcomings in this work or for any of the opinions I express.

Chapter 1

ELITE INTEGRATION AND

HUNTINGTON'S CRITERIA

OF INSTITUTIONALIZATION

The purpose of this monograph is to take two theories concerning the political system, Samuel Huntington's on political institutionalization[1] and my own on elite integration,[2] relate them and, when they are applied in a variety of specific contexts,[3] see whether their application is enlightening. The process of application and their combination will also, I trust, refine and test them.

Huntington's theory, which will be specifically summarized as the book proceeds, is principally concerned with evaluating the capacity of the formal institutions of government and certain closely associated organizations (such as political parties) to mediate social demands and to carry through policies. Its orientation is toward the capacity of government to govern. Institutional elite integration is concerned with the degree and form of elite[4] recruitment from one unit of government to another and its effect on the political system. This theory of elites centers on the role of those occupying positions of power in social mediation and policy implementation. There is no requirement that each political actor goes through *all* the possible positions in the career ladder, only that there is movement among them.

Let us orient ourselves by taking an overview of Huntington's model of institutionalization and seeing how it relates, in general terms, to elite integration. Huntington suggests four criteria of institutionalization: complexity, autonomy, coherence, and adaptation.[5] Concerning the criterion of complexity, Huntington argues that "the more complicated an organization is, the more highly institutionalized it is."[6] An organization having a variety of subunits is better able to meet a variety of demands, internal and external, than is a monolithic organization. It has enhanced capacity for flexibility and resilience. This is evident from the comparative history of simple and complex institutions when they are challenged. Simple organizations such as monarchies in India or Europe were less resilient than those having more complex bureaucratic systems such as the Roman Catholic Church[7] or those bureaucracies existing throughout Imperial Chinese history.[8]

In more general terms, of course, institutional elite integration requires a certain amount of complexity for it to exist at all. I am speaking here about the actual movement of elites from one position to another: for example, whether and to what degree central cabinet members are recruited from state cabinets, or from political party central committees, or perhaps from military bureaucracies, or whether they are even recruited from outside the institutional political structure. Clearly, if there are only a very few institutions among which the elite can travel, there will be little or no movement, and the whole question of elite integration becomes moot. There can be no elite integration in a village in which nearly all the power is concentrated in a hereditary headman. On the other hand, a village where there is a bureaucracy of sorts, a council, and an elective headman permits at least the possibility of an institutionally integrated elite.

Elite integration among political institutions clearly serves to differentiate the political system from the larger social system. Within a larger polity, such as a state, elite integration may also serve to make that political system complex by establishing differentiated units within it.[9] Karl Deutsch has defined boundaries among political regions by information flow analysis.[10] The same approach could, in theory, be taken within a polity, but it would present quite substantial practical problems. It may be adequate and certainly more economical to observe the pattern of elite integration in a society. Just as Deutsch noted and measured how information overspilled a boundary, so it is possible to measure to what extent leaders move from one institution to another. Where recruitment boundaries are defined, as, for example, between the federal bureaucracy and the elective officers whom it serves, the society has greater differentiation than if officials commonly moved from "career" bureaucratic offices to elective ones. Of course, there is the inevitable contradiction here that elite integration, by its very nature, serves to differentiate and perhaps divide as much as it integrates. There is consequently a constant tension between integration and diffusion wherever there is a high level of elite integration.[11]

Elite integration is not, however, a simple function of complexity but is a separable variable. The Indian Civil Service[12] under the British Empire illustrates a complex organization with a high degree of institutional elite integration. Officers entered the service at the bottom of the officer class and over a lifetime worked their way to higher positions. Lateral entry was rare. This system of internal elite recruitment was in marked contrast with the Mughal system of elite recruitment which preceded it. Although the British largely patterned the organization (and hence much of the formal organizational complexity) of their system on the Mughal, they injected a different form of elite integration. Of course, several radical innovations were added to the Mughal pattern, such as competitive entrance examinations and compensation by fixed salary, but for our purposes the notable point is that the Mughal system, though formally complex, by and large lacked elite integration. Lateral entry was common, and there was little idea of starting out and working one's way up within a bureaucratic system.

Huntington, in discussing the autonomy of the political system (the second criterion of institutionalization) from the larger society, argues that this partial separateness from the pressure of social forces is essential for the political system to mediate these forces.[13] Organizations that are easily penetrated and coerced are incapable of mediating those forces which push in upon them. In this regard, Huntington comments:

> In every society affected by social change, new groups arise to participate in politics. Where the political system lacks autonomy, these groups gain entry into politics without becoming identified with the established political organizations or acquiescing in the established political procedures. . . . In a highly institutionalized political system, the most important positions of leadership can normally only be achieved by those who have served an apprenticeship in less important positions.[14]

This process of apprenticeship and integration is what we are concerned with here. Internal recruitment is of the very essence of autonomy. A group that chooses its own members and its own leaders is in the best possible position to resist interference from the larger society. Indeed, no factors are more relevant than internal recruitment and cross-elite self-selection in determining the degree of autonomy an institution has. Elite integration consists of more than vertical integration (recruitment from within), but this process is at the very heart of a well-integrated and developed political elite system.

Parenthetically, the same characteristic is well noted in the larger society as well. Professional organizations, political or otherwise, seek first and foremost to control the numbers and quality of membership as well as the distribution later of professional honors.[15] Physicians in the United States are the most notable example of this, but it is also found in other groups such as bricklayers and dockworkers. In politics, presently and historically, successful (which is to say autonomous) organizations have been extremely jealous of this prerogative, and have fought for self-selection when they have felt it necessary to give up all else.

The way of assuring this self-selection has varied over time. The earliest and simplest form in monarchical and feudal societies was through heredity. The ruling group was largely self-selecting merely on the basis of birth. Although such a system had considerable elite integration in social terms, it lacked full elite integration in institutional terms. A person did not pass through a variety of lesser positions before becoming a duke; he was born a duke. On the other hand, there was the possibility (though seldom realized in practice) of a member of the elite going from one position to another at the same level but in a different organization. Thus Thomas á Becket went directly from a high secular feudal post to a high ecclesiastical one. This, like a feudal lord changing his geographical area of domain, was always rather rare and much more characteristic of feudalism in its less-developed earlier stages.

Elite integration arises most notably with the development of bureaucracy. The Medieval Catholic Church, with both a high degree of institutional elite integration and autonomy, is perhaps the outstanding example. In this bureaucracy as in any other, the criterion for advancement was essentially achievemental—the display of the social and technical skills that the organization values. The extension of bureaucratic systems in the West, first from the quasi-political church organization to government and later to political parties, was at all points accompanied by those institutions enjoying a high level of elite integration. Most notable is the case of political parties. Those political parties that were not only hierarchical (as was also the feudal system) but vertically and hierarchically integrated have been the most successful.[16] The analogous resiliency of communist parties—the best articulated, complex, and autonomous of all contemporary political parties—in states where the larger and more diffuse nationalist parties have gone under is well documented.[17]

As will be discussed in more detail later, elite integration in institutional terms where unmodified by some form of integration with the social forces it seeks to mediate, results in that institution or political system becoming isolated from the society, stagnating, and eventually falling into decay. The problem is not one of too much autonomy, however, but autonomy unaided by other types of integration.

The autonomous character of elite integration in institutional terms not only concerns a political system's relation to the nonpolitical aspects of a society, but is also relevant for the internal effectiveness of the system. The political system enjoying elite integration is not simply an autonomous and complex unit—effective though that would be—but consists of a variety of "cells," each one coherent and semi-autonomous itself.

This is best illustrated by comparing an autonomous and coherent system with little internal differentiation by way of elite integration, with its opposite. Well-established military dictatorships such as Ayub's in Pakistan come to mind.[18] This system ranked if not high at least not very low in autonomy from the larger polity. It was also characterized by complexity, though not by adaptability. Despite its autonomy vis-à-vis the larger polity, it lacked internal units of autonomy. Its later history demonstrated that defects that became evident at one point could not be confined, but rather spread quickly. Had this organization had autonomous subunits, it would have been more effective and resilient. Again to return to two notably successful and resilient organizations—the Roman Catholic Church and the Communist Party—these organizations are made up of a variety of semi-autonomous subunits. The ability of many of these units to survive even after the organization as a whole suffered severe reverses permitted such resiliency.[19] Likewise, their multiplicity of subunits, each largely looking to itself for recruitment and leadership, accounts for the institutions' remarkable flexibility and problem-solving capacity despite their overall autocratic orientation.

The internal semi-autonomous character of these organizations also results in their avoidance of one of the greatest ills of large-scale organizations—apathy and alienation. The morale of the organization is stimulated by the unity that shared backgrounds and shared futures are associated with.

This aspect of autonomy brings us to the third of the developmental characteristics, that of coherence. "Coherence" refers to the consensus within an organization as to its procedures for resolving disputes and the definition of the boundaries of its functions. It is very similar in its effect to what is called community, esprit, morale.[20] Huntington notes that though autonomy and coherence are separable theoretically, they seldom are in practice. Autonomy is to a large measure a function of internal elite integration. This relationship of autonomy to elite integration is quite evident when an organization is suddenly faced with large numbers of new members or when new leadership is forced upon it. In such circumstances, coherence, community, esprit, and morale disappear very rapidly, whether the polity is a defeated nation like Germany after World War II or a department in a university forced to change its leadership and student clientele.

Another point concerning the coherence of a political system should be made here. Coherence is very much a psychological attribute involving the feeling among its members that an institution's goals are worthwhile and that success is being achieved in reaching them. A group that is tied by common career patterns will have a higher level of psychological unity than one that is not. This is evident in the case of military morale, where camaraderie rests on common postings and experiences, as well as being found in political organizations such as political parties and labor unions, where even if the leaders did not fight in the same battles, they fought in the same sort.[21]

There are some apparent exceptions, though marginal and minor ones. Temporary charitable organizations often have a high level of coherence and low internal elite integration. The same is often the case in spontaneous political action groups. These groups, however, are of short duration and are supported not only by whatever stimulated their formation in the first place,[22] but also by noninstitutional integrative factors such as shared social background.[23]

As Huntington points out, adaptability is one of the outstanding characteristics of politically effective organizations. The world changes, and nothing lasts that cannot change with it. The characteristics just described of coherence, autonomy, and complexity are important for such adaptation. More specifically, Huntington offers three other variables that indicate an institution's capacity for adaptation—all based on the institution's previous record for adaptation. These are the chronological age of the institution (how long it has existed), its generational age (how many sets of leaders of different generations it has had), and its functional age (how many times it has changed its principal goals). Organizations that score high on these criteria are considered to have high adaptability.[24]

Elite integration presupposes a fairly high chronological and generational age of the institution in question. In all but the very least stable societies, the process of becoming an elite at one level or in one institution inevitably takes time. There is always a certain amount of learning to be done, opportunities to be waited for, etc., and also of course a certain amount of resistance of older elites at the highest level. Although an organization's strong traditions and procedures for selecting its members from certain other elite organizations, as described above, may have no direct effect on its eventual chronological or generational age, the characteristic of coherence, autonomy, and complexity, will have an indirect effect by making that organization better able to carry out its functions. In other words, effective organizations tend to become older, generationally and chronologically, than others, and institutions of high institutional elite integration tend to be more effective than otherwise.[25]

Concerning functional age, elite integration may be a positive variable. An organization that has and continues to draw its own leadership elements from a variety of institutional elites external to itself may have greater capacities to take new directions than one whose leadership has a narrower background of experience and clientele. The future always has been, in the final analysis, imponderable. For an organization to meet these challenges, there is no substitute for a leadership cadre that at least in part has ties and experience with these new forces.[26] On the other hand, other aspects of integration can have negative consequences which will be discussed in Chapter 3.

Examples of successful elite integration are not difficult to find. The remarkable adaptability of the British House of Commons and that of the U.S. political system as a whole is in large measure due to those systems, at their policy-making level, being open to new elites.[27] Entry of industrialists, non-Anglo-Saxons, nonwhites, the unpropertied, labor leaders, etc., has characterized the historical development of these institutions. At times the system has not moved fast enough and has suffered for it as in the initial effective exclusion of organized labor in the United Kingdom in the latter part of the nineteenth century. By and large, though, the record has been a good one, due in large measure to the complementary electoral mechanisms of the ballot and the political party, which have greatly facilitated the entire process of elite integration. Nor is the other side of the picture difficult to find. The Chinese Empire decayed and fell due in large part to its exclusion of the "un-Chinese" and often gross mercantile and Western-educated elements that might have permitted the old order to make some type of transition to the modern world.[28]

Within a polity, the same situation can be noted, whether in the business enterprise that only hires a certain type of engineer or salesman, or in a political party such as the Federalists that persist in only appealing to regions and classes which become progressively less significant. Of course, an institution can draw on only one type of group and ignore all others if its role and immediate environment is a stable one. This organization may, with luck, last a long time, as did the British Empire in its relience on a small British social class for its higher colonial bureaucracy.[29] The same narrow base of recruitment worked reasonably well in the Roman Catholic Church's recruitment to its priesthood in Latin America in much of the nineteenth and early twentieth centuries,[30] drawing on European and conservatively oriented priests until the political tone of Latin America progressively changed in this century. In this case, other very considerable resources of the Church have been sufficient to avoid extensive damage.

So much for introductory comments on elite integration and Huntington's criteria for institutionalization. Let us turn now to a comparison of elite integration in its various forms with each of the criteria in particular political contexts. First, we will look at elite integration within and between bureaucracies.

NOTES

1. The two leading works in this regard are Samuel Huntington, "Political Development and Political Decay," *World Politics,* 17 (April, 1965) pp. 386-430, and *Political Order in Changing Societies* (New Haven: Yale University Press, 1968). Citations on this work will be from the fourth printing, 1970 edition.

2. Robert S. Robins, "Political Elite Formation in Rural India: The Uttar Pradesh Panchayat Elections of 1949, 1956, and 1961," *Journal of Politics,* 29 (November, 1967) pp. 838-860, "Elite Career Patterns as a Differential in Regional Analysis: A Use of Correlation Techniques and the Construction of Uniform Strata," *Behavioral Science,* 14 (May, 1969), pp. 232-238, "Institutional Linkages with an Elite Body," *Comparative Politics,* (October, 1971) pp. 109-115.

3. There are a variety of studies dealing with the contextual aspects of institutional behavior. The publications of the Duke University Commonwealth-Studies Center, especially those by and under the editorship of Ralph Braibanti, are especially useful. Among the leading works, see Ralph Braibanti and Joseph J. Spengler (eds.), *Tradition, Values and Socio-Economic Development* (Durham, N.C.: Duke University Press, 1961); the "Introduction" by Ralph Braibanti to Braibanti (ed.), *Asian Bureaucratic Systems Emergent from the British Imperial Tradition* (Durham, N.C.: Duke University Press, 1966); and Braibanti "External Inducement of Political-Administrative Development: An Institutional Strategy" in Braibanti (ed.), *Political and Administrative Development* (Durham, N.C.: Duke University Press, 1969). Other leading scholars in this revival of institutionally oriented studies are Milton J. Esman and Fred C. Bruhns, especially their *Institution-Building in National Development* (Pittsburgh: University of Pittsburgh Press, 1965); Fred W. Riggs, "Structure and Function: A Dialectical Approach," a paper prepared for delivery at the Annual Meeting of the American Political Science Association, September, 1967; Talcott Parsons' *Essays in Sociological Theory* (rev. ed. Glencoe, Ill., Free Press, 1954) is a very useful basis for analysis; Joseph LaPalombara, "Parsimony and Empiricism in Comparative Politics" in Robert Holt and John Turner (eds.), *The Methodology of Comparative Research* (Glencoe, Ill.: the Free Press, 1969). Taking a somewhat different but complementary approach, see the works of S. N. Eisenstadt, *Modernization: Protest and Change* (Englewood Cliffs, N.J.: Prentice-Hall, 1966). A study that makes a conceptual analogy between economic and political development in terms of the productivity of their respective "goods" is K. de Schweinitz, "Growth, Development, and Political Modernization," *World Politics,* 22 (July, 1970), pp. 518-540.

4. The three most useful works offering an overview of elite studies are Lewis J. Edinger and Donald D. Searing, "Leadership: An Interdisciplinary Bibliography" in Lewis J. Edinger (ed.), *Political Leadership in Industrialized Societies: Studies in Comparative Analysis* (New York: John Wiley, 1967), pp. 348-366, which is a carefully selected and well annotated bibliography of approximately 200 leading works; a more comprehensive, and consequently less selective, bibliography is Carl Beck and J. Thomas McKechnie, *Political Elites: A Select Computerized Bibliography* (Cambridge, Mass.: MIT Press, 1968); and for a very perceptive commentary on the general trends in elite studies, see Dankwart A. Rustow, "The Study of Elites: Who's Who, when, and How," *World Politics,* 18 (July, 1966), pp. 690-717. The following works are especially relevant to our study. Harold Lasswell et al., *Comparative Study of Elites* (Stanford: Stanford University Press, 1952) is one of the most seminal works. There have been a large number of elite studies of national, state, and community elites in America. Robert Dahl's *Who Governs?* (New Haven: Yale University Press, 1961) has been perhaps the most

influential, along with works by Robert Presthus and Floyd Hunter, among others, in community studies. Robert E. Agger, et al., *The Rulers and the Ruled: Political Power and Impotence in American Communities* (New York: John Wiley, 1964) contains several essays. Curiously, there have been relatively few studies of the national political elite. Donald R. Matthews, *U.S. Senators and Their World* (Chapel Hill: University of North Carolina Press, 1960) is a classic study of an elite institution. A useful book, despite the fact that it accomplishes less than it sets out to do is Leonard Ruchelman, *Political Careers: Recruitment Through the Legislature* (Cranbury, N.J.: Fairleigh Dickenson Press, 1970); Floyd Hunter, *Top Leadership, U.S.A.* (Chapel Hill, N.C.: University of North Carolina Press, 1959) is another excellent major work dealing with a national elite. The quality of many of the non-Western studies has varied perhaps even more than those dealing with the United States and other Western nations. Frederick Frey's *The Turkish Political Elite* (Cambridge, Mass.: MIT Press, 1965) is an excellent study, both methodologically and substantively, of a single, institutionally defined, national elite. Among other superior studies are Lester G. Seligman, *Leadership in a New Nation: Political Development in Israel* (New York: Atherton, 1964) and Michael Brecher, *Political Leadership in India* (New York: Praeger, 1969). A very good recent survey, which gives special attention to the Kornhauser, Sartori, Schumpeter revisionist approaches is that of Geraint Parry of the University of Manchester: *Political Elites* (New York: Praeger, 1969). For a careful in-depth historical analysis, see Gerald Caplan, *The Elites of Barotseland 1878-1969* (Berkeley: University of California Press, 1970). Among the best discussions of the Indian bureaucratic elite cadre are Ralph Braibanti, "Reflections on Bureaucratic Reform in India" in Braibanti and J. J. Spengler (eds.), *Administration and Economic Development in India* (Durham, N.C.: Duke University Press, 1963), pp. 3-68; and David C. Potter, "Bureaucratic Change in India" in Braibanti (ed.), *Asian Bureaucratic Systems Emergent from the British Imperial Tradition,* pp. 141-208.

Concerning the Marxian class and the Pareto group emphases in elite theory, see Vilfredo Pareto, *The Mind and Society.* 4 vols., Arthur Livingstone (ed.), trans. A. Livingstone and Andrew Bongiorne (New York: Harcourt Brace, 1935); and for the best review and evaluation of Marxist elite theory see T. B. Bottomore, *Elites and Society* (New York: Basic Books, 1964). For a general overview of the role of ideology, with special reference to Italy and Great Britain, see Robert Putnam, "Studying Elite Political Culture: The Case of 'Ideology' " *American Political Science Review,* 65 (September, 1971), pp. 651-681.

5. These criteria are discussed in general in the first chapter of Huntington, *Political Order in Changing Societies,* pp. 1-92, especially pp. 12-24. For a critique, see Mark Kesselman, "Order or Movement?: The Literature of Political Development as Ideology" *World Politics,* 26 (October, 1973) pp. 139-154.

6. Ibid., p. 17.

7. The most comprehensive treatment of religion and political development, including institutional development, is that of Donald Eugene Smith, *Religion and Political Development* (Boston: Little, Brown, 1970). This topic will be discussed at greater length in Chapter 4. Also see S. N. Eisenstadt, "Religious Organizations and Political Process in Centralized Empires," *Journal of Asian Studies,* 21 (May, 1962); J. Milton Singer, *The Scientific Study of Religion* (New York: Macmillan, 1970).

8. Ping-Ti Ho, *The Ladder of Success in Imperial China: Aspects of Social Mobility, 1368-1911* (New York: Columbia University Press, 1962).

9. The complexity of subunits, where this complexity is accompanied by multi-functionality, may result in a more institutionalized but less flexible political system, as

is argued in Sigmund Neumann, "Toward a Comparative Study of Political Parties" in Neuman (ed.), *Modern Political Parties* (Chicago: University of Chicago Press, 1956), pp. 403-405.

10. *The Nerves of Government* (New York: Free Press, rev. ed., 1966). His work owes a substantial debt to that of Talcott Parsons, *The Social System* (Glencoe, Ill.: Free Press, 1951).

11. Institutional political elite integration, the topic of this monograph, is of course only one form of elite integration—there are also varieties of *social* integration among elites. For a description of a fragmented Western political culture see Joseph LaPalombara, *Interest Groups in Italian Politics* (Princeton: Princeton University Press, 1964), especially pp. 55-63.

12. For a study dealing with the formative stages, see Barnard S. Cohn, "Recruitment and Training of British Civil Servants in India, 1600-1860" in Braibanti (ed.), *Asian Bureaucratic Systems,* pp. 87-140; for a more contemporary study see in the same volume, David C. Potter, "Bureaucratic Change in India," pp. 141-208.

13. Although the focus here is on political institutionalization, and hence on autonomy, within a state, it should be noted that less institutionalized polities are particularly sensitive to events outside their borders. For a study of the demonstration effect of violence among less institutionalized political systems, see Samuel P. Huntington, "Patterns of Violence in World Politics" in Huntington (ed.), *Changing Patterns of Military Politics* (New York: Free Press, 1962), pp. 44-47.

14. Huntington, *Political Order in Changing Societies,* pp. 21, 22.

15. See Wilbert E. Moore, *The Professions: Roles and Rules* (New York: Russell Sage Foundation, 1970), especially "The Professional and His Peers: Identification and Self-Regulation," pp. 109-130. A summary of the "state of the art" in organizational sociology is found in O. Grunsky and George Miller (eds.), *The Sociology of Organization* (New York: Free Press, 1970).

16. For the historical development of political parties, see R. M. MacIver, *The Modern State* (London: Oxford University Press, 1964); for a contemporary-oriented but historically based study, see Leon D. Epstein, *Political Parties in Western Democracies* (London: Pall Mall Press, 1967); for an early, and critical, evaluation see M. Y. Ostrogorski, *Democracy and the Organization of Political Parties* (London: Macmillan, 1902).

17. The literature here is quite extensive. The most useful for the present purposes is the section on "Leninism and Political Development" in Huntington, *Political Order in Changing Societies,* pp. 334-343. Also see Franz Schurmann, "Organizational Principles of the Chinese Communists," *China Quarterly,* 2 (April-June, 1960); Douglas Pike, *Viet Cong* (Cambridge, Mass.: MIT Press, 1966). Pike's study makes a particularly notable contribution.

18. For a general study, see Wayne Wilcox, *Pakistan: The Consolidation of a Nation.* (New York: Columbia University Press, 1960); for a study of the origins of the Ayub regime, see Guy Wint, *The 1958 Revolution in Pakistan,* St. Antony's Papers, No. 8 (London: Chatto and Windus, 1960). For a study of the instutitionalization of the Ayub regime, see Richard Wheeler, *The Politics of Pakistan* (Ithaca: Cornell University Press, 1970), especially pp. 232-283.

19. For Communist organization, see Pike, *Viet Cong;* for the Church, see Smith, *Religion and Political Development,* p. 52.

20. Of the briefer works with a specific focus, Herbert McCloskey, "Consensus and Ideology in American Politics," *American Political Science Review,* 18 (June, 1964) is among the best. For another approach to the problem of societal consensus, see Susanne Hoeber Rudolph, "Conflict and Consensus in Indian Politics," *World Politics,* 13 (April, 1961).

21. Despite the growth of personality theory, relatively little has been done in regard to the personality aspects of elites. Jean Meynaud, "Introduction: General Study of Parliamentarians," *Internal Social Science Journal*, 12 (1961), pp. 513-543, is a very good overview of the literature, with interpretive comments. His section on "Influence of Personality" is quite helpful. Also see the works of Erik Erikson, especially his *Young Man Luther* (New York: Norton, 1958); "Hitler's Imagery and German Youth," *Psychiatry*, 5 (1942), pp. 475-493; *Gandhi's Truth* (New York: Norton, 1969); Robert E. Lane, *Political Life. Why People Get Involved in Politics* (Glencoe, Ill.: Free Press, 1959); John B. McConaughy, "Certain Personality Factors of State Legislators in South Carolina," *American Political Science Review*, 44 (December, 1960), pp. 897-903; Lewis Bowman and G. R. Boynton, "Recruitment Patterns Among Local Party Officials: A Model and Some Preliminary Findings in Selected Locales," *American Political Science Review*, 60 (September, 1966), pp. 667-676. P. M. Sniderman and J. Citrin, "Psychological Sources of Political Belief," *American Political Science Review*, 65 (June, 1971), pp. 401-417.

22. A series of essays dealing with the initiation of spontaneous movements, in a variety of ways is found in S. M. Lipset (ed.), *Students and Politics* (New York: Basic Books, 1967).

23. Social integration is, of course, a broad and important topic, which is beyond our scope here. The most useful works for complementing the present study of institutional elite integration are Kenneth Prewitt and Heinz Eulau, "Social Bias in Leadership Selection, Political Recruitment, and Electoral Context," *Journal of Politics*, 3 (May, 1971), pp. 293-315. Studies that deal with the process of leadership and recruitment in a somewhat broader context are Dwaine Marvick, "Political Recruitment and Careers," *International Encyclopedia of the Social Sciences*, 12 (New York: Macmillan and Free Press, 1968), pp. 273-282; Joseph Schlesinger, *Ambition and Politics: Political Careers in the United States* (Chicago: Rand McNally, 1966); Kenneth Prewitt, *The Recruitment of Political Leaders: A Study of Citizen-Politicians* (Indianapolis: Bobbs-Merrill, 1970).

24. Huntington, *Political Order in Changing Societies*, p. 13 ff.

25. William H. Starbuck, "Organization Growth and Development," in James G. March (ed.), *Handbook of Organizations* (Chicago: Rand McNally, 1965), p. 453: "The basic nature of adaptation is such that the longer an organization survives, the better prepared it is to continue surviving," as quoted in Huntington, *Political Order in Changing Societies*, p. 13.

26. For an application of this principle on the national level, see Lee Benson, *The Concept of Jacksonian Democracy: New York as a Test Case* (Princeton: Princeton University Press, 1961).

27. A brilliant analysis of the course of political development in the United States and in Europe, especially the United Kingdom, is found in Huntington, *Political Order in Changing Societies*, "Political Modernization: America vs. Europe," pp. 93-139.

28. Ping-Ti Ho, *The Ladder of Success in Imperial China*.

29. Cohn, "Recruitment and Training of British Civil Servants in India, 1600-1860" Potter, "Bureaucratic Change in India."

30. Lloyd J. Mechan, *Church and State in Latin America: A History of Politico-Ecclesiastical Relations*. (rev. ed. Chapel Hill, N.C.: University of North Carolina Press, 1966). A book that discusses the attitudes toward social change held by contemporary Catholic leaders in Latin America is Frederick C. Turner, *Catholicism and Political Development in Latin America*. (Chapel Hill, N.C.: University of North Carolina Press, 1971).

Chapter 2

BUREAUCRATIC INSTITUTIONALIZATION
AND ELITE INTEGRATION

The relation between Huntington's four criteria of institutionalization and elite[1] integration has been described and illustrated in general terms and the conditions under which these relations may occur—where elite integration is possible—have been indicated. Let us turn now to a more detailed analysis of how these criteria apply to elite integration in the case of bureaucracies.[2]

Assuming that there is a significant degree of elite integration in a society, the next question concerns its form. There are two general forms of elite integration, vertical and horizontal. Let us turn to the horizontal first.

Elite Integration at Equivalent Levels in Public
Bureaucracies: Horizontal Elite Integration

Horizontal integration refers here to the process by which elites in one bureaucratic organization move to positions of equal or similar authority in another. An example would be a Brigadier General leaving the army to take an active role on a board of directors of a large government corporation such as the TVA. Here the individual would be transferring at approximately the same level from a military elite (an elite of force) to an elite of economic power.[3] Horizontal elite integration to the same type but organizationally distinct institutions is also possible. An example would be a city manager from Durham, North Carolina, becoming the city manager of Reading, Pennsylvania. Here the individual would remain the same type of elite but would transfer to a different geographic area.[4]

There is a distinction to be made clear here between simple transferability of skills within an organization and horizontal elite integration. Elite integration always assumes the existence of at least two organizationally distinct elites. Movement must be from one to another. Policemen being transferred from one beat to another within a city, or judges changing venue would not be considered as cases of elite integration. For elite integration to occur, a shift to a different area of source of proximate legitimacy and authority and a different decision-making structure is necessary.[5] One might argue that all personnel movement is a case of transferability of skills, vertically as well as horizontally. This is so, but institutional elite integration also involves movement to a different institutionalized group.[6]

Movement from one organization to another is much less common. Such intragovernmental, horizontal bureaucratic elite integration may be best illustrated in the foreign affairs-military area.[7] Here the military bureaucracies are usually the sending units, entering the intelligence and diplomatic service at middle and higher ranges, as for example in the case of Admiral Raburn becoming the Director of the Central Intelligence Agency and General Marshall becoming Secretary of State.

This type of horizontal integration occurs especially at the higher levels because there are strong technical and social ties at these levels—i.e., noninstitutional forms of integration are strong.[8] Such ties take a long time in the making, and that is probably why it has been in the mature and complex societies that such horizontal forms of integration are most common. This is not necessarily to say developed countries, only mature and complex ones. Such integration is not only characteristic of contemporary American society,[9] but also characterized that of Europe in the late Middle Ages[10] and China in various periods.[11] It does not characterize societies where the institutions are new or in rapid change. It did not characterize nineteenth-century America,[12] and it does not characterize present day India.[13]

The situation is not different outside the bureaucratic elements of the political system. Curiously, there is no word to differentiate the nonbureaucratic part of the political system from the bureaucratic. Here, by "nonbureaucratic," I am referring to what is generally referred to as politics— the more or less entrepreneurial open market search for power, through elections, support of candidates, or even the use of force. This type of activity is usually designated as "political," and I will use this term, though recognizing that bureaucratic politics are not any the less political in its broader sense.[14]

Noting this distinction, the principal bureaucratic elites in a society may be categorized as the civil service, the military, the quasi-governmental economic bureaucratic elite, and, where highly disciplined and bureaucratized, the political party organizations.[15] Economic and political party bureaucracies are relevant to our discussion of societies, such as the Soviet Union, where they form an intimate and highly institutionalized part of the governmental apparatus.[16] In certain societies, such as Meiji Japan, the political parties, such as they were, cannot be considered in this way, though the economic bureaucracies may.[17] On the other hand, in states such as Nasser's Egypt, the political party may be considered part of the government bureaucracy, but by and large economic organizations may not.[18] Of course, there is some overlap and not all types of elites are fully represented in every society. Moreover, it is a rare polity within which some type of elite movement of all kinds does not occur. It is the dominant characteristic, however, which is being described here.

It should be stressed that it is not merely an alliance between the institutions which is being referred to, but actual elite movement. There are, for example, a great deal of cooperation and many ties between high-level German industrialists and high-level German civil servants, but because industrialists do not actually become high-level civil servants, there is no elite integration in institutional terms.[19]

Having made the categorization between institutionally integrated and non-institutionally integrated elites, what is its utility? Unless these new categories do more than describe, they are simply a theoretical nuisance. In fact, of course, a fairly cursory analysis suggests that high elite integration in institutional terms is systematically related to certain political characteristics.

States with relatively high levels of horizontal elite integration such as Meiji Japan,[20] India under the ICS,[21] the Medieval Roman Catholic Church,[22] Nazi Germany,[23] the United States,[24] and the USSR,[25] all reflect complex, and, with the possible exception of Nazi Germany, politically effective societies. The Nazi German case is something of a puzzle here, because of the difficulty of categorizing it. The illustrative method of demonstrating a proposition is, however, insufficient without reference to a larger theory and more detailed analysis. So let us turn here to the four criteria of institutionalization discussed earlier to give ourselves theoretical direction.

COMPLEXITY

Concerning complexity—the multiplication and differentiation of subunits —the existence of interorganization horizontal movement among a polity's bureaucratic elites suggests a low level of differentiation at those levels.[26] Instead of several units, each with its own set of leaders and functions, there may still be a multiplicity of units but the personnel boundaries among them will be indefinite.

Hence, although horizontal elite integration may complement the multiplication of subunits' dimensions of complexity, at the same time it lessens the differentiation among those units. Differentiated units are apt to have differentiated elites in terms of specific technical and administrative resources. The movement of individuals from one unit to another at equivalent levels, however, both requires and encourages a broad homogeneity not only of personnel but of function among those units.

Such a lack of differentiation at lower levels is characteristic of less institutionalized and less politically developed states. This is not so much the case at higher levels, where quasi-political skills are more evident among the elite and are functionally more interchangeable. The reason for the utility of horizontal elite integration at higher governmental levels concerns problems of routinization of decision-making and information availability peculiar to those levels.[27]

At the level where the ultimate power of a bureaucracy is for a particular problem, the type of decision that has to be made is not of a routine nature. In other words, where the techniques for mediating disputes that have been regularized within the system are inadequate, the dispute rises to or above the level of that institution. For example, a military bureaucracy will be able to solve a variety of military problems, whether of a disciplinary or battlefield type, at all levels where the type of solution has been routinized. Where the problem is not a routine one, it is necessary, whether the decision is how to deal with a new form of widespread indiscipline or whether to enlarge the limits of a war, to share the decision-making among a larger group. This is a matter of information availability (forms of knowledge may be needed that the bureaucracy has had inadequate occasion to acquire), and extraorganizational support (the level of support which the rest of the society—its elites—has contracted for) may have to be extended and their previous support must be gained. Where horizontal elite integration is established at the higher levels, the possibility for such political, analytic, and technical support is of course enhanced: the effective and relevant elite base is that much larger.[28]

AUTONOMY

The pressures on an organization's autonomy are greater on its top elites than at lower levels. At lower levels, a leader can naturally and, more important, profitably look up in his own organization for preferment and advancement. When a person is at, or near, the top of his organization, it is inevitable that he will be inclined to look outside for further advancement. Thus it is that whereas lower-level leaders might find organizational chauvinism useful for advancement, it will become less so, as they rise, and the more ambitious and clever will totally eschew it as they reach the top.[29]

The principal consequence is that, at the higher levels of each functional unit, external influences are more likely to penetrate than at other levels, and this is most striking at the very highest levels. Autonomy is a necessity for organizational effectiveness, but unless it is itself modified, the institution would not merely be autonomous, but also be separate and out of contact with the larger society and in the discussion here, the rest of government.[30] In such a situation, the autonomous institutions would be effectively muscle-bound—a situation that Karl Deutsch refers to as immobilism would occur. There are several mechanisms for modifying this autonomy (such as budgetary control), and the inclusion of new elites, though not one of the most common, is sometimes used and is certainly one of the most effective.

Horizontal integration by bureaucratic elites, rather than horizontal integration by nonelites, also has the considerable advantage of bringing in leaders who have themselves been socialized, if not into that organization, at least into the larger governmental system. Also, they have acquired organizational and leadership skills that make their inclusion less disruptive than unsocialized and unskilled leaders.[31]

This relation can be seen most strikingly in times of major social disruption when the group called in to aid or replace the civil bureaucracy is generally the military bureaucracy—a situation more conducive to order and continued governmental autonomy than the inclusion of civil "revolutionary" bureaucracies.[32] There are obviously additional reasons for military bureaucracies being a stabilizing force, aside from their bureaucratic experience and previous socialization, but their experience and socialization are also important factors. As will be seen in the next chapter, the Roman Catholic Church played a similar role in civil assistance in the Medieval period.

In other words, the dilution of autonomy by horizontal elite integration is sometimes a necessity for a political system's maintenance and the mechanism of horizontal elite integration is one of the least disruptive of all modifications of any part of the system's autonomy.

COHERENCE

These examples are also instructive in noting the relation of horizontal institutional elite integration to coherence (the level of agreement in an organization concerning methods of conflict resolution and toal definition, and their reflection in organizational morale).[33] Undoubtedly, the lateral entry of external elites at a high level of organization tends to lessen the coherence of that organization.[34] The fact that leaders from other organizations are put over an organization inevitably damages morale to some extent, though the prestige of the lateral entrant can modify this considerably.[35] The vital point here is not that lateral elite integration in institutional terms lessens cohesion—it does—but what the effect of this coherence lessening is.

From time to time, organizations must change their methods of dispute resolution and goal orientation. From time to time, they must also be shaken out of socially unmerited high levels of morale or self-satisfaction. A nation sometimes has this done for it by losing a war (losing a small war is thus a very useful piece of instruction) or having a major economic crisis.

Institutions that are not essential may retain their coherence as they become irrelevant and obsolescent, disappearing slowly, as did the cavalry in the armed forces or the poor houses in most developed countries. Where a bureaucratic institution, such as the police or an educational system, is essential for society, that organization must be revived, by force if necessary, its morale at least temporarily shaken, old methods of conflict resolution suspended, and goal limits adjusted.[36] The simplest and least disruptive manner is for the leadership of the organization to be forced to accept some counterparts from the outside. In this way, the social forces—to use Huntington's phrase—are prevented from directly impinging upon the institution. The new members, though outsiders, have themselves been socialized through the political process and are apt to be much less disruptive than non-elites. In other words, horizontal elite integration is here the minimum-force-necessary approach to organizational reform from the outside. What is an apparent instance of political decay in one part of the political system is actually a reflection of the adaptive capacity of the larger political system.

Three examples of this process come to mind. The first concerns the reform of Oxford University—a quasi-public bureaucracy—in the middle of the nineteenth century.[37] By the second half of the nineteenth century, Oxford University was autonomous, coherent, fairly complex, and ranked high in adaptation by Huntington's criteria of past adaptive performance. However, the curriculum was almost exclusively classical and various exclusions, quotas, and reserved places made both the students and faculty of lower quality than a more meritocratic system would have produced. Parliament in alliance with a body of academic liberals at Oxford forced changes in this system by forcing the old regime to accept the appointment of faculty and administration that favored the more modern policy. The same sort of situation occurred in the Turkish Army under Ataturk,[38] and to the East India Company Civil Service in the early nineteenth century.

ADAPTABILITY

Turning to adaptability, it is awkward, in Huntington's terms, to find a direct relationship between horizontal elite integration and adaptability. This is in part because his definition refers to past achievements rather than directly to present capacity. A powerful indirect relationship is evident when one views elite integration as an aid to the general effectiveness of the institution. That is, a healthy, complex, autonomous, cohesive organization, regardless of its history, is more likely to adapt itself to new forces than one lacking these qualities. There are, however, some direct relationships that should be considered.

Concerning chronological age, it is evident that older institutions tend to have older leaders than do younger ones.[39] The two characteristics—old institutions and old leaders—are of course separable variables, but their empirical covariance suggests that one of the reasons that older institutions are more adaptable is that their leaders may have certain characteristics, of temperament particularly, that distinguish them from the younger leaders of younger organizations. In a developed polity, a fairly young institution, by bringing in external elites (who will be on the average older) will obtain the benefit of their age. In this way, younger institutions (scoring low on chronological age) can obtain, ironically, a transfusion of old blood and in that way acquire at second hand a part of the advantages of being chronologically old.

This relationship is most frequently noted in the development of reform and revolutionary bureaucratic organizations such as priests-militant or bureaucratic "ginger groups." These groups generally are characterized by a fairly young leadership—ordinarily in their late twenties and early thirties. Their eventual success largely hinges on their ability to expand their base of leadership. The expansion of the base is not in numbers alone, and certainly not in lowering the average age of the elite. Quite the contrary, the adaptability of the organization—its capacity to make the transition from a reformist/revolutionary group to a ruling one, involves its gaining the support of the (older) leaders of other organizations. New organizations must acquire the support of older elites, and this is characteristically accomplished by bringing the older into the decision-making structure of the younger generation. To at least some degree, the Chinese Cultural Revolution involved conflicts of this type, involving Red Guards and the army.[40]

The same general argument applies to the effect of horizontal elite integration on a society's functional age. New elites are unlikely to have the identical function in a society, and so their inclusion in another elite would bring some of the advantages of functional age. Again, it is to be assumed that at least part of the functional age advantages rests in certain elite characteristics. To illustrate, assume an organization that faces the problem of making a transition from one primary goal to another. Also assume that the organization has never made such a transition before. In this case, it would obviously be useful for it to have at least a small part of its elite structure composed of elites from organizations that have made such a transition. It would also be useful for it to have among its members some elites who were familiar with the new function that institution is about to take up. One reason—among others—for the success of military regimes in securing power is that a military bureaucracy has members enjoying a wide variety of skills.[41]

The horizontal transfusion or transplantation of elites is also evident in the measure of an organization's generational age (how many generations of leaders an organization has had). It is difficult for most organizations to make the transition from one generation to another. For personal reasons and also through concern that the new generation can not carry forward their work, older elites are reluctant to give way to newer ones. Where the leading elite contains some outside members of another generation, its homogeneity and hence resistance to new members is apt to be lower. One reason that bureaucracies that have been in a stable environment find it difficult to adapt in terms of making a generational transition is that its leadership has been stratified by the normal workings of seniority. A bureaucracy in a more demanding environment will have undergone a variety of vicissitudes—including expansions and occasional sudden contractions—and so have a generationally more diffuse elite structure.

SUMMARY OF HORIZONTAL BUREAUCRATIC ELITE INTEGRATION AND POLITICAL INSTITUTIONALIZATION

In summarizing the effect of horizontal elite integration on institutionalization, evaluated in Huntingtonian terms, we have seen that three of his cour criteria are affected by the operation of horizontal elite integration. In these cases of coherence, complexity, and autonomy, horizontal elite integration served to modify, for the most part, these characteristics in part of the political system for the purpose of enhancing the political effectiveness of the system as a whole. Under certain circumstances, the effectiveness of the organization in mediating social forces—its political development—may be enhanced by these characteristics, ordinarily associated with development, declining. Furthermore, even where there is not an argument to be made for their decline per se, a temporary lack of coherence, complexity, and, especially, autonomy may be a necessary condition for future effectiveness. In such a case, horizontal elite integration may be the least disruptive way to effect these reforms.

This is not to reject Huntington's arguments, but rather to modify and refine them. Unmodified, coherence, complexity, and autonomy would, despite their more general utility, result in the destruction of the political system which they would otherwise so well maintain. There can be in politics, as in most other matters, too much of a good thing.

Elite Integration Involving Different Levels in Public Bureaucracies: Vertical Elite Integration

Elites may not only be integrated horizontally, but also—and actually more commonly—integrated vertically. Vertical elite integration, like horizontal elite integration, assumes the existence of several elites. In this case, the elites are integrated by virtue of the fact that elite strata enjoying higher access to the values of a society than subordinate strata are characteristically occupied by former members of these subordinate elites.[42] As in the previous discussions, the two (or more) elites must be different—that is, the movement may not be along an undifferentiated continuum in one organization—though one organization may be divided into several elites. Also, the movement must be systematic and characteristic. It may not be by chance or rare. It must be a stable relation among the several elites.

The difference between a single organization composed of merely administrative subunits and a single organization composed of subelites, like Justice or Beauty, more easily discerned than defined. It would be possible, though not very productive, to define the elites in various ways by viewing an organization on several levels of analysis. For example, one could state accurately that all members of the armed forces are elites of violence and then go on from there, dividing and subdividing by the type of function toward violence that a particular group might carry out. Interest, however, is principally in those individuals in a society who can make policy in a systematic way. The distinction within an institution between who makes policy and who does not largely must be derived from an analysis of that institution, noting of course that groups of organizations—whether military establishments or national post offices—have at minimum certain functional characteristics in common. In fact, the problem of categorization and subdivision is made much simpler in that organizational leaders are very well aware of the differences between policy-making elites (principal and subelites) and non-policy-making positions. The analyst can in almost all cases adopt these self-defined organizational distinctions himself.[43]

For example, in practically every (if not every) army, there is a distinction among four ascending groups: the enlisted men (non-elite), officers up to rank of lt. colonel or equivalent (subelites), officers above this level (institutional elite), and a few officers at the very highest positions such as the Joint Chiefs of Staff or special advisers to the chief executive, such as Maxwell Taylor held in the Kennedy Administration. Where the elite group is recruited from those elites below it, we would speak of vertical elite integration.

Vertical elite integration is not confined to movement within an organization, but also extends to movement among several institutions. This movement is often, and rather confusingly, referred to as "lateral advancement."

This is really, of course, vertical advancement and is seen in the case of a charitable foundation's official being given a subcabinet post in Washington, or where a colonel or brigadier general becomes a well-paid and influential member of a major corporation. Note that this latter case is to be distinguished from horizontal elite integration, due to the person involved having a relatively lower position in the previous organization—here, the armed forces.

There are even some quasi-governmental institutions that depend almost exclusively on external vertical elite integration for their higher personnel. Most major charitable foundations in the United States draw on university administrative elites for their leadership, and this is a well established pattern. In these cases, vertical elite integration is well established.

COMPLEXITY

The effect of a well-established system of vertical elite integration on the institution's complexity is important. Empirically, those institutions that are highly differentiated and complex are also characterized by high internal levels of vertical elite integration.[44] The armed forces of a modern state, the Roman Catholic Church especially since the thirteenth century, and the Communist Party of the Soviet Union come to mind. It is not sufficient to say that such complexity makes vertical elite integration possible—certainly it does—but vertical elite integration could, and does exist in many simpler organizations such as a small-town school system.

In fact, vertical elite integration is essential for the maintenance of any system of high complexity. Could such institutions as the Roman Catholic Church, the Communist Party of the Soviet Union, the U.S. army, or the Indian Administrative Service function if they had to continually depend, at almost all levels, for new leaders recruited from external sources?

Most large complex organizations have certain duties which, in the broad sense, may be called technical. That is, there are certain techniques—whether in ecclesiastical ceremonies, military tactics, or legal procedures—that can only be learned, or at least learned best, in that organization.[45] Though it is true that there are certain general social skills, of aggregation particularly, that are universally useful at almost all levels—and in many cases at all levels— a practical knowledge of how the organization carries on its work is very useful and often necessary, for successful leadership.

Probably even more important than technical knowledge for leadership success in an organization is what might be called social knowledge of that organization. This social knowledge consists of knowing the unwritten tabus of the organization, knowing the effective organizational hierarchy (who can be relied upon to get a job done, who can be relied upon for effective political support, and who are the dead wood). This type of organizational knowledge can only be gained by working within an organization over a period of time.[46] An organization that recruits its subelites—and even its top elites—from outside is likely to find itself with a leadership that is incapable of controlling, developing, and exploiting the organization.

Furthermore, the elites who are selecting new colleagues must have adequate information on the technical, social, and personal capacities of their prospective colleagues. The best way to secure their information is by having worked with these men over a period of time. There are a variety of methods that can be used supplementarily, from peer ratings to civil service type examinations. All these may be useful, but in the final analysis the elite members tend to be the best judges as to what characteristics—personal as well as strictly organizations—are needed for being an effective member of what, lacking a better phrase, they want in a team member.[47]

Different organizations and different units of organization would vary in their need for vertical elite integration. A large business enterprise selling, for example, steel products, would be able to bring in high-level salesmen whose skills would not so much depend on experience within the organization and whose expertise may have been gained equally as well in another organization. It would be, however, in most cases, more important for them to appoint a sales manager from within the organization. This may not be a true exception because it is debatable whether even a very high-level salesman can be considered an elite in a policy-making sense. So also, the fund-raising elements of political parties need not be as integrated into the political organization as would be those positions which distribute patronage or make policy. In a military organization, it is essential that higher members have strong social and personal qualities, as well as technical-military ones, before they are given authority; otherwise their general effectiveness would greatly lessen.[48]

Consequently, one can see that a complex organization not only is characterized by but requires high levels of internal vertical elite integration. Vertical elite integration from *outside* the organization, on the other hand, is not a requirement and, indeed, may damage that organization. This is why complex modern organizations recruit few members from the outside, horizontally or vertically. The modern organizations that do—such as the Ford Foundation and the Office of the U.S. President—are relatively less complex, and indeed rely on more complex organizations (which have high levels of internal vertical elite integration) for their supply of new elite members.

AUTONOMY

The relation of autonomy to vertical elite integration has already been discussed, where it was pointed out that autonomy is more closely related to internal selection than to any other characteristic,[49] and more likely to be damaged by its violation than by any other event.

Would there be any other way to preserve this essential autonomy other than by elite integration? There is, but through fulfilling the formal requirement of autonomy it would damage that organization's capacity to mediate social forces. An organization may find itself in the seemingly happy position of having an independent source of income and a captive clientele. The situation is not as rare as it might at first glance seem. Oxford University found itself in that position in the nineteenth century, for example. Due to historical accident, the university—that is, the group of colleges—was independently wealthy. Though there were other institutions of higher learning—Edinburgh and Cambridge, for example—that competed with it, various traditions and Oxford's geographical location made it the preeminent institution of higher learning. Victorian society and a key group—the educable (or semi-educable) sons of the ruling class—were forced to rely upon it.[50] Another example, to be discussed at greater length in the next chapter, is that of the Medieval Church. The Church was also wealthy, not only by its property holdings but also by its traditional freedom from heavy taxation and its customary power of tithing. Furthermore, the population of almost all of Europe, its clientele, was no more Christian by choice then than most people are citizens by choice today. The Church's clientele was a captive one.[51]

Institutions of this type may retain their autonomy indefinitely if the larger polity remains fairly stable. In fact, of course, societies do not remain stable. Where the institutions are necessary for the existence of the larger society—or where they are perceived to be necessary—the institution is either reformed, or the society falls and out of the wreckage a functionally equivalent institution is created.

Many institutions avoid a sudden and catastrophic loss of their autonomy by virtue of the normal process of elite recruitment. Elites, when they can choose their own recruits, do a fairly thorough job of recruiting members like themselves.[52] No screening process is perfect, however, and inevitably the elite lets members in who have been affected—probably beneficially—by forces operating in the larger society. Consequently, although vertical elite integration moderates the effect of social forces on its own membership, it does not prevent the institution from slowly accommodating itself to social forces. An extreme though perhaps unfortunate example may be seen in the evolution of various monastic orders, such as the Benedictines and even the Franciscans[53] later, from an emphasis on austerity, when austerity was a high social value in the early Medieval society, to increasing affluence as the society as a whole became more prosperous and worldly.

COHERENCE

As mentioned above, vertical elite integration aids coherence by giving an organization a social as well as a technical unity. It also aids coherence by virtue of the fact that the assumption of role, method of conflict resolution, and agreed functional limits are acquired at lower levels, or at least conflicting attitudes are not acquired. Elites at lower levels not only share the same experiences and expect, more or less, the same future; they also have had the same values ingrained upon them. People are deeply affected by the values of the organization in which they work, and even more affected when their promotion and success has been due, at least symbolically, to these values.[54] A general in the armed forces is not likely to think that discipline and other military virtues are foolish and irrelevant—quite the contrary, he will feel a sense of personal obligation and even affection toward them and the institution that rewards them.

Vertical elite integration is certainly not the sole cause for coherence in an organization—tradition, a clear but flexible organizational structure, societal support in the sense of admiring the institution, and past success are at least as, if not more, important. On the other hand, it would be very difficult to maintain cohesion in a complex organization without vertical elite integration.

Two ways that such coherence could be maintained without vertical elite integration should, however, be noted. In the first place, some larger organization could enforce—by the giving and withholding of resources and by putting its own members in key positions—the limits of function and the methods of resolving disputes. This is how, for example, universities are controlled by government in most of the developing (or decaying) countries of the world.[55] Obviously, such techniques may be destructive of morale. Furthermore, it is questionable whether in this case the subject institution can be considered a separate organization at all. It is more a subsidiary organ of whatever controls it. Morale, which is vital here, is not just a reflection of how well an institution's functional boundaries are defined or how clear, and even agreed upon, is the institution's conflict resolution procedure.

Where the procedure and the limits are set outside the organization by a separate elite—where there is no internal vertical elite integration—then that institution will have low coherence and will be less effective in mediating social forces. Perhaps as Huntington suggests the problem of morale is in the organization's complete lack of autonomy, which brings us full circle.

The other method of creating coherence without any reliance on elite integration, horizontal or vertical, is by the total commitment to a shared ideal. The ideal—whether humane treatment of animals, the establishment of a classless society, or the defeat of a communal enemy—defines the object, and the selflessness of the elite obviates most if not all normal internal conflicts in an organization. It would be unrealistic to say that such organizations do not exist. They do now and have throughout history. At times they have helped effect major political changes and ameliorated great social ills. The

Society of Jesus in its earlier stages particularly was one such organization, and several of the anti-slavery groups in Europe in the early nineteenth century constitute another example.[56]

This type of organization is the exception, and it is instructive to note that the two examples given above, both successful, were very well structured. Another group, consisting of the anarchist organizations of the turn of the century, are undoubtedly more typical. The anarchists illustrate the defects of this transcendent method of cohesion. Where the more prosaic aspects of organization, such as an articulated hierarchy and the systematic self-regeneration of the organization from within or its symbiosis with other elites, do not take place (as they did in the Jesuits and did not in the anarchists), the organization soon dissolves.[57]

An ideal is a sufficient source of coherence only for a short period in an organization. However, it may last longer if that organization is a small sub-unit of a much larger one. For example, there can be monastic orders of perpetual silence in the Catholic Church, and these orders may last centuries and be quite successful in their own terms, but only so long as they are nourished by the larger body. Similarly, military organizations have their place for special high-risk, high-morale units. These organizations exist without regard to the normal correlates of cohesion but show high cohesion. They can continue because they are supported by the highly institutionalized parent body.

Another reason that organizations depending on a strongly shared ideal for their coherence do not last is that so long as they are successful, they have a tendency to expand into other areas, where they have little expertise, and that process saps their reason for being. Of course, more conventionally organized institutions do the same, but their organizational structure and their more complex elite structure both retard a precipitate progress and also—by virtue of the more widely applicable advantages of institutionalization—make them more effective in new areas.[58] On the other hand, revolutionary or millenarian organizations that find themselves in power tend to go forward into other areas rapidly, and with notable lack of effectiveness, eventually destroying themselves in the process. The religio-military Mahdi Movement in the Sudan in the 1880s is a striking example of this tendency. Elan—among other factors—was not enough over the longer run.[59]

ADAPTABILITY

Vertical elite integration plays the same significant, though not central, role in adaptability as it does in coherence. Chronological age is indirectly enhanced and also engendered by vertical elite integration, particularly when this integration is from outside the organization. Elites, even second-ranking ones, will themselves tend to be chronologically older than non-elites.[60] As described above, a chronologically old elite is not the same as a chronologically old institution, but the two tend in fact to be empirically related. One of the virtues of a chronologically old institution is its older elites, which, contrary to popular wisdom, are often more flexible and effective than their younger counterparts who have not spent decades in the political system. Bringing in chronologically older members—as would to a limited extent be the case with vertical as well as horizontal integration—is a substitute, albeit an incomplete one, for institutional chronological age.

Vertical elite integration, however, is on the average less successful in this regard than horizontal elite integration, because subordinate elites will in the normal course of things be younger than their superiors. There is an exception here: in an institution that depends on subordinate elites outside the organization—such as do large foundations or governmental advisory groups—the new elite's age usually is about the same as the receiving elite's. The question as to whether this may be a case of horizontal integration can only be settled by reference to the particular case.

Vertical elite integration is, however, unquestionably an aid in enhancing generational age. Changing leadership from one generation to another is always difficult, regardless of the organization, and, like most difficult things, it is often more easily done in bits and pieces, gradually, over time. The transition is consequently made somewhat easier by power being passed on, in many cases to proteges, and to others who worked with, and usually sought to please, their seniors.[61]

In terms of functional age—which reflects the capacity to make a functional change—external vertical integration would be useful, as it would bring members to the elite that had experience, and perhaps a clientele and contacts with other functional areas. Obviously, an organization having elements of this type of leadership is more likely to try, and more likely to succeed, in changing its function than an organization that did not have this personnel resource.[62] Vertical elite integration that is internal, which is what we have been emphasizing in this section, would on the other hand not be useful for improving the organizational level of functional adaptation. Although the younger members of the organization would have been exposed to somewhat different influences—simply by virtue of their age and different bureaucratic position—it cannot be expected that they will have much greater functional versatility or a more various clientele than their seniors.

A classic case of an organization—here, virtually the entire structure of government—relying only upon vertical elite integration is that of Tokugawa Japan.[63] Under the shogunate, the government was closely controlled by one group, promoting members, but strictly excluding outsiders. The system lasted, even with occasionally considerable success, for about two hundred years. It did this by creating a level of isolation for the country unequalled in any other time for such a major nation. When the outside world finally pushed in upon Japan in the mid-nineteenth century, transition was affected by promoting marginal elites. The vertical system became inadequate.

SUMMARY

This chapter has been principally concerned with the relation between bureaucratic elite integration, horizontal and vertical, and levels of institutionalization as measured by Huntington's four criteria of coherence, complexity, autonomy, and adaptability. The effect on institutionalization of members of one elite moving in the course of their careers in systematic and characteristic patterns to other levels is a mixed one, seen in terms of these criteria. At points such movement apparently decreases the directly affected unit's level of institutionalization and at other points increases it. Generally, though, the effect of elite integration on bureaucratic institutionalization is positive. Furthermore, this effect is systematic; that is, it is consistently effective in certain circumstances and not so in others. It is a stable variable.

It was also noted that in some cases the negative effect of elite integration on a unit's level of institutionalization is not, on balance, negative on the effectiveness of the larger system. The relationship between the variables used to define institutionalization and political development is not completely uniform. That is, in certain cases, some of the components of institutionalization may have to be temporarily weakened to increase the level of institutionalization, just as, metaphorically, temporarily tiring the body is essential for building it up.

This relationship was seen in the analysis of autonomy. We demonstrated that an organization's autonomy is closely related to the extent to which it can control who enters it and who leads it. Vertical elite integration consequently was seen as a strong indicator of an institution's level of autonomy, as well as being a principal support for such autonomy.

On the other hand, it was noted that very high levels of autonomy based on high vertical elite integration would make the institution less and less effective in mediating social forces. It would become more than autonomous; it would become isolated. Sometimes such organizations simply decline and die, but in other cases they may be able, for a time, to maintain their position while carrying out their function less and less well. It was pointed out that, when such reform is necessary, it is most effective and least disruptive where it is carried through by imposing external bureaucratic elites upon the institution (horizontal elite integration) or by an external elite choosing certain sympathetic, subordinate elites within the overall autonomous organization and giving them power.

This method of dealing with a moribund but essential institution is functionally superior to a direct external, nonbureaucratic takeover of the institution, or its destruction and rebuilding. Hence, in this case, one can see where the violation of an institution's autonomy (by forcing external elites upon it, or by requiring it to accept certain of its own subelites) is essential to the maintenance of political development in the system as a whole.

Coherence is another variable where elite integration can be of value. An organization where the leadership shares an institutionally common past and looks forward to a common future is apt to enjoy high coherence. Vertical elite integration is an aid here, although horizontal elite integration may be harmful. Although we have discussed at some length how important elite integration can be to coherence, it was also emphasized that on balance a shared ideal and a history of progress in fulfilling that ideal are even more important variables.

The relationship of elite integration to adaptation is a more involved one, due in part to the indirect relation of Huntington's criteria to adaptation. Functional, generational, and chronological age are not present capacities (as is differentiation and socialization with regard to complexity), but part of the institution's history, which it may be assumed indicates that the organization has some unidentified characteristics that account for this adaptation.

The concept is thus not quite parallel with the other criteria, and is, thus, more difficult to work with. Nevertheless, it has the great attraction of being the best guide available. The connection between adaptation and elite integration is determined by noting that elites of organizations that are high in chronological, generational, or functional age have some of those useful characteristics. Consequently, an institution that has members who have served in institutions with a high adaptability rating will be itself more adaptive than would otherwise be the case. Horizontal integration for low adaptability organizations would be useful, and vertical elite integration would be of relatively less value.

In conclusion, a society characterized by bureaucratic organizations with high levels of vertical elite integration and moderate levels of horizontal elite integration will be more highly institutionalized, and for the most part more politically developed than a society not so characterized.

NOTES

1. The appropriate definition for elites must be determined in terms of the purpose of that study. No definition is better than another; each is a tool, appropriate to a particular problem. The definition of elites here must be in terms of institutions, not because it is the only definition or the "right" definition, but because it is the definition that will best permit complementing the concepts of political development and institutionalization. The three major methods of operationalizing the concept of elite are by defining (actually measuring) the elite in terms of specific institutions, by reputation as

determined through some questionnaire method, and by the analysis of some decision-making process. The institutional method has been most commonly used in national elite studies (for example, see Matthews, *U.S. Senators and Their World*, and Frey, *Turkish Political Elite*) and the decisional and reputational approaches are characteristic of community studies (see here Dahl, *Who Governs?*, and Presthus, *Men at the Top*).

2. The aspect of bureaucracy that is most relevant here is, of course, that of developmental administration, and its associated theory. The two theorists which will be depended upon primarily in this chapter are Ralph Braibanti and Fred W. Riggs. For Braibanti, especially see his "Comparative Political Analytics Reconsidered," *Journal of Politics*, 30 (February, 1968), pp. 25-65. Note section IV, pp. 49-63. Other works by the same author that are notable in this regard are "Administrative Reform in the Context of Political Growth" in Fred W. Riggs (ed.), *Frontiers of Development Administration*. (Durham, N.C.: Duke University Press, 1970), pp. 227-246; "The Relevance of Political Science to the Study of Underdeveloped Areas," in R. Braibanti and J. Spengler, *Tradition, Values, and Socio-economic Development*. (Durham, N.C.: Duke University Press, 1961), pp. 139-180; "Reflections on Bureaucratic Reform in India" in R. Braibanti and J. Spengler, *Administration and Economic Development in India* (Durham, N.C.: Duke University Press, 1969), pp. 3-68; and the "Introduction" to *Asian Bureaucratic Systems Emergent from the British Imperial Tradition* (Durham, N.C.: Duke University Press, 1966), pp. 3-22. For Riggs, see "Structure and Function: A Dialectical Approach"; "The Idea of Development Administration" in Edward W. Weidner (ed.), *Development Administration in Asia* (Durham, N.C.: Duke University Press, 1970), pp. 25-72; *The Ecology of Public Administration* (Bombay: East Asia Publishing, 1962); "The Theory of Political Development" in James Charlesworth (ed.), *Contemporary Political Analysis* (New York: Free Press, 1967); "Modernization and Development Administration," *CAG Occasional Papers* (Bloomington, Ind.: Indiana University, 1966); and especially his *Administration in Developing Countries: The Theory of Prismatic Society* (Boston: Houghton Mifflin, 1964).

There are, of course, a wealth of other notable works on development administration, which will be cited where appropriate, but the principal orientation will be toward the works cited above.

3. There are a variety of ways in which elites within a society may be categorized. The preferable system is that one which best exploits the data and fits in best with the larger theoretical model.

Watunuki, Organski, and Lipset argue that elites, for comparative purposes, may be best categorized in terms of a tradition-modernity classification, but even here the essential plurality of elites within these categories remains. Joji Watanuki, "White Collar Workers and the Pattern of Politics in Present-Day Japan" in S. M. Lipset and Stein Rokkan (eds.), *Cleavage and Consensus: Cross National Perspectives* (New York: Free Press, 1965) as cited in S. M. Lipset, "Political Cleavages in 'Developed' and 'Emerging' Politics" in Erik Allardt and Yrjo Littunen (eds.), *Cleavages, Ideologies and Party Systems* (Helsinki: Westermarck Society, 1964), p. 47. Fred R. von der Mehden, *Politics of the Developing Nations* (Englewood Cliffs, N.J.: Prentice-Hall, 1964) divides the national elites into a traditional elite, a new (modernizing) elite, and a foreign economic elite. Thus, one part of the dichotomy is itself dichotomized here. Numerous categorizations can be found for different types of elites. If the writer has a particular interest in the ideological attributes of the elites, he may follow Apter in terms of civil servants (theory-oriented), managers (pragmatic), brokers (compromise-oriented), and political entrepreneurs (ideologically oriented). *The Politics of Modernization* (Chicago: University of Chicago Press, 1965). Chapter 5 "Innovation, Professionalism, and the Formation of Careers," pp. 152-178, esp. p. 177. Apter stresses the conflicts among these elites.

Aron, "Social structure and the Ruling Class" offers a typology suitable to industrialized societies. There is, of course, no "right" typology any more than one of the three methods of operationalizing the elite concept is "right." The right one is the one relevant to the solving of the problem that the researcher has set himself. Its rightness can only be evaluated in terms of its utility.

A.F.K. Organski, *The Stages of Political Development* (New York: Knopf, 1965), pp. 38-41. Organski stresses what he perceives as the role of the traditional elite in both an intermediary capacity between the Westernized modernizing elite and the masses and, concurrently, as an obstacle to the Westernized elite. Robert S. Robins, "Political Elite Formation in Rural India: The Uttar Pradesh Panchayat Elections of 1949, 1956, and 1961" *Journal of Politics,* 29 (November, 1967), p. 841, argues this problem has been most successfully dealt with, as in the case of British Imperial India and in Tokugawa Japan, by creating and working through a parallel, centrally oriented, traditional, local elite alongside the obstructive, local, traditional elite. See Harumi Befu, "Village Autonomy and Articulation with the State," *Journal of Asian Studies,* 25 (November, 1965), pp. 19-32, and Hugh Tinker, *The Foundations of Local Self-Government in India, Pakistan and Burma* (London: Athlone Press, 1954). Also see Leonard Binder, "National Integration and Political Development," *American Political Science Review,* 58 (September, 1964), pp. 630-631.

In Lipset, "Political Cleavages in 'Developed' and 'Emerging' Polities," pp. 44-47, the author argues that the Western-perceived left-right divisions are relevant to elite conflict in new nations only to the extent that they can be articulated in traditional-modern terms. Bottomore, *Elites and Society,* stresses in his section on "Tradition and Modernity: Elites in the Developing Countries," pp. 93-111, the role of formal organizations such as the political party in helping to resolve elite-elite and elite-mass conflicts. William H. Friedland, "Some Sources of Traditionalism Among Modern African Elites" in William J. Hanna (ed.), *Independent Black Africa* (Chicago: Rand McNally, 1964), pp. 363-369, states that the traditional elites (principally tribal) in Africa will weaken in power as modernization becomes less associated with colonialism. Lloyd I. Rudolph and Susanne H. Rudolph, *The Modernity of Tradition: Political Development in India* (Chicago: University of Chicago Press, 1967) stress the role of the caste group (jati) in bridging the traditional-modern gap.

4. A discussion of horizontal bureaucratic mobility in the Indian bureaucracy may be found in B. S. Khanna, "Bureaucracy and Development in India" in Weidner (ed.), *Development Administration in Asia,* pp. 236-238.

5. For a discussion of the role of legitimacy in general terms in regard to bureaucracies, see Carl Beck, "Bureaucracy and Political Development in Eastern Europe," in Joseph LaPalombara (ed.), *Bureaucracy and Political Development* (Princeton: Princeton University Press, 1963), pp. 299 ff. Like Beck, we follow Lipset in defining legitimacy as "the capacity of a political system to engender and maintain the belief that existing political institutions are the most appropriate or proper ones for the society." "Some Social Requisite of Democracy: Economic Development and Political Legitimacy," *American Political Science Review,* 53 (March, 1959), p. 86. Fritz Morstein Marx, "The Higher Civil Service as an Action Group in Western Political Development" in LaPalombara (ed.), *Bureaucracy and Political Development,* pp. 75-77, offers an analysis of the symbiosis between the concepts of legitimacy and bureaucracy.

6. That is, following our earlier analysis, a group that is somewhat autonomous from the larger bureaucracy and is distinctively coherent. A further important attribute for our analysis is that it have a stable elite structure.

7. Among the very large number of works dealing with the role of the military in nominally civilian roles, see Huntington, *Political Order in Changing Societies,* pp. 192-

263; Dankwart A. Rustow, "The Army and the Founding of the Turkish Republic," *World Politics,* 11 (July, 1959); on the Ayub regime, Karl von Vorys, *Political Development in Pakistan* (Princeton, N.J.: Princeton University Press, 1965); P. J. Vatikiotis, *The Egyptian Army in Politics* (Bloomington, Ind.: Indiana University Press, 1961); Martin C. Needler, "Political Development and Military Intervention in Latin America," *American Political Science Review,* 60 (September, 1966). A work that deals with the conflict of political and bureaucratic modes of behavior, and stresses the role of institutionalization in Huntingtonian terms is Edward Feit, "Pen, Sword, and People," *World Politics,* 25 (January, 1973), pp. 251-273.

8. Elite theory, principally for certain normative reasons, has been dominated by a concern with the social background characteristics of the elite, in relation to one another and in relation to the larger society. Observed similarities among the elite (educational level, family ties) that distinguished it from the larger society would serve as integrative factors. See note 22, Chapter 1 for some leading works on this topic.

9. The principal work that outlines this position, though in a perhaps simplified and exaggerated form is C. Wright Mills, *The Power Elite* (New York: Oxford University Press, 1959).

10. See Chapter 4.

11. For the period 1368-1911, Ping-Ti Ho, *The Ladder of Success in Imperial China;* also see Yung-Teh Chow, *Social Mobility in China* (New York: Atherton Press, 1966); Wolfram Eberhard, *Social Mobility in Traditional China* (Leiden: E. J. Brill, 1962). For the separate character of the bureaucracy as a continuing and characteristic feature of Chinese civilization, see Etienne Balazs, *Chinese Civilization and Bureaucracy* (New Haven: Yale University Press, 1964), especially "China as a Permanently Bureaucratic Society," pp. 13-27.

12. There is no work that has a theoretical focus on nineteenth-century political institutions that is compatible with ours. An excellent study that examines the institutionalization of a major institution and whose model approximates Huntington's is Nelson Polsby, "The Institutionalization of the U.S. House of Representatives," *American Political Science Review,* 62 (March, 1968), pp. 144-168.

13. See Chapter 6.

14. For a discussion of the distinctions and the overlaps between the "political" and "nonpolitical" aspects of a polity, especially in developing countries, see Fred W. Riggs, "Bureaucrats and Political Development: A Paradoxical View," in LaPalombara, *Bureaucracy and Political Development,* pp. 120-167.

15. For a discussion of the categorization, definitions, and models of bureaucracies and their components see, LaPalombara, "An Overview of Bureaucracy and Political Development" in LaPalombara, *Bureaucracy and Political Development,* pp. 6-9; in the same volume, see John Dorsey, "The Bureaucracy and Political Development in Viet Nam," pp. 318-359, which takes an information-availability approach to the phenomenon; Bert Hoselitz, "Levels of Economic Performance and Bureaucratic Structures," pp. 168-198, takes a structural-functional approach, as does S. N. Eisenstadt, "Bureaucracy and Political Development," pp. 96-119; Merle Fainsod, "Bureaucracy and Modernization: The Russian and Soviet Case," pp. 233-267, takes an approach that essentially defines a bureaucracy in terms of how it relates to the exercise of coercion. In Braibanti, *Asian Bureaucratic Systems Emergent from the British Imperial Tradition,* a functional approach is taken, in terms of the bureaucracy's role in "the maintenance of compatibility between the spirit and substance of statutory law and administrative discretion"; "the role of the bureaucracy as an institution with the capability of converting political and social demands into programs and action"; and "the bureaucracy as a social institution for a large segment of employed population," pp. 5, 6.

16. A study which is strongly oriented to the party professional, the *apparatchiki*, and demonstrates the highly institutionalized form of the Soviet Communist Party through elite analysis is Michael P. Gehlen, "The Soviet Apparatchiki," in R. Barry Farrell (ed.), *Political Leadership in Eastern Europe and the Soviet Union* (New York: Aldine, 1970), pp. 140-156.

17. Fujii Jintaro (compiler and editor), *Outline of Japanese History in the Meiji Era* (translated and adapted by H. K. Colton and K. E. Colton; Tokyo: Obunsha, 1958). See section on "Political Party Movements," pp. 220-225, and "The Three Great Issues," pp. 230-237. Jintaro notes that soon after the Imperial Rescript of 1881 pledged a National Diet, "political parties and societies sprung up in many places like bamboo sprouts after a rain," p. 220. These parties, however, and other extra-governmental organizations were excluded from the government and were soon virtually abolished. The bureaucratic structure of the government was kept decidedly separate. See also G. B. Sansom, *The Western World and Japan* (London: Crescent Press, 1950), pp. 369-391.

18. A sociologically oriented study of the non-party bureaucracy in Egypt is Morroe Berger, *Bureaucracy and Society in Modern Egypt* (Princeton: Princeton University Press, 1957). The military's decision to establish a cadre-type party was an effort to insulate the military from politics. Huntington, *Political Order in Changing Societies*, p. 248; see also Vatikiotis, *The Egyptian Army in Politics.*

19. The mechanism for business influence on the government, in terms of elite movement, is principally through the legislature. Gerard Braunthal, *The Federation of German Industry in Politics* (Ithaca: Cornell University Press, 1965) especially see pp. 150-191. For a study that indicates that the German bureaucratic elite, at least compared to the British, lacks a general corporate sense, see Bruce Heady, "The Civil Service as an Elite in Britain and Germany," *Integration Review of Administrative Science*, 38 (1972), pp. 41-48.

20. Jintaro, *Outline of Japanese History in the Meiji Era*, pp. 220-225, 230-237; and Sansom, *The Western World and Japan*, pp. 369-391.

21. There is not a recent full-length treatment of the I.C.S. Two useful works are L.S.S. O'Malley, *The Indian Civil Service* (London: Murray, 1931); and Philip Mason, *The Men Who Ruled India.* Two volumes. (London: Jonathan Cape, 1953, 1954).

22. See Chapter 4.

23. For a study of the remarkable fluidity of membership in a single politically sensitive institution, see George H. Stein, *The Waffen S.S.* (Ithaca: Cornell University Press, 1966). See especially pp. 119-196 for the foreign element in its membership. A study that stresses the continuity of German bureaucratic tradition under National Socialism is Arnold Brecht and Comstock Glaser, *The Art and Technique of Administration in German Ministries* (Cambridge, Mass.: Harvard University Press, 1940).

24. For a study taking an evaluatory point of view, see Grant McConnell, *Private Power and American Democracy* (New York: Knopf, 1967).

25. Gehlen, "The Soviet Apparatchiki." Gehlen notes that "there has been a steady increase in the number and percentage of persons co-opted into the higher echelons of the apparat who have functional specializations in the economic sector of Soviet society" (p. 147) though co-optation also comes from other sectors as well.

26. A bureaucracy that would be differentiated would for the most part in Riggs' terms conform to a "diffracted" (in his earlier works, a "refracted") model. Riggs, *Administration and Development*, pp. 19-30. For a discussion of the distinction between differentiation within bureaucracies and differentiation between bureaucracies and political institutions, see Riggs, "Bureaucrats and Political Development," pp. 122-127. See Braibanti, "External Inducement of Political Administrative Development,"

pp. 52-66 for an analysis that integrates the concepts of specialization of function and differentiation of structure with the concept of institutionalization.

27. For a discussion of the relative importance of perceived political potential in choosing entrants to a bureaucracy in more- and less-developed bureaucracies, see Riggs, *Administration in Developing Countries,* pp. 272-273. For a discussion of strict compartmentalization and its deleterious effect on the decision-making process, see Ralph Braibanti, "Public Bureaucracy and Judiciary in Pakistan" in LaPalombara, *Bureaucracy and Political Development,* pp. 390-395.

28. Dorsey, "The Bureaucracy and Political Development in Viet Nam," takes an information availability approach to the evaluation of public bureaucratic institutions. See also Karl W. Deutsch, *Nationalism and Social Communication* (New York: John Wiley, 1953), and his *Nerves of Government.*

29. Carl Beck, "Bureaucracy and Political Development in Eastern Europe" in LaPalombara, *Bureaucracy and Political Development,* pp. 268-300, notes the increasing importance of autonomy within even highly centralized, disciplined, and authoritarian polities, see especially, pp. 288-289.

Riggs defines autonomy thus: "The extent to which a social system can influence its environment and its reactions upon the system are a measure of its *autonomy* (discretion)." "The Idea of Development Administration," in Weidner (ed.), *Development Administration in Asia,* p. 34. Riggs goes on to distinguish autonomy as discretion, from autonomy as a measure of freedom of role, which Riggs refers to as "autogeny," pp. 35-36. See his section on "Autogeny vs. Discretion: Contrasting Forms of Autonomy," pp. 37-39. The concept of autogeny is a useful distinction for Riggs' purpose, but it appears to be an unnecessary complication for the present study, so autonomy will be defined principally in terms of an institution's ability to resist external pressures.

30. There is an important distinction to be made between institutions that are separate from the larger society in social as well as political aspects, and those that are only separate in one or the other of these aspects. For example, the higher bureaucracy of Pakistan, like that of the British institution that preceded it, is somewhat separate in social terms from the larger society; a necessity in a society where ascriptive pressures are so strong. See Braibanti, "The Higher Bureaucracy of Pakistan" in Braibanti, *Asian Bureaucratic Systems Emergent from the British Imperial Tradition,* pp. 209-353. On the other hand, it is possible to have a bureaucracy that is well integrated, socially, into the polity, but is somewhat out of touch with the broader demands that that society makes upon it. The "Mandarin" (scholar-official) quality of much of Chinese history illustrates this point. Balazs, *Chinese Civilization and Bureaucracy,* emphasizes the bureaucratic essence of Chinese history, and notes the political, though not the social, distance of the bureaucracy from the larger society. Balazs notes how this attitude is also a characteristic of Chinese historiography, wherein individuals are uniformly perceived as members of groups, and events are reported without interpretation. For a fuller discussion of this topic, see in the above volume, "History as a Guide to Bureaucratic Practice," pp. 129-149.

For an analysis of the persistence of the Chinese bureaucratic phenomenon today, see A. Doak Barnett, *Cadres, Bureaucracy and Political Power in Communist China* (New York: Columbia University Press, 1967).

31. In Riggs' terms: "Here analysis . . . presupposes the existence of a polity, or of some widely accepted myths and formulas which legitimize the input-output framework," which takes place "in a setting of group structures and operating principles which are taken for granted." *Administration in Developing Countries,* pp. 195-196. An attempt to evaluate the influence of leadership on organizational performance may be found in

S. Lieberson and James F. O'Connor, "Leadership and Organizational Performance," *American Sociological Review*, 37 (April, 1972), pp. 117-130.

32. A volume that makes this point in a variety of ways with a variety of authors and countries is John J. Johnson (ed.), *The Role of the Military in Underdeveloped Countries* (Princeton: Princeton University Press, 1962).

33. The relevant section in Riggs is his chapter on "Social Structures: Poly-Communalism and Clects," pp. 157-173 in *Administration in Developing Countries*. Riggs is principally interested in the role of bureaucracy in a polycommunal society, and analyzes the role of these units in their various forms in integration and disintegration.

Braibanti approaches the problem of the group basis of integration in a more formal fashion, identifying what he calls "sectors," which are very similar to what we will later characterize as subinstitutions. Braibanti, "External Inducement of Political-Administrative Development: An Institutional Strategy," pp. 58 ff.

34. Arnold J. Toynbee, *A Study of History* (abridgement of Vols. I-VI by D. C. Somervell, New York: Oxford University Press, 1947) pp. 176-177, notes how the Ottoman Empire, despite its other shortcomings, maintained, until near the end, its administrative integrity by specialized training of its administrative leaders.

35. For example the entry of Eisenhower over the regular Republican organization, though accompanied by substantial complaint in some quarters, was fairly well accepted due to his very high prestige.

36. A revolution is such an instance on a grand scale. See the effect of the Communist revolution on the old bureaucracy: Barnett, *Cadres, Bureaucracy and Political Power in Communist China*. On a less dramatic scale, the reader should consult the record of the administrative and policy reforms on Oxford University in the latter half of the nineteenth century.

37. W. R. Ward, *Victorian Oxford* (London: Cass, 1965). This volume emphasizes the politics of the time. See especially the chapter "The Triumph of Reform and the Executive Commissioners," pp. 180-209. For the politics of an earlier and more stable period see W. R. Ward, *Georgian Oxford* (London: Oxford University Press, 1958). Also see E.G.W. Bill, *University Reform in Nineteenth-Century Oxford: A Study of Henry Halford Vaughan* (London: Oxford University Press, 1973).

38. Richard D. Robinson, *The First Turkish Republic* (Cambridge: Harvard University Press, 1963); and especially Bernard Lewis, *The Emergence of Modern Turkey* (London: Oxford University Press, 1961).

39. It may well be that a more precise indication of the elite's age is a measure of the duration in politics of its members rather than their chronological age. In many cases the distinction is apt to be a relevant one. Of course, an elite member's total age is apt to be proportional (during and especially after middle age) to the length of his political experience. See Robins, "The Indian Upper House and Elite Integration," pp. 23-24, which emphasizes the length of political experience; similarly, see W. L. Guttsman, *The British Political Elite* (New York: Basic Books, 1963), p. 201; Guttsman's principal emphasis is on parliament. Philip W. Buck, *Amateurs and Professionals in British Politics,* 1918-1959 (Chicago: University of Chicago Press, 1963), pp. 27-28, demonstrates that, excepting minor parties, members are similar in age (35-39) at first contest, and also similar in age at the termination of their careers. Frey, *Turkish Political Elite,* 59, demonstrates that the greater amount of education, the sooner a person was likely to enter politics. Also see Austin Ranney, *Pathways to Parliament: Candidate Selection in Britain* (Madison: University of Wisconsin Press, 1965).

There is no single work which ties together the various writings on the relation between age and institutionalization. Further works that are useful are Mattei Dogan, "Political Ascent in a Class Society: French Deputies, 1870-1958," in Dwaine Marvick (ed.), *Political Decision Makers* (New York: Free Press, 1961), p. 61; Matthews, *U.S. Senators and Their World*, p. 56. A particularly interesting work is that of Hans Gerth, "The Nazi Party: Its Leadership and Composition," *American Journal of Sociology*, 45 (1940), pp. 530-531; the age structure of the Nazi Party was similar to that of new institutions (that is the members were younger) in developing states, and different from the German institutions that preceded and followed it. For an analysis of the role of age in political change in a conservative regime see Paul H. Lewis, "The Spanish Ministerial Elite, 1938-1969," *Comparative Politics*, 5 (October, 1972), pp. 83-106.

40. An excellent analysis of the institutional relation between the party and the army, as structured by the Cultural Revolution, is John Gittings, "Army-Party Relations in the Light of the Cultural Revolution," in John W. Lewis (ed.), *Party Leadership and Revolutionary Power in China* (London: Cambridge University Press, 1970), pp. 373-403.

41. This point has been made in a variety of contexts. See Lucian W. Pye, "Armies in the Process of Political Modernization," in Johnson (ed.), *The Role of the Military in Underdeveloped Countries*, pp. 76-79; for a more extended discussion of the same topic, see Morris Janowitz, *The Military in the Political Development of New Nations* (Chicago: University of Chicago Press, 1964). For a broader view of the role of the military role in political development, see Huntington's chapter on "Praetorianism and Political Decay," in *Political Order in Changing Societies*, pp. 192-263. Two closely associated studies are David Rapoport, "A Comparative Theory of Military and Political types," in Samuel Huntington (ed.), *Changing Patterns of Military Politics*, pp. 71-100; and Amos Perlmutter, "The Praetorian State and the Praetorian Army: Towards a Theory of Civil-Military Relations in Developing Polities," (unpublished paper, Institute of International Studies, University of California, Berkeley) as cited in Huntington, *Political Order in Changing Societies*, p. 195.

42. Riggs, "Channels of Elite Recruitment," in *Administration in Developing Countries*, pp. 134-136, which discusses the active role of vertical bureaucratic elite recruitment in prismatic societies.

43. For a systematic elaboration of the necessity for viewing any concept within a specific context, particularly as it pertains to bureaucracy and development, see Braibanti, "Comparative Political Analytics Revisited."

44. A very instructive study of the development of this concept in nineteenth-century America is Leonard D. White's classic *The Republican Era* (New York: Macmillan). See especially pp. 32-45.

45. Riggs approaches the problem of technical efficiency and effectiveness by distinguishing the two concepts and relating them both to the political power of the bureaucracy—his conclusion being that the "degree of administrative efficiency of a bureaucracy varies inversely with the weight of its power," *Administration in Developing Countries*, p. 263. See the entire section pp. 263-267.

46. In viewing a bureaucratic organization as a social organization and the bureaucratic process as a social process, Herbert Simon's *Administrative Behavior: A Study of Decision-Making Processes in Administrative Organization* (2nd ed., New York: Macmillan, 1957) is a seminal work. For a specific application (by a sociologist) see Peter M. Blau, *The Dynamics of Bureaucracy: A Study of Interpersonal Relations in Two Government Agencies* (Chicago: University of Chicago Press, 1955).

47. See Blau, *Dynamics of Bureaucracy*, especially for the role of compatibility in internal elite selection.

48. Morris Janowitz, *The Professional Soldier: A Social and Political Portrait* (Glencoe, Ill.: Free Press, 1960).

49. "In every society affected by social change, new groups arise to participate in

politics. Where the political system lacks autonomy, these groups gain entry into politics without becoming identified with the established political organizations or acquiescing in the established political procedures." Huntington, *Political Order in Changing Societies*, p. 21.

50. For a discussion of Oxford and its political relationship to rapidly changing Victorian society, see Ward, *Victorian Oxford*. Also see note 37 and associated text above. On the use of external elites for reorganizing bureaucracies, see N. D. Milder, "Some Aspects of Crozier's Theory of Bureaucratic Organizations," *Journal of Comparative Administration*, 3 (May, 1971), pp. 61-82.

51. Southern, *Western Society and the Church in the Middle Ages*, remarks that "the church was a compulsory society in precisely the same way as the modern state is a compulsory society. Just as the modern state requires those who are its members by the accident of birth to keep its laws . . . so the medieval church required those who had become its members by the accident . . . of baptism to do all these things and many others," pp. 18, 19.

52. In Riggs' terms, in a diffracted society, the principal mode of recruitment is one in which familistic considerations are dominant, though there may be formal testing, etc., *Administration in Developing Countries*, p. 273. In other words, a person's loyalty and power potential are most important for his recruitment. Riggs' discussion here applies equally to the recruitment into the system and promotion thereafter. Thus, the ascriptive and personalistic considerations continue for promotion among the elite.

53. Southern, *Western Society and the Church in the Middle Ages*, the sections, "The Benedictines," pp. 217-239; and "The Friars," pp. 272-299.

54. Janowitz, *The Professional Soldier*. On this affective aspect of elite integration and bureaucracy, see M. P. Smith, "Self-Fulfillment in a Bureaucratic Society: A Commentary on the Thought of Gabriel Marcel," *Public Administrative Review*, 29 (January/ February, 1969), pp. 25-32.

55. A very useful survey of this topic may be found in David Abernathy and Trevor Coombe, "Education and Politics in Developing Countries," *Harvard Education Review*, 35 (Summer, 1965).

56. A perceptive and often overlooked work is David A. Wilson, "Nation-Building and Revolutionary War," in Karl W. Deutsch and William Foltz (eds.), *Nation-Building* (New York: Atherton Press, 1963), pp. 84-94, which discusses the institutionalization of the transcendent and charismatic attributes of Communist insurgency movements.

57. A study that indicates the necessity of institutionalization for effective political action—using nineteenth-century France, is David Stafford, *From Anarchism to Reformism* (London: Weidenfield and Nicholson, 1971). On the organized opposition to the slave trade, see L. Bethell, *The Abolition of the Brazil Slave Trade* (Cambridge: Cambridge University Press, 1970).

58. The best work on the expansion of bureaucratic institutions directly and also their adoption by exotic countries is that of Ralph Braibanti, cited above. An important contribution in this respect, and relevant to our argument, is that the expansion of any institution into a new area, and especially into a new culture requires a complex reciprocity of changes in political/cultural norms. See especially Braibanti, "The Relevance of Political Science to the Study of Underdeveloped Areas."

59. P. Holt, *The Mahdist State in the Sudan, 1881-1898* (Oxford: Oxford University Press, 1958); Alan B. Theobald, *The Mahdiya* (London: Longmans, 1951).

60. See note 39 in this chapter.

61. Although there is a substantial literature on the communal nature of elite advancement in less-developed areas (see for example the section on "Communalism, Clects, and Bureaucratic Enclaves," in Riggs, *Administration in Developing Countries*,

pp. 274-276, there is very little in the way of studies indicating in a systematic fashion the temperamental affinities that affect such advancement. Even studies in the administration-as-social-system tradition do not offer such a systematic study. In many ways, studies such as Lucian W. Pye, "The Non-Western Political Process," *Journal of Politics,* 20 (August, 1958), pp. 468-486 is most useful, as indeed is Pye's longer work (which includes the article above in another form), *Politics, Personality, and Nation Building.*

62. Several works, which Huntington also draws upon, that demonstrate the capacity of organizations to change functions and indicate, with varying specificity, the role of a functionally complex elite structure are David L. Sills, *The Volunteers* (Glencoe, Ill.: Free Press, 1957), especially see Chapter 9; Sheldon L. Messinger, "Organizational Transformation: A Case Study of a Declining Social Movement," *American Sociological Review,* 20 (February, 1955); Mayer N. Zald and Patricia Denton, "From Evangelism to General Service: The Transformation of the YMCA," *Administrative Science Quarterly,* 8 (September, 1963); Joseph R. Gusfield, "Social Structure and Moral Reform: A Study of the Woman's Christian Temperance Union," *American Journal of Sociology,* 61 (November, 1955).

63. The four classes (soldier, farmer, artisan, trader) were clearly delineated, and movement within each of the classes was much more common than movement between. The establishment of stability was, of course, the whole point of the Tokugawa regime. George Sansom, *History of Japan, 1615-1867,* (Stanford: Stanford University Press, 1963).

Chapter 3

ELITE INTEGRATION BETWEEN

BUREAUCRATIC AND POLITICAL ELITES

Earlier it was mentioned that it is often useful to make a distinction between bureaucratic elites and what are generally called "political" elites. This latter category is ill named, in that the bureaucratic elites are also political in the general way in which this word is often used, but it does emphasize a difference. The political elites are those in a society whose style in politics is entrepreneurial and who join bureaucratic organizations—if they join them at all—for the purpose of fairly short-term and rapid advancement. They do not make a lifelong commitment to that organization. More important, these elites are oriented toward what is known as policy-making even more than is the case with the bureaucratic elite, who have a greater orientation toward such elite rewards as security and deference.[1]

The point of this chapter is to explore, first, the integration of bureaucratic and political elites. Here the focus will be on the elite integration relation between such institutions as bureaucratized political parties and high-level government positions (such as, for example, the organizational-ministerial split in many Indian states, especially before the Congress split), or the relation between state bureaucracies and less bureaucratized political elites, such as that between the British higher civil service and the cabinet.

The interest has shifted from the relation between two bureaucratic elites (which has already been examined), to that between a bureaucratic elite and a political elite. Furthermore, it is the institutional aspect that is being emphasized. It is, for example, the relation between a bureaucracy as an institution and, say, a cabinet as an institution that would be examined in terms of the type or existence of elite movement between them.

Frame of Reference

To return to the frame of reference, the assumption is made that societies examined have more than one elite, and that of the two or more at least one will be bureaucratic and one will be political. As discussed above, almost all societies have some sort of bureaucratic organization, whether a priesthood or some institutionalized military force such as the Ottoman Janisseries. A bureaucracy, it should be emphasized, is principally defined not only by the Weberian[2] criteria of hierarchy, emphasis on rationality, etc., but whether in the normal course of events its leaders would expect to look to it as an institution for their rewards and achievements. They would receive this reward as a consequence of spending a major portion of their lives working their way up in the hierarchy.

In such terms, national political parties in the United States are not bureaucracies, though in certain American cities they may be. A charitable foundation is a very weak bureaucracy, and the post office is a strong one. An institution can change from a political organization such as the higher officer corps in Cromwell's army in the 1640s to a bureaucratic one, such as the armed forces in Britain today. The point here is that, in making the delineation, one must be guided not only by the conceptual definition but also by the configuration, to use Ralph Braibanti's phrase, of the institution and the society being studied.[3]

The political institutions are not so evident or so obvious, or their structure so explicit as that of the bureaucratic ones. Some institutions—stable patterns of valued interaction—are, if not invisible, difficult to discern. This is the case, for example, in noting the patterned but largely implicit structure of elite recruitment into the politically active sector of the elite through family arrangements, charitable institutions, social clubs, etc.

Such processes are all legitimate units of analysis, but are difficult to handle conceptually because of the imprecision of the data and, in some cases, the multifunctionality of the institution. Consequently, what is best known will be emphasized: government positions that are not open to bureaucrats in the normal course of events and which are valued for their policy-making functions. Where certain extralegal organizations that are nonbureaucratic in the present terms are effectively integrated into the government system, they will be included as well. National political parties in the United States would fit this characterization.[4]

However, the focus will be on government positions. The reason for this emphasis does not spring from a narrow conception of politics, but rather from a realization that we do not have the conceptual tools to make precise delineations between the political and nonpolitical components of a society. Because the borders cannot be precisely drawn is not to say, however, that there are no borders or that there are not certain institutions that are clearly in one or the other area. The formal institutions of government are clearly within the political area, and are indeed central to it.

Not only is the focus appropriate conceptually, equally important is the fact that there is a large body of reliable information on government institutions and their elites. Regardless of a scheme's conceptual clarity or cleverness, it is useless unless it is complemented by a body of applicable, reliable data. The situation otherwise is like having a fine automobile with an empty gasoline tank.

The first area of discussion is elite integration between the bureaucratic system of a state and its political system. The near universality of bureaucratic elites extant not only in modern developed states, but in most premodern ones as well has been discussed. Is there always a political elite, in the terms in which it has already been defined? For most cases, there obviously is one, subdivided into many subelites—the national cabinet, local legislatures, office of the chief executive, national and local legislatures, etc. The problem arises in the consideration of so-called bureaucratic states.[5] In states such as the Soviet Union or British India under the Indian Civil Service, is there not a society where all positions are tied into some overarching organization? This organization is hierarchical, rational, etc., and, moreover, its members may have to spend their lives working their way up the hierarchy, whether the apogee might be the lt. governorship of the Punjab or membership on the Presidium.

There are two points to be made here. First, the organization itself—here the Communist Party of the Soviet Union or the Indian Civil Service—is a policy-making, specialized organization. An analysis of its higher positions at each political level indicates that the style of politics, and consequently the skills required, are of a dominantly entrepreneurial type. Success here requires moving from position to position—being in charge of a backwater district at one stage, advising a local ruler on subversion at another, overseeing the administration of a large enterprise at another. Its political entrepreneurial nature is also illustrated by the prevalence of sudden reverses in fortune, and the accompanying demotion of high political officials to essentially technical positions. Malenkov's fall from central power to the status of manager of an eastern hydroelectric plant is an illustration of this.[6]

The second point, related closely to the former, is that, in many cases, the positions at the top, though nominally bureaucratic, are not so in fact.

The leadership is brought in from the oustide or the elite effectively leave the bureaucratic organization when they take these positions. The Indian Civil Service illustrates this situation. The viceroy was a political appointee of the Crown, and not a member of the civil service. Even the selection of the lt. governors and other high positions—including the secretariat and commander-in-chief—was deeply involved in political considerations, not surprisingly. Another case is the common one in which a clearly political elite is replaced, generally through extralegal coercion, by a bureaucratic elite—in most cases, the armed forces. In this case, the armed forces' leadership, often reluctantly, is changed into a political elite, not definitionally by virtue of its new position (which would be a case of circular reasoning) but by virtue of the pressures and demands placed upon it and its response.

Field Marshall, later President, Ayub of Pakistan illustrates this process.[7] When the military regime took power in the late 1950s, replacing a quasi-elected body of politicians, initial efforts were made to run the country the way the army was run—with technical efficiency and honesty and largely without regard to sectarian or other narrow interests. The "nonpolitical" system did not last beyond a few months. The leadership—though not the army as a whole—took on the essential characteristics of conventional politics —balancing interests, seeking allies of convenience, etc.

Second, it should be noted that only rarely does a true bureaucratic elite come to power. Where military elites seize power (or have it thrust upon them), they have in almost all cases been courted by and previously involved in the political system.[8] The military does not break upon the political scene from its barracks, but has been increasingly involved in politics for some time. The Japanese military before World War II, in the 1920s and increasingly in the 1930s, involved itself in assassination and less extreme pressures upon the government until it seized effective power not many years before the attack on Pearl Harbor.[9]

Thus, though the division between political and bureaucratic organizations is not less real in so-called bureaucratic states as in more conventional ones, it may often be far less obvious. Because they are more difficult to discern and of no extra theoretical utility, by and large the examples will be limited to the type of state that is most characteristic in the world today: that is, states in which there is an explicit differentiation (though frequent inter-action) between bureaucratic and political components. The difference between the conventional and the bureaucratic states is more apparent than real for the present purposes; nevertheless, the reader may wish to exclude the bureaucratic polities from the conclusions of this book.

Political-Bureaucratic Elite Integration and Huntington's Criteria of Institutionalization Complexity

The first criterion of institutionalization is complexity. It must be examined in light of its relation to elite integration, vertical and horizontal, between the bureaucratic and the political institutions of a state. The question here is whether a polity in which there is substantial movement of elites between bureaucratic and political institutions is or tends to be more or less complex than where there is little or no such movement. The situation may be that the bureaucratic elite moves to the political, the reverse, or a more or less equal mutual exchange.

Of these three possible relations, the first is by far the most common and the one to be emphasized. Political elites very rarely become bureaucratic elites, though there was such an apparent movement in seventeenth- and eighteenth-century Britain, but then the civil bureaucratic organizations were poorly developed and still very political.[10] A simple and continuing interchange was characteristic of the Soviet Union in the 1920s, but this was a temporary case. More common is the case of military men moving into political positions, civil servants reaching cabinet rank, and church leaders acquiring effective political direction in religiously integrated societies.

The general thesis in this section is that political-bureaucratic elite integration, horizontal and vertical, damages the complexity of the political system, and that though this lessening of complexity may be useful in terms of political development at the higher levels of government, it is damaging at all other levels. It is not possible for a political system to be characterized by differentiation and specialization of its subunits where the elites of those subunits are constantly shifting between bureaucratic organizations and political institutions. As discussed in the previous chapter, vertical elite integration is essential to complexity within an organization. That is, the army or the post office must recruit the bulk of their elites from within, else they will lack a leadership with the social and technical skills that only tutelage in their organization can provide. In almost all cases, horizontal elite integration would be disruptive of this complexity.

Two general aspects of government—the bureaucratic and the political—are under discussion here. It is of course a cliché—and a truth, as many clichés are—that the political and the bureaucratic aspects of politics overlap, that the administrative (policy carrying-out) and political (policy-making) areas of government are not sharply differentiated. Again, to note that a sharp line cannot be drawn between two types of organizations is not to say that no distinction is possible. Bureaucratic organizations do indeed carry out, typically, different sorts of functions in societies than do nonbureaucratic organizations. Furthermore, to note that all members of one category are not congruent with each other is not to say that there may not be approximate congruence among them, and that noting this similarity is not useful. Bureaucratic organizations are typically charged with the implementation of policies.[11]

It has been noted how the bureaucratic elements must specialize to accomplish their ends, must develop techniques of organization and procedure, and we have seen how vertical elite integration is essential to this capacity. The same situation applies to the political organizations of a polity. Political organizations also require social knowledge of their clientele, and the fact that the skills of aggregation and articulation are more commonly found among older leaders and older institutions reflects the fact that the successful practice of policy-making involves techniques that must be learned.

Briefly, it is the function of the political organizations to make policy, to say that something may or must be done. The procedures are also generally laid down as well, but the bureaucracy is the institution that implements the policy.[12] This is obvious, perhaps too obvious, and something of a simplification. Nevertheless, it is important that essential distinctions be noted. For many years there has been movement in India to establish a system of land reform, principally land redistribution. Political parties, including both the Old and to a greater extent the New Congress Parties have publicly approved of this policy, and laws have even been passed to this effect in many states. The distribution has only been partially carried out, principally because, through design or inadvertance, the bureaucracy has been put in a position to "interpret" the law and, at times, frustrate its nominal end. Of course, this frustration may have been with the connivance of parts of the legislature.[13] The point here is that policy-making and policy implementation are not the same, but are two different forms of power.

Let us first look at the case of bureaucratic elites shifting to political elites. This would be illustrated by civil servants in Malaysia becoming elected officials in the national legislature or in America by career military officers resigning or retiring to run for office. There is little if any reason to believe that such integration, where it occurs at the high levels of a major organization, has a significant negative effect on complexity (though it may have other unfortunate consequences). Complexity is not lessened in the bureaucracy because, at the higher levels of a bureaucracy, as mentioned earlier, there is by definition no place to go but to the political elite. In other words, the new position cannot be seen as in any way a substitute for a parallel bureaucratic one. Nor is a bureaucratic position being eliminated. The complexity of the bureaucratic organization—its subdivision and specialization—is not affected.[14]

The situation changes, however, when considering the case of elite movement at levels below the highest. Here, complexity would be severely damaged. The advantages of complexity are, first, that the institution is better able to stand strains by virtue of redundancy, and second and even more importantly, that it permits the development of expertise, social and technical, and the regularization of procedures.

The advantages of redundancy will be discussed below when autonomy and elite integration are discussed. Here, the emphasis is on the deleterious effect on complexity of elite integration between bureaucratic and political institutions. Knowledge specific to an organization and necessary for its effectiveness requires sustained membership. This is less so for its technical aspects (which in at least some cases can be learned easily and quickly enough), than for what has been described above as the social knowledge of an organization. Not only would the person entering from the outside lack this information, but the organization itself would, by virtue of its disruption, have less of this social knowledge to give—it would be less structured and regularized. This takes us back to the principles earlier discussed, that complexity requires vertical elite integration, and a violation of this principle results in a decline of institutionalization.[15]

Huntington describes what happens when an effective civil service is rapidly expanded by new members: the organization loses its capacity to carry on its work; it decays.[16] Huntington discusses this in terms of the institution's loss of coherence, and indeed it does lose its coherence. The point being added here is that not only the morale of the institution is destroyed by such an influx, but so is its muscle. The new members lack the technical and social knowledge necessary for their work, and even if they could agree on the functional limits of the organization and on the methods of resolving disputes, and even if their morale was of the highest, the organization would still decay simply through a lessening of administrative competence. Even if the new entrants are themselves elites of other organizations, though the situation would be somewhat—even substantially—better, the essential problem would remain.

There have been many examples of such decay in the process of decolonization. Probably the most striking case was that of Pakistan in 1947. The British-established Indian Civil Service was one of the great civil services of history. By 1947, the majority of its elite were native to the subcontinent, but only a minority were Muslim and only a portion of this minority went to Pakistan. New members—mostly drawn from the elite of the organizationally separate provincial civil services—were brought in, but the organization's capacity declined. The same decline occurred when elements of the military bureaucracy moved into political positions a decade later.

Coherence

Turning to elite integration and coherence, the same general pattern is noted: the effect of elite movement from bureaucratic institutions to political institutions, or vice versa, lowers the level of institutionalization. Concerning the aspect of coherence involving the procedures for the settling of disputes, no specific method is being referred to, nor is the effectiveness of a method in the sense of its functional effectiveness involved. The question is simply whether there is agreement as to the method by those who are most influential in an organization.

Of course, it is possible to imagine a situation where a method of settling disputes was accepted within an organization, but resulted in a decline in the organization's effectiveness in mediating social forces. In point of fact, one could argue that the entire pre-modern system of aristocratic privileges by birth was an nonrational method of solving disputes as to who should own what land and occupy what seats of power.[17] It was better than no system, but it was less satisfactory than the more bureaucratic or democratic systems that replaced it.

Probably the most damaging effect of political-bureaucratic elite integration on cohesion concerns the elaborate system of rules and procedures that almost all large bureaucracies have. The elaboration of these rules and procedures for dispute settlement is much better established within organizations than between or among them. Where members of an organization have a reasonable expectation of leaving their own organization, and do so, it is much more likely that disputes will overspill the organization's boundaries into less-structured areas.[18]

This situation is often noted where the personnel procedures of a school district, though well defined, are readily subject to appeal to an elected school board, upon which are found former teachers and students of the school system. In such circumstances, conflicts concerning promotion and other personnel matters frequently enter the larger political system with consequent decline in school morale and general effectiveness.

To state the principle more bluntly: if individuals in an organization can profit by frustrating the rules of that organization by going outside its jurisdiction, they will do so. This will happen more frequently when those in a bureaucratic organization see themselves as in that organization only temporarily, and when former members are in the superior external organization. There can be no agreed upon procedures for settling disputes without authority for making those procedures apply consistently. Without such a proximate source of authority, the coherence and morale of an institution rapidly decline.

In fact, such lack of authority and high elite mobility are very rare. Elites of the bureaucratic and the political institutions seldom actually change positions. This is not to say that conflicts between political elites and bureaucratic elites are not common, and violation of the autonomy of the bureaucracy does not occur and does not result in a decline in cohesion. It does. The situation of the Indian Army when Krishna Menon was minister of defense, the army's decline in elite morale, even before the Chinese punitive expedition of 1961, and the case of the U.S. State Department under McCarthyite pressure are examples of decline in cohesion due to political pressure; they are not examples of elite integration, because there was no major exchange or movement of elites.[19]

The other aspect of coherence concerns the setting of limits on functional boundaries—those functional boundaries within sectors (within the bureaucratic division of the government and within the political division). In both sectors, there are very few completely parallel, or redundant, organizations. There is one post office, one social security bureau. There may be other ways to get parcels or mail from one place to another and there are institutions other than the Social Security Administration to take care of one in old age, but not within the government.

Whereas such organizations are not redundant, they do overlap (marginal redundancy) and conflict, especially as new areas of authority arise. There may only be one armed force in a state, but its components will vie as to whether a mission is carried out by the army or the navy. The same conflicts occur within and between the components of the civil bureaucracy. Similarly, in the political area, where rival legislative branches, and particularly the executive and the legislature, will be in conflict. This is especially the case in presidential systems, but exists in parliamentary systems as well.[20]

The clash of social forces is frequently—in fact, usually—reflected in institutional conflict. In a politically developed system, this institutional conflict is a method of shifting the clash of social forces into the political arena, mediating and perhaps resolving or at least alleviating them. The American Civil War, of course, is an outstanding case where social forces became associated with certain institutional concepts involving the practice of federalism. The question here is, however, whether movement of elites between the bureaucratic and political institutions damages or enhances the institutions' ability to set functional limits internally.

Initially, it would seem that that elite movement—elite integration—would lower the intensity of the conflict, though at the same time weakening the regular procedures necessary for its resolution. The problem here, unlike most of the earlier examples, is especially difficult to solve because there is relatively little empirical evidence to guide us. Exchange of elites between the bureaucracy and political institutions is not characteristic of stable developed polities. Thus, it is difficult to ascertain whether when this exchange occurs (as when political elites become high officers in the military during war, especially civil war) it is causative or reflective of a larger breakdown. What evidence and theory there is suggests that such elite integration would be harmful if it precedes a breakdown, but there is very little evidence that it often does.[21]

Where there is a history of bureaucratic, particularly military, officers becoming political leaders, the functional boundaries of that organization tend to break down. The institutions are consequently less capable of mediating social forces because the procedures for mediating this type of conflict are not regularized and so do not evoke discipline within the organization. The damage is particularly severe on the receiving institution—on the political elites. If agreements and procedures settled upon by them are likely to be overturned by the inclusion of what will be hostile elites, they cannot function effectively.

But again it must be noted that such situations in developing polities are not very common and occur when the breakdown of cohesion has already taken place. It is important to note, however, that the breakdown in cohesion is most evident in the receiving (here, the political) institutions, and the sending (the police or military) generally are reacting to a concern that the coherence (and autonomy) of their social sector is threatened. They see the established methods of conflict resolution as already inadequate, and so the threat, if not the actual use, of force is likely to be invoked to meet the larger crisis. The elite integration—the coup of a military or the much milder instance of a police chief running for office—is very often an effort to restore the essential effectiveness of the system, not to destroy it. Looked at from a different perspective, these violations of societal coherence may be seen as attempts to establish or, better said, reestablish, the coherence (morale, boundaries, conflict resolution procedures) of the "aggressing" institution. In other words, what appears to be political decay might actually be the response of a part of a system to arrest that decay.

It is necessary to adopt a configurational approach with emphasis on the temporal relation between cohesion violation by, say, the military and subsequent coherence deterioration. If a situation of low morale, poor internal conflict resolution, and poor boundary delineation precedes the type of elite integration we have just been discussing, then it is reasonable to say that the elite integration involved is an attempt to reestablish an effective political system, including its coherence.[22]

Looking at the historical record, one notes that coherence violation cases of elite integration have occurred when an outside agency has suddenly forced a major change in the political system, and though it may not be in crisis, the former continuity has been broken. The most outstanding and recent example has been during the period just after decolonization, where cohesion-violating elite integration has been quite common and much commented upon by Huntington, among others.[23] Other examples of elite integration across bureaucratic lines are less specific to a particular country or time. The military has moved into power in many states—Turkey,[24] Korea,[25] Pakistan[26]—because the morale, functional boundaries, and conflict resolution procedures of the state have already decayed. The movement of military here is not a cause of lack of coherence, but a response to it. This relation is generally quite obvious to all participants, but less so at a distance, particularly when viewed in terms of normative anti-military, anti-police prejudgments.

It should be added that damaging as such a movement may be in certain cases, it is preferable in terms of stability and effectiveness to a mass movement into the institutionalized area. The elites at least are technically skilled in governance, enjoy some social skills, and in most cases have been somewhat socialized into the previous political system.

Autonomy

The effect on the autonomy of bureaucratic organizations when substantial numbers of their elites—at all levels—move on to political positions and become political elites will be examined first. Obviously, this type of mobility damages the essential procedural elements of a bureaucracy's well-being, even threatening its existence. The regular procedures for promotion, carrying on work, etc.—indeed, the very ethos of a bureaucracy—require its members to make a commitment for much of their lifespan and to look toward that organization for their career satisfaction. The bureaucracy, to protect these procedures and expertise, sets up barriers of various sorts against the political system—to some extent rationality and expertise are valued not only for their worth in getting the bureaucracy's job done, but also for their effectiveness in preventing extrabureaucratic involvement.

Where a member of the bureaucratic elite looks outside the organization to institutions more closely attuned to and affected by social forces, he will likely adjust his behavior while still in the bureaucratic organization to those forces at the expense of bureaucratic values.[27] The social forces thus penetrate directly into the bureaucratic system, lessening or even eliminating that institution's capacity to mediate those social forces. In point of fact, this lessening of autonomy coincides with or soon follows a lessening of institutional coherence. A case of this sort can be seen in examining the various regulatory boards and institutions in the United States. Members of these institutions frequently leave these boards to accept positions in the industries they regulate and often run for elective office later. The effect is not disastrous on the system, but few would deny that this type of elite movement is damaging to the board's autonomy and effectiveness in mediating the social forces that conflict in the regulation of industry.

Another autonomy-decreasing effect of bureaucratic-political elite integration concerns the rise in political pressure that accompanies such integration. Of course, most political scientists and historians are familiar with the "house of cards" or "rotten house" analogy, in which some political institution or political system collapses under the first strains put upon it. The analogy is a false one in the great majority of cases because there are very few instances where important institutions are not under constant stress. The government of Tokugawa Japan may be appropriate to the falling house of cards metaphor (but even here only in terms of exotic pressures).

By and large, however, most institutions are under a variety of pressures, and this certainly includes autonomy-threatening action by the political institutions on bureaucratic elites. Nevertheless, the bureaucratic institutions, like other social organisms, have a limit to what they can tolerate, not only in crisis terms (due to a sudden onslaught, as the U.S. State Department suffered in the late 1940s and early 1950s), but also to steady pressure, such as a police force would have to contend with if operating under an elected government influenced by organized crime.

Where members of the bureaucratic elite are also, at several levels, prospective recruits for the political elite, the pressures on this bureaucratic elite will be greater. How this type of elite integration would weaken the bureaucratic organization's capacity to resist attacks on its autonomy has already been discussed. The combination of its weakness, the attraction of that weakness, and the prospective involvement (the expectation of this involvement) of the bureaucratic elite in the political elite would be a potent combination. In fact, competing political elites would feel impelled under such circumstances to exercise themselves in influencing the bureaucratic elite through such conventional political means as offering rewards and sanctions for adjusting bureaucratic action—in promotion and policy application—to their demands. Before long, the autonomy of the bureaucratic elite would be deeply compromised, coherence would decline, complexity would weaken, autonomy would lessen, and the capacity for adaptation would be nearly eliminated.

The penetration of social forces into the fabric of the bureaucracy follows quickly behind the breakdown of bureaucratic-political elite differentiation. Bureaucratic organizations do not have the capacity—the temperamental resiliency, the organizational flexibility—to mediate these conflicts once they have entered into their own structure. Especially, they do not have the capacity to bring in the new elites of these new social forces. The need for technical qualifications and social knowledge of the organization prevent the elites from being rapidly given commensurate positions; in some cases, it is difficult for them to enter at all. This situation is illustrated by the continuing disruption in many urban school systems in the United States. In New York City particularly, the bureaucratic elite—the principals and other high administrative positions—is the liaison between the bureaucracy (the teachers) and the policy-making elite (especially the Board of Education). In the clash between the social force of Black demands for greater authority and the desire of the existing bureaucracy (dominated by non-Blacks) to resist, the penetration of political elements has had the effect of weakening and disrupting a school system that already had severe social problems.[28]

The effect on political elite autonomy of political-bureaucratic elite integration is similar, though not so extreme. Where members of the bureaucratic elite enter the political elite through established institutions and methods, the loss of autonomy may be only marginal. The institutions are maintained and the political elite, though perhaps weakened, is not replaced.

A striking example of this situation can be found in the comparison of France and the United States in crises in the mid-twentieth century. In the United States in the early 1950s and in France in the mid-1950s, there was a substantial demand for a major change in leadership. In both countries, the figure having the most political support was a general, a leader in World War II. In France, it was DeGaulle; in the United States, it was Eisenhower. The American political system made it possible, due to the party structure being open at the highest levels to extrapolitical elites, for Eisenhower to be brought in. This was done, of course, by his being given the Republican Party's nomination for the presidency. Although there was some criticism of a career military man being nominated for the presidency, there was no constitutional or political crisis. Even—perhaps especially—within the Republican Party, there was little significant resentment at an outsider being chosen. A tradition of elite integration and the mechanism for doing it permitted the political system to function effectively. On the other hand, France had no peaceful legal tradition or mechanism for bringing a major military figure having political support into the political system at a high level. Consequently, France had to disrupt its political process for a time and even came near to civil war.

Where such well-institutionalized patterns of political-bureaucratic elite integration do not exist, the bureaucracy becomes, by virtue of its double position of elite supplier and implementer of policies (the latter capacity declining) an element that the political elite must contend with, to some extent on its own terms. Generally, the political elite is dominant, but at times agreements worked out on the political level are subject, from inception to completion, to the effects of bureaucratic veto and adjustment.[29]

The situation is worse than it would first appear, however. The bureaucracy, disrupted in its procedures and political now in its orientation, is not a reliable partner for negotiation. Institutionalization has declined, and the political system as a whole is inadequate for what becomes greater demands calling on lessening capacities.

It is difficult to offer examples of a situation where an initially effective political system is tied to an inadequate bureaucratic system, which then pulls both down. In fact, political systems are so interrelated in terms of their policy-making/policy-administering components that both tend to improve or degenerate together. One could argue that perhaps certain advisory circles in the period in France[30] and Russia[31] just before their revolutions, when enlightened policies were enacted but not implemented, fit the situation of adequate policy elites combined with inadequate administration.

Adaptation

Adaptation is the fourth and final criterion that will be looked at in terms of bureaucratic-political elite integration. We will examine this criterion in some detail due to the fact that it is highly reflective of the other criteria (coherence, complexity, and autonomy) as well as being notable in its own terms. This criterion will be analyzed in three dimensions: chronological age, generational age, and functional age.

CHRONOLOGICAL AGE

In the earlier discussion of chronological age, it was indicated that the advantage of chronologically old institutions in adaptation was to a significant degree due to characteristics of their elite members. One pertinent characteristic—though undoubtedly not the sole one—was that there was a correspondence between older institutions and older elites, especially at the higher levels. Older elites, on the average, tended to have developed the skills that facilitated adaptation.

It is thus now appropriate to turn our attention to the age structure of those elites who shift from the bureaucratic to the political elites. If the shift only takes place among the very top, who will also tend to be the very oldest, the effect on the bureaucracy will be minor. Although the fact of elite integration here will to some extent be associated with diffusion and will consequently damage the political elite's autonomy, cohesion, coherence, and, hence, autonomy, this effect will be limited by the small numbers involved. It will also be limited because the new elites will be socialized into the political system as a whole, and, by virtue of their long relation to the political elite, being marginally socialized into that elite as well.

In developed polities, the shift, when it does occur, is at the higher levels. In France and the United States, for example, it will only by the very highest officers and leaders—a DeGaulle or an Eisenhower—who makes this shift, rarely majors or lieutenant colonels. In less-developed systems, the situation, like most other matters in systems that are underdeveloped, is more diffuse. Not only do high officials—principally military—make a shift as General Amin in Uganda or General Ayub in Pakistan, but lower-level and less-socialized officials do the same. There are not only coups by generals, but by colonels and majors as well. Batista of Cuba was only a sergeant when he led his coup, and Lumumba of the Belgian Congo was a mere postal clerk.

The capacity of the bureaucracy and the political elite to adjust to new demands and to maintain their organization in unstable times is consequently lessened by this political-bureaucratic mobility. Armed forces wherein this sort of integration occurs become less suitable for not only facing new military challenges but also for adapting to new roles, such as counterinsurgency and national development. Civil bureaucracies are likewise weakened, and corruption—both political and economic—is encouraged, which may be functional and even an indication of a measure of adaptability, but at least in the short run lessens the institution's capacity to meet new demands. The political institutions behave likewise. Political institutions such as the legislatures and the institutionalized political parties are unable to form stable governments capable of enacting new and appropriate laws when their elite structures are constantly being disrupted by the direct entry of the military into politics, or the presence of a highly politicized bureaucracy.[32]

It is now clearer why the oldest continuing polities such as the United States, Switzerland, or the United Kingdom are marked by low levels of bureaucratic-political elite integration. They are old because they are adaptable, and this adaptability requires not only a formal differentiation, but also a substantive dimension of low bureaucratic-political elite integration.

GENERATIONAL AGE

The second dimension of institutional adaptation, its generational age, is an even more complex topic. Both political and bureaucratic organizations require continuing procedures to replace each generation of leaders as it moves on. Let us look at the political elite's problems here in light of bureaucratic-political elite integration. Generational replacement operates on the same principles as does promotion: the protege and the formal key institution link system. Of course, violent revolution is also a method of generational replacement, but, aside from it being, despite its drama, not very common, it, too, in fact, is conditioned by previous institutional and personnel histories. More to our point, it is the avoidance of such violent replacement that we have accepted as our norm, and is consequently to be viewed as an instance of the breakdown in institutionalization, not an example of it.

Where the generational transition takes place in a context of high bureaucratic-political elite integration, the protege[33] system will typically involve a mentor in the political elites and a protege in the bureaucratic. Each works within his own organization but each bears a special relation—albeit an indirect one—to the other organization in terms of favors given and received. The obligation is typically higher from the bureaucratic to the political. For the relationship to be significant to the participants, in their own self-interest, and to us, for the purposes of this book, the normal procedures that would exist between them if they were not protege and mentor must at times be suspended. Otherwise there would be no purpose to such a relationship.

These rewards of a characteristic bureaucratic-political relation are generally of an informational and priority nature. That is, the two individuals give each other types of information and preferences that they would not normally give their protege or mentor's counterparts. This type of exchange enhances the position of each—especially that of the protege because he usually, though not always, has relatively less to give. Typically, the favors will also extend to other types of direct aid, such as discrimination in promotions and treatment of policy decisions—giving some greater priority or perhaps frustrating others. On a small scale, such a relationship may be functional in carrying on business.

To the extent that this system is vigorous and widespread, however, it is highly violative of established bureaucratic norms. The bureaucratic elite member (the protege) does not look to his own organization for advancement, and his loyalty does not lie there. He is to a substantial degree an agent of a portion of the political system, and the autonomy of the bureaucracy is consequently proportionally lessened. Furthermore, the effect of this relationship, when it is common enough to have an impact on the system, is likely to be known. Morale consequently declines. In the fullest form of such a protege system, it is expected that the protege will enter the political elite himself.[34]

This mentor-protege system is especially common in societies where rewards are based principally on ascriptive considerations. Here proteges are selected on the basis of family, racial, or regional ties. Prussia in the eighteenth century and Tokugawa Japan are two such cases.[35] But the most common instance today, as elsewhere in much of this analysis, is in newer polities, involving the military and other bureaucracies of force. High members of the Soviet political elite have such proteges in the secret services, and Krishna Menon, it was feared by some, was attempting to establish such preferential links with certain elements of the Indian armed forces.[36]

The other method of generational replacement, the key institutional link system, is less common for bureaucratic-political linkage. As will be discussed in Chapter 5, all developed (and most less-developed) political systems have certain routes for advancement defined in institutional terms. They may be more or less rigid, but they are discernable everywhere. In the United States, the path to the presidency is generally from the Congress to the presidency today, or from a governorship to the presidency.[37] An ambitious politician would do well to avoid, in most cases, city positions or even cabinet-level posts. In Britain, the route to the prime ministership necessarily involves the Parliament, subcabinet posts, and then cabinet posts.[38] In India, high positions are reached almost invariably through achieving influential state-level positions first.[39] In China, certain posts in the Chinese Communist Party are essential.[40]

If these positions can be bypassed or only held nominally, the normal course of promotion is short-circuited. The inclusion of new positions—bureaucratic here—vitally changes it. The political system, if so integrated into the bureaucracy in terms of key institutions for advancement, loses an element of its autonomy, and the method of selecting new leaders—making generational transition—becomes more difficult. It becomes more difficult, simply, because it is now integrally related to an external system—the bureaucracy. The process is consequently less regularized; more factors have to be taken into account; and, since the bureaucratic member has been largely outside the political elite structure (in close contact perhaps with only one or a few of its members), less is known about him. Where the political system has a substantial number of such entrants, it is consequently much more likely that force and other forms of direct coercion rather than regularized procedures will enter in this selection and even treatment as part of the process of generational renewal. Normative considerations aside, force is obviously disruptive to organizational stability.

The situation in terms of the bureaucracy is even more difficult. Political elites, though institutionalized in terms of procedures for generational renewal, are inherently more flexible in bringing in new elites for generational renewal than are bureaucracies. Bureaucracies require not only regular, but explicit and time-consuming procedures for determining promotion. Where there is a constant movement of members between the bureaucratic and political elite structures, the characteristic bureaucratic methods of elite selection are severely damaged, if not eliminated.

A situation of high bureaucratic political elite integration may be described thus: promotion in the bureaucracy is determined to a major degree not only by the acquisition of certain skills, long service in the organization, loyalty to organizational leaders, and occupying key positions in terms of the bureaucracy's function: it is greatly influenced by certain relations with extra-bureaucratic elites. Bureaucratic elites will be promoted on the basis, first, of whether they have as a mentor outside the bureaucracy and who it is. As the more senior generation moves on, the influence of political elite members would be decisive in choosing new members, as with postings. Certain subinstitutions, certain offices of the bureaucracy, would be considered as crucial to advancement in the bureaucracy and would be under special political elite influence. Elements of the bureaucratic elite, depending on the closeness of the relationship to the political elite, would move on to policy-making political institutions as elites.

Clearly, the situation described here is one of low bureaucratic autonomy with presumably low coherence. Its complexity may be high, but it is to be expected that its adaptability will be low. In terms of the present discussion, however, its effectiveness in generating new elites will depend on certain factors external to the entire elite structure.

In periods of general social stability, the political-bureaucratic elite integration system may be a stable one. Although promotion and generational renewal will be more difficult (because of the greater number of external pressures), an effective and integrated political elite can make the generational renewal adequate in its bureaucratic counterpart. Effectiveness and morale in the bureaucracy will be less satisfactory than in an autonomous system, but such relations have and do occur with frequency, and the political system as a whole does not collapse nor is it even vitally damaged.

Examples are most to be found in undeveloped polities, such as that of eighteenth-century Britain or contemporary Nepal.[41] In developed polities, especially those where the political elite is under severe stress, the political-bureaucratic elite integration as discussed tends to the decline and demoralization of the bureaucratic system, and particularly toward its near breakdown when an old generation is passing away. An example here is that of urban areas of the United States. These areas have passed through two crises in the past century. The first was in the late nineteenth century with the development of industry and high immigration, especially from Europe. The other crisis is that beginning in the late 1950s and still continuing, also associated with a heavy urban influx of migrants (Blacks from the South) and, conversely, the decline of urban-based industry.[42]

During both crises, there has been a high degree, relatively speaking, of bureaucratic and political elite integration. In the late nineteenth century, there was a strong relationship between the politicians (political elite) and the police and other key city employees (bureaucratic elite). Protege systems, often based on ethnic and family considerations, and key institution links (police precinct captain, and the various officials responsible for allocating city contracts) were the heart of politics. Police seldom moved directly into political positions, but good service in key patronage-associated positions in the bureaucracy were rewarded with political appointments and influence. This system had certain advantages in integrating new elites into the political system, though that end was achieved at the expense of bureaucratic effectiveness and probably at the expense of certain liberal norms.

By the turn of the century, a reform movement had developed to better institutionalize the bureaucracy through civil service procedures, and this tendency continued into the next great urban political crisis, that of the 1960s.

In this period, the autonomy of the civil service made it in many areas difficult for a generational transition to take place between the older, predominantly white ethnic elite, and the new generation of Blacks. In this case, once again, the attempt of political elites to mediate the social forces involved resulted in incursions into the promotion and generational renewal system of the bureaucracy, especially in the schools and the police. It may be argued that such incursions are necessary in the larger cause of overall system stability and effectiveness, but there can be little doubt that the immediate effect has been to lessen the bureaucracy's adaptability and cohesion.[43]

FUNCTIONAL AGE

Another continuing problem of renewal that large institutions face is that of functional change, the periodic necessity of an institution to take up a new mission, a new job. In relating political-bureaucratic elite integration to this capacity of functional change we will look first at the political elite.

Of course, the essential function of the political elite as a whole, and, indeed, of any part of it, cannot change and still be designated as the political elite. The political elite must continue to make policy and mediate social forces, or it becomes something else. What we are referring to here is not the essential change of function, but (1) how the forces are mediated—e.g., the use of majoritarian procedures, the development of political parties, the manipulation of public opinion (another phrase for this quality of adaptation is "institutional innovation"); and (2) what groups are mediated—the middle class, working class, mountain people, organized labor, previously excluded tribal groups, etc. This dimension may refer to the scope of the mediation, but also refers to specific groups mediated. It is possible for an institution to adapt by excluding groups as well as by expanding—though expansion has been more the norm in the modern era. Institutional elites that reject a vital new group—as the British Liberal Party did organized labor—or refuse to develop or accept institutional innovation—as several European monarchies refused to accept any form of parliamentarianism in the early nineteenth century—fail to adapt and are greatly weakened or destroyed.

Institutional innovation by majoritarian political parties was characteristic of the nineteenth century, but has been less so in the twentieth. Where such institutional innovation has occurred, it has been preceded by major social stresses. The principal innovation in the twentieth century has been the development of highly disciplined, highly organized authoritarian conspiratorial or semi-conspiratorial organizations, the principal model being that of the Communist Party.[44] Earlier examples of major institutional innovation has been the development of parliamentary government and participatory political parties.[45] Until this century, there has been a steady growth of institutions mediating social forces through the use of majoritarian principles, develution of authority on legislative and executive committees, and the use of political parties for the purposes of public aggregation and articulation.

These developments—the parliamentary constitutional ones of the past and the tightly organized authoritarian ones of this century—proceeded with a close correspondence between their respective bureaucratic and political elites. This is not to say that the two always cooperated, but that the same social pressures affected both and so both were in constant reaction not only to one another, but to these social forces. The same process of evolutionary institutional innovation has occurred many times in the past, in the development of the classical empires, and in the development of European feudalism. It is a process that continues today—in a less dramatic fashion—in such institutional innovations as the ombudsman[46] in the developed European nations or in the *panchayati raj* system in India.

What is the effect of bureaucratic-political elite integration on this process of institutional innovation? The answer is a rather anticlimactic one, but probably is that political-bureaucratic elite integration has very little effect on this type of institutional innovation.

It may be argued that the effect is considerable, though indirect, because of the general weakening of all political institutions that accompanies—as we earlier demonstrated—political-bureaucratic elite integration. This is a plausible argument, but not a conclusive one. There is good reason to believe that smooth transition of a political elite from one institutional form of mediation to another, from one type of clientele to another, is impossible.[47] There are apparent limits to people's social capacities, limits imposed by their history and limits imposed by their very nature. Obviously, the author does believe that people can adjust and improve their social environment and can create more politically developed states. If it were not so believed, a book of this nature would not be written. However, to say that people are in control of their political fate is not to say that they are in absolute control; it is not to say that though battles may be won, they may be won without cost.

In fact, successful institutional innovation can only come out of circumstances in which the previous institutional arrangements have completely or nearly completely failed. This is not an argument for institutions' failing, far from it. What it is is an acknowledgement that the elites of societies are not likely to make major changes at high risk where these changes are not forced upon them.

Arnold Toynbee and Barrington Moore, Jr., two rather dissimilar historians, both note that societies in major crisis and on the point of social change are often better off in terms of future government effectiveness if they suffer a major breakdown rather than piecemeal reform and adaptation.[48] The relative smoothness of the Japanese[49] and Prussian shifts from a feudalistic to an industrial form of society were both at relatively low initial but at high eventual cost—later paid in mass suffering through war and fascism. The same situation may be occurring in India.[50] Certainly the parliamentary system of government in its modern form and even the establishment of imperial hegemony in much of the world grew largely out of a breakdown of earlier systems of bureaucratic and political elite integration. This type of strife and suffering may be greatly modified by an understanding of its dynamics, but it must remain an open question as to whether it may be eliminated.

Another form of functional adaptability of political institutions and elites concerns the clientele of politics—those whose interests are to be mediated.

First, a distinction between mediating an interest of a new group, and actually letting members of that group into the elite—a distinction between elite responsiveness and elite integration—must be noted. There are cases of an elite noting the demands of a group in a society and going a considerable distance toward satisfying those demands without letting members of that group into the elite. This has occurred in many colonial areas—such as in the former Belgian Congo—wherein a colonial elite has often taken genuine note and care with popular interest and demands without letting members of the subject group make a significant entry into the elite.[51]

Conversely, there are cases where leaders of excluded groups are co-opted into the ruling elite, with little regard to the welfare of their parent group. This is the so-called Uncle Tom or tokenism technique, perhaps used by the French in Algeria.[52] The two techniques just described are in fact not so dissimilar from one another as they are from the type that most concerns us: the inclusion of new elites representing new social forces in the political elite.

This last described technique is in fact the most common. In the first place, the established elite will only take new members who will be of some use to it. It will take pre-established elites from previously unrepresented groups—and the new elite member not only will have established himself by building a clientele in his own group but will have to tend this clientele to maintain it. In cases of significant social pressure by such a group, an Uncle Tom solution will not be effective. Where the pressure is slight, there is little incentive for the existing elite to let new members in; where it is greater, they must let in a member who will have influence over his own clientele.

It is important to note that political elites expand under pressure; they do not expand by members looking about for new groups to exploit. The major expansion of elites in the West—entrance of middle-class and later organized labor—obviously came after these groups pressed their claims, not before; such was also the case with the opening of the U.S. political elite to Blacks in the middle decades of the twentieth century. A similar analysis can be made for the limited inclusion of Untouchables in the Indian political elite.[53] In other words, the group involved was politicized well before its members achieved elite status.

An apparent exception here is the case of those who sought to politicize a group—Blacks in the early twentieth century, laborers in the late eighteenth, peasants in much of the twentieth—and ride, or lead to political power, a social movement involving that group. In the first place, those involved in politicization at this stage are not themselves elites, but individuals wishing to be elites. At most, they are counter-elites. Second, in the rare cases where a previous elite is overthrown, the new elite is notorious for either rapidly selling out to the previous power structure, or for ruthlessly exploiting their original supporters in the name of some ideal.

Where the bureaucratic elite supplies members to the political elite, it can assist the process of the political elite widening its membership only if those it contributes are from the previously excluded group. To some extent, the political elite in the United States was expanded by ethnics using the bureaucracy—especially in the cities in the late nineteenth and early twentieth centuries—to rise.[54]

Conversely, a bureaucratic-political elite integration system can damage social mediation where the political elite prevents entry into the bureaucracy from politically socialized but unrepresented groups. The political elite—in cooperation with higher members of the bureaucracy—can do this by requiring a certain social background, or specialized schooling acquired at an early age. The British higher civil service may be an example of this exclusion, though its members have very rarely gone directly into the political elite. A dominant group in a government can carry on the same exclusion on ethnic grounds, as when the leader of Pakistan before that country's partition effectively kept Bengalis out of the armed forces.

The actual situation that obtains is associated principally with the previous extent of political development in the polity. In underdeveloped states, the principal method of stable entry into politics is the protege system. The political elite, dominated as it is by ascriptive factors, will have chosen its proteges on these factors as well. Consequently, little can be expected in the way of new groups entering the elite through political-bureaucratic elite integration. This situation is illustrated by the family-oriented protege system in present-day Nepal[55] and also by the caste/communal-connected or caste/ communal-oriented protege system in village politics in India.[56]

Where the polity is somewhat more developed, there will be a greater latitude for previously excluded elites to enter the bureaucratic elite, and hence enter the political elite, where political-bureaucratic elite integration exists. There is a point in the development of many states where the bureaucracy is modern and developed enough to let in new groups, but the system is still undeveloped and undifferentiated enough to permit elite transfer from the bureaucracy to the political areas. In such societies, the bureaucracy is often very much the home of ambitious and aggressive individuals, rather than the "weak career choice" it becomes later in the polity's history.[57] In such polities, the security services—the army in Egypt (lower-middle class), the secret services in the Soviet Union (non-Great Russians)—may especially serve as a point of entrance for formerly excluded groups.

Although there are further exceptions (the role of the Germanic levies in the Roman armed forces is a classic example), by and large bureaucracies do not serve as an efficient means of political elite adaptation in terms of bringing in new groups. The situations when such elite integration may take place are not very common, but where such political-bureaucratic elite integration does exist, and where the bureaucracy has been opened to previously excluded groups, it can be very effective.

The effect of political-bureaucratic elite integration on the adaptation of bureaucratic elites is not much different from its effect on its political counterparts. Bureaucratic elites are even more constrained with regard to institutional innovation than are political elites. The creation of new bureaucracies is almost exclusively within the capacity of the political elite—whether a new farmers' aid bureau or a new type of security force, the decision and authority for its foundation must come from the political elite. Bureaucratic elites may often resist such innovation. When faced with a clear necessity—a demand from the political elite, itself reacting to pressure—the bureaucratic elite generally prefers to have the new function carried on by existing organizations.[58] This is a method of preserving influence and control, of course, but in our terms it is a preference for coherence over complexity.[59] Two examples from this century are the U.S. State Department's desire to retain control of intelligence activities rather than permit the establishment of a Central Intelligence Agency in the late 1940s, and the desire of the U.S. army at about the same time to retain control over the air force. These are cases of innovation-limitation policies.

A second characteristic of bureaucracies under pressure is that of innovation prevention. Although bureaucracies are notorious for growth, or empire-building, within the confines of their institutional structures, civil bureaucracies seldom are very favorable to major innovational expansion—as, for example, the nationalization of industry or the institution of new types of welfare programs. Similarly, professional soldiers are seldom in favor of major wars. In both cases, the risk to the bureaucratic elite—which is already established—is too great.

Consequently, bureaucracies are rarely able to innovate by creating new institutions if they so desired, and also rarely desire to do so in any event. Only rarely does political-bureaucratic elite integration make any difference in this general situation. In a situation of high political-bureaucratic elite integration, a different sort of person—politically oriented and ambitious—is likely to be attracted to the bureaucracy rather than the more cautious type. Temperamentally, such an individual will be more likely to be innovative and build his own empire.[60]

Innovation takes place here most commonly in periods of social stress. This is not only the case with armed forces—where the innovation is usually during and just before war—but in civil agencies as well, such as the development of various new bureaucracies in time of economic depression. Even here, however, the institutional innovation came very little from the bureaucratic elite.[61]

Bureaucracies have a better adaptive record with regard to admitting new elites—elites from previously excluded groups. This has been particularly the case where there has been a civil service "merit" system. Mention has already been made of the role of the military bureaucracy in many formerly colonial areas in admitting formerly marginal groups. The civil bureaucracy has also served the same function even in an earlier stage of development.

The integration of ethnic groups in the United States in the late nineteenth and twentieth centuries was to a significant extent mediated through non-civil service urban bureaucracies. A less-known example would be the various groups, previously excluded by the Hindu *kshatriya* ruling caste that the Mughals brought into their bureaucracy. In much of North India, for example, a sub-caste called the *kayastha,* of middle to low status, was brought into the lower levels of the Mughal bureaucracy, particularly as village accountants, and it time rose in prestige, until in modern India one of their members, Lal Bahadur Shastri, became Prime Minister.

In very many cases, however, it should be noted that though much of the bureaucracy, and even much of its elite structure, may be opened to previously excluded groups, very often the very top positions are reserved for the previous elite. This was the case with the opening of the British civil service in the nineteenth century and remains the case with the Japanese Tokyo University-dominated bureaucracy. Of course, the bureaucracy that has acquired the major reputation for admitting new elites and "sending them on" to political elite status has been the military. By and large, however, the higher—and in most cases the lower as well—officer corps is strongly reflective of political elite features and is not likely to admit previously excluded members to its elite. The Pakistani army, as previously noted, discriminated against non-Punjabis just as the political elite did, and the U.S. navy tended to favor groups of higher social standing, especially those of Western and Northern European extraction.

In fact, though exceptions are more dramatic, high political-bureaucratic elite integration is more characteristic of situations where the bureaucracy and political elites are socially integrated than where they are not. Political and bureaucratic elites tend to be homogeneous in terms of groups represented in all but a few polities. In short, political-bureaucratic elite integration can play and has played a significant role in adaptation through the admission of new groups, but this role has been fairly uncommon.

In summarizing the effect of bureaucratic-political elite integration on adaptability, the primary stress is that such integration is fairly uncommon. By the time a society has developed a substantial bureaucracy as a specialized unit, the differentiation has generally extended to the prevention of movement of elites between the components. Where it has occurred—in the time period between the establishment of a bureaucracy and its differentiation in elite terms, or during periods of severe social stress—the impact, though notable, has not necessarily been great.

Chronological age is one of the measures of adaptability. As noted earlier, political-bureaucratic elite integration, where it takes place, may mimic a situation of a chronologically old institution by adding elite bureaucratic members (who will tend to be older given bureaucracies' emphasis on seniority) into a political elite that may be younger. This is a marginal and infrequent relationship. By and large, bureaucratic-political elite integration has little direct specific effect on the chronological age of an institution.

Concerning generational age, a distinction was made between the protege and key institutional link systems of generational renewal in stable polities. The institutional method was emphasized. In both instances, however, political-bureaucratic elite integration complicated and hindered generational renewal—excluding certain specialized cases. The problem was especially damaging in the bureaucratic sector.

Functional age was defined in terms of the capacity for institutional innovation and the acceptance of new elite groups. It was stressed that here, above all, a smooth transition is difficult if not impossible. The form of the major elite institutional structure and especially of the groups directly represented in the elite is not changed at low social cost.

Political-bureaucratic elite innovation is by and large marginal to such a major movement. Bureaucratic elites have little inclination and little capacity to innovate institutionally. In some cases, however, they have served to admit new elites, and where these elites could move on to the political elite, as in the case of some post-colonial armies, their effect in adaptation has been significant. Where this integration takes place, the bureaucracy is likely to be more politically sensitive and perhaps more generally innovative.

In short, political-bureaucratic elite integration is worth noting in considering a political system's capacity for adaptation, but it must remain a lesser variable.

Summary

In this chapter, the relation between elite integration—bureaucratic and political—and Huntington's criteria of institutionalization was systematically examined. A clear trend was evident. It was indicated that this form of integration is fairly uncommon, especially in developed, modern polities. This infrequency was notably in contrast to the very high frequency of elite integration, especially vertical elite integration, which we discerned among bureaucratic elites.

Though uncommon in stable modern polities, political-bureaucratic elite integration is characteristic of pre-modern states—such as Europe in the middle ages—and unstable modern polities, such as decaying post-colonial governments. It was pointed out that such political-bureaucratic elite integration is characteristic of periods of transition—mostly characteristic of periods of decay, but also of periods of development, where this elite integration, and the disruption that accompanies it, may be necessary to re-establish or develop stable patterns of social mediation. Wherever political-bureaucratic elite integration is chronic, however, it is an indication of political ineffectiveness.

In this chapter, as in the two that preceded it, the key role of elite movement, or its lack, is emphasized as an element of institutionalization and political differentiation. The nature of a political system, as well as its elite system, is not only a product of who speaks to whom about what, or even who pays whom. A political system is also very much defined in terms of who in power goes where, from where.

NOTES

1. The same general distinction is made by Riggs, *Administration in Developing Countries,* pp. 54-57. "*Politics,* as I see it, refers to the process by which the major policies of any organization are chosen—that is, how its available wealth, rights, and duties are authoritatively allocated. *Administration* refers to the process by which such policies are implemented by an organization" p. 54. Riggs further notes that "the normal condition in human history has not been to separate politics and administration. Rather such separation is a recent phenomenon, characteristic of more highly industrialized, and especially the more democratic, countries" p. 54.

2. Two studies on Weber that relate his models to contemporary developmental theories are Robert A. Packenham, "Approaches to the Study of Political Development," *World Politics,* 17 (1964) pp. 108-120; and Alfred Diamant, "The Bureaucratic Model:

Max Weber Rejected, Rediscovered, Reformed," in Ferrell Heady and Sybil L. Stokes (eds.), *Papers in Comparative Public Administration* (Ann Arbor: Institute of Public Administration, 1962), pp. 59-96. A favorable evaluation. of Weber's work in social-psychological terms, based on empirical data, is I. Miller, "Social-Psychological Implications of Weber's Model of Bureaucracy," *Social Forces,* 49 (September, 1970), pp. 91-102.

3. Braibanti, "Comparative Political Analytics Reconsidered."

4. Hugh Bone, *Party Committees and National Politics* (Seattle: University of Washington Press, 1958). See especially Chapter II, "The Headquarters Bureaucracy," pp. 36-68.

5. The reference here is to those states in which the decision-making process and the process of elite recruitment are characterized by clear hierarchical structures and explicit and regularized procedures. Huntington discusses more traditional bureaucratic states in his chapter, "Political Change in Traditional Polities," in *Political Order in Changing Societies,* pp. 140-191. Works that should be consulted in this regard are Gaetano Mosca, *The Ruling Class,* p. 80 ff.; Apter, *Politics of Modernization,* pp. 81 ff.; Eisenstadt, "Political Struggle in Bureaucratic Societies," *World Politics,* (October, 1965), pp. 18-19, all of which Huntington consults. Two works that deal with the question of a modern bureaucratic state are Carl J. Friedrich, "The Theory of Political Leadership and the Issue of Totalitarianism," in Farrell, (ed.), *Political Leadership in Eastern Europe and the Soviet Union,* pp. 17-27, and in the same volume, see Andras Hegedus, "Marxist Theories of Leadership: A Marxist Approach," pp. 28-56.

6. This despite the fact that Malenkov was the leader of the managerialist forces. For a discussion of the managerial/anti-managerial conflict in Soviet society, see Jeremy Azrael, "The Managers," in Farrell (ed.), *Political Leadership in Eastern Europe and the Soviet Union,* pp. 224-248, and especially pp. 236-238 for a discussion of the Malenkov rise and fall.

7. For the Ayub regime, see von Vorys, *Political Development in Pakistan;* Wint, *The 1958 Revolution in Pakistan;* Wheeler, *The Politics of Pakistan,* especially, pp. 232-283.

8. Ibid.; Vatikiotis, *The Egyptian Army in Politics;* Needler, "Political Development and Military Intervention in Latin America."

9. See Edwin O. Reischauer, *Japan: Past and Present* (New York: Knopf, 1946), "The Nationalistic and Militaristic Reaction," pp. 157-185.

10. A good study of how eighteenth-century politics came to differentiate the bureaucratic and the political into the nineteenth century, is that of Asa Briggs, *The Age of Improvement* (London: Longman's, 1959).

11. Although there may seem to be a strong element of conflict between the bureaucratic and the political organizations, in fact, in more developed polities they are symbiotic. As Huntington points out, "The parties which at first are the leeches on the bureaucracy in the end become the bark protecting it from more destructive locusts of clique and family," *Political Order in Changing Societies,* p. 71.

12. Riggs, *Administration in Underdeveloped Countries,* pp. 54-57.

13. A good comprehensive study of the problem is Baljit Singh and Shridhar Misra, *A Study of Land Reform in Uttar Pradesh* (Honolulu: East-West Center Press, 1965).

14. Another argument should be considered: that the very highest levels of a bureaucracy have nearly all the substantive (lacking only the formal) aspects of a political position and so the high-level bureaucratic elite has already passed into political elite status. Policy-making is frequently involved at the highest levels of a bureaucracy, and in many cases the agent of selection is not the bureaucracy itself, but the political elite. This argument is less than completely persuasive, however, because in very many cases the leader

is chosen by his peers, as in the election of a Pope, and in other cases the top position may be effectively chosen by (on the recommendation of) the previous incumbent. Furthermore, the top of a major bureaucracy is still a bureaucracy in function and style; though the distinction is generally blurred, it is not eliminated.

15. As Huntington comments, in fact, a society's level of development is principally characterized by its level and extent of association, and the stability of that association. Huntington, *Political Order in Changing Societies*, p. 31.

16. Some countries are better examples of this decay than others: certainly Burma, (Pye, *Politics, Personality and Nation Building*); Pakistan soon after independence, perhaps (see, for an overview of this topic, Braibanti, *Research on the Bureaucracy of Pakistan*); and probably not India (Taub, *Bureaucrats Under Stress*).

17. D. W. Brogan, *The Price of Revolution* (London: Hamish, 1951). The book relies principally on the American experience just after World War II, but does emphasize the value of a set of agreements over a lack of such agreements.

18. The longest, most detailed study of political-bureaucratic elite integration appears in Fred Riggs, *Thailand: The Modernization of a Bureaucratic Polity* (Honolulu: East-West Center PRess, 1966). See especially Chapter IX, "Politics, Administration, and High Finance," pp. 242-310. Another worthwhile study of this highly bureaucratized political system is by William J. Siffin, *The Thai Bureaucracy* (Honolulu: East-West Center Press, 1966). The Siffin book has a greater emphasis on historical background, and the Riggs book is more analytically oriented.

19. The same relation exists looking at elite integration from the policy-making elite's perspective. Diffusion here can lead to policies being determined by the majority of the political elite, but then frustrated by a minority of the political elite and the bulk of the bureaucratic elites. Conservative governments overthrown by radical ones often give rise to a situation where the policy-making elements are in the hands of the radicals, but the structure of the state still is dominated by conservatives. The situation need not be the left in power and the right in the bureaucracy, but something of the reverse. For an instance of where a conservative regime (the Republicans under Eisenhower) felt their policies would be sabotaged by a liberal bureaucracy, seen from the standpoint of its bureaucratic consequences, see Eleanor Bontecou, *The Federal Loyalty-Security Program* (Ithaca: Cornell University Press, 1953).

20. A discussion of how these institutional conflicts were modified in two similar but significantly divergent systems, see Huntington's chapter, "Political Modernization: America vs. Europe," pp. 93-139 in *Political Order in Changing Societies.*

21. In modern, developed polities, a violation of functional limits between bureaucratic and political elites are likely to occur only in extreme cases, and those instances, of course, are very specific and concrete as to circumstances. Normal rules of functional limitation do not necessarily apply in extraordinary situations. The problem is that exceptions tend to become precedents. An interesting analysis of self-generated (for the most part) functional limitation is found in Edwin Lieuwen, "Militarism and Politics in Latin America," in Johnson (ed.), *The Role of the Military in Underdeveloped Countries*, pp. 131-163.

22. There are many examples of this effect. Pakistan's 1958 military takeover is in many ways a model example. See Wint, *The 1958 Revolution in Pakistan.*

23. Huntington, *Political Order in Changing Societies*, pp. 192-263.

24. D. Rustow, "The Army and the Founding of the Turkish Republic" *World Politics*, 11 (July, 1959); and also see, for a longer account, Bernard Lewis, *The Emergence of Modern Turkey* (London: Oxford University Press, 1963).

25. Robert A. Scalapino, "Which Route for Korea?" *Asian Survey*, 11 (September, 1962).

26. Wint, *The 1958 Revolution in Pakistan.*

27. One of the best analyses of the relation between members of the bureaucratic and political elites, concerning reform, is John D. Montgomery, "Sources of Bureaucratic Reform: A Typology of Purpose and Politics," in Braibanti (ed.), *Political and Administrative Development,* pp. 427-471. Montgomery examines autocratic, Western Democratic, and developing systems in terms of a threefold typology of sources of reform (upward, lateral, and internal).

28. On the other hand, the major problem in most developing areas may be the independence of the bureaucracy from public control. Joseph LaPalombara stresses this argument in his "An Overview of Bureaucracy and Political Development," in LaPalombara (ed.), *Bureaucracy and Political Development,* pp. 55-61. For a somewhat contrary view, see Lee Sigelman, "Do Modern Bureaucracies Dominate Underdeveloped Polities?" *American Political Science Review,* 66 (June, 1972), pp. 525-528.

29. The best examination of such a polity is Riggs, *Thailand.* See especially his chapter, "Cliques and Factions in the Thai Cabinet," pp. 211-241. "Cliques and factions consist of individuals who are often bound by ties of friendship and long-standing acquaintance. . . . Members typically hold official positions in the bureaucracy, whether military or civil. . . . Increasingly, they have been military officials, but civilian bureaucrats have also played decisive roles in these cabinet groups. They can augment their capacity to exercise bureaucratic power by coopting members drawn from different agencies," p. 213.

30. See Huntington, *Political Order in Changing Societies,* pp. 366 ff., for a discussion of the relation between reform and revolution. Huntington follows the Tocquevillian approach. For France in the pre-revolutionary period, Crane Brinton, *Anatomy of Revolution* (London: Cape, 1953) is still a vastly informative work. See the chapter, "Types of Revolutionists," pp. 101-133.

31. Stolypin was such an adviser in Czarist Russia. For this period, see Jerome Blum, *Lord and Peasant in Russia* (Princeton: Princeton University Press, 1961).

32. Like any other generalization that takes in a major segment of history, there are apparent exceptions. Japan, Thailand, and Prussia appear to violate the generalization. Certainly Hans Rosenberg, *Bureaucracy, Aristocracy, and Autocracy: The Prussian Experience, 1660-1815* (Cambridge, Mass.: Harvard University Press, 1958) demonstrates how a politicized bureaucracy effected changes in this "developing" state not only in itself, but in a wider polity. Riggs makes the same sort of analysis in his *Thailand.* Perhaps the work of Barrington Moore, Jr., in his *Social Origins . . .* provides the key, wherein he argues that the transition to industrial development (and those few social aspects necessarily associated with it) may be accomplished smoothly in the short run by a united aristocratic elite—with a price to be paid later. In any event, the Thai, Prussian, and Japanese examples are in the nature of exceptions, instructive and suggestive as they may be.

33. For the patron-client model in the study of Soviet politics, see John Armstrong, *The Soviet Bureaucratic Elite: A Case Study of the Ukrainian Apparatus* (New York: Praeger, 1959); Frederick Barghoorn, *Politics in the USSR* (Boston: Little, Brown, 1966), pp. 184-185; the patron-client model and the rational technical models of Soviet recruitment are evaluated in P. D. Stewart, R. L. Arnett, W. T. Ebert, R. E. McPhail, T. L. Rich, and C. E. Schopmeyer, "Political Mobility and the Soviet Political Process," *American Political Science Review,* 66 (December, 1972), pp. 1269-1290. Also see John Powell, "Peasant Society and Clientalist Politics," *American Political Science Review,* 64 (June, 1970), pp. 411-425; P. Lemarchand and K. Legg, "Political Clientalism and Development," *Comparative Politics,* 4 (January, 1972), pp. 149-178; Richard

Sandbrook, "Patrons, Clients, and Unions: The Labour Movement in Kenya," *Journal of Comparative Political Studies,* 10 (March, 1972), pp. 3-27.

34. This is not to say, however, that the politicization of the bureaucracy results in a lower level of performance in all circumstances. Riggs argues that the general effect of politicization is to make the bureaucrats arbitrary and unresponsive. "Bureaucrats and Political Development," in LaPalombara (ed.), *Bureaucracy and Political Development,* pp. 120-122. Pye, however, argues that the problem is a lack of politicization. "The Political Context of National Development," in Irving Swerdlow (ed.), *Development Administration: Concepts and Problems* (Syracuse: University of Syracuse Press, 1963), p. 34. The real conflict here appears to be in a difference of perception of the source of the politicization.

35. Rosenberg, *Bureaucracy, Aristocracy, and Autocracy: The Prussian Experience;* Sansom, *History of Japan,* 1615-1867.

36. Frederic Fleron, "Representation of Career Types in the Soviet Political Leadership," in Ferrell (ed.), *Political Leadership in Eastern Europe and the Soviet Union,* especially, pp. 116, in which Fleron, with considerable documentation, evaluates the literature on the institutional and "interest group" approach to Soviet leadership with the social background approach. For Krishna Menon and the Indian army, see Neville Maxwell, *India's China War* (London: Jonathan Cape, 1970), pp. 185-199.

37. See, for a comprehensive approach, Schlesinger, *Ambition and Politics: Political Careers in the United States.*

38. For a comprehensive study of movement within the British political elite, see W. L. Guttsman, *The British Political Elite;* Buck, *Amateurs and Professionals in British Politics, 1918-1959;* and Ranney, *Pathways to Parliament.*

39. See Chapter 6.

40. An excellent study, which stresses the importance of routine career ladders, is Michel Oksenberg, "Getting Ahead and Along in Communist China: The Ladder of Success on the Eve of the Cultural Revolution," in Lewis, *Party Leadership and Revolutionary Power in China,* pp. 304-347.

41. For eighteenth-century Britain, see Max Beloff, *The Age of Absolutism* (London: Hutchison, 1954). For Nepal, see Leo E. Rose and Margaret Fisher, *The Politics of Nepal* (Ithaca: Cornell University Press, 1970), pp. 63-83; B. L. Joshi and Leo E. Rose, *Democratic Innovation in Nepal* (Berkeley: University of California Press, 1966), see especially pp. 475-477.

42. There is extensive literature of the Black migration into urban areas of the United States, especially since World War I. A comprehensive evaluatory summary of the effects and consequences of this migration is that of Edward Banfield, *The Unheavenly City* (Boston: Little, Brown, 1970).

43. For an evaluation of the positive aspects of bureaucratic politicization, see Pye, "The Political Context of National Development," p. 34; and, for a somewhat contrary view, Riggs, "Bureaucrats and Political Development," pp. 120-122.

44. For a discussion of the capacity of Leninist Communist Parties for effective governance and political activity, see the section "Leninism and Political Development," in Huntington, *Political Order in Changing Societies,* pp. 334-343.

45. Ibid., pp. 93-139.

46. An excellent study of the ombudsman, viewed in terms of the transfer of institutions, is that of Larry Hill, "The International Transfer of Political Institutions: A Behavioral Analysis of the New Zealand Ombudsman," (unpublished dissertation) Department of Political Science, Tulane University, 1970.

47. Brogan, *Price of Revolution.*

48. See the section, "Challenge and Response" I: 271-299 in Arnold Toynbee, *A*

Study of History. Ten volumes. (London: Oxford University Press, 1934). Also see Moore, *Social Origins.* . . . For the "necessity" for social disruption, see the section, "Independence and the Price of Peaceful Change," pp. 385-412, where Moore is especially dealing with India, but the point is more broadly made. For a discussion on Japan in the same volume, see pp. 228-313; the discussion of Germany is spread through the book, but especially see pp. 435-442.

49. The case of Tokugawa Japan is an especially interesting one, where the shogunate set up a parellel, Tokyo-oriented, administrative structure within the villages, being careful to staff the new service with prestigious villages. See Harumi Befu, "Village Autonomy and Articulation with the State," *Journal of Asian Studies,* 26 (November, 1965), pp. 19-32.

50. Moore, *Social Origins* . . . pp. 314-412.

51. There is, of course, no necessary causal nexus between the attitudes of the elite member and those of the population as a whole. Elite recruitment is thus not necessarily the basis for constituency control. For an excellent analysis, both substantive and methodological, of this point, see Charles F. Cnudde and Donald J. McCrone, "The Linkage between Constituency Attitudes and Congressional Voting Behavior: A Causal Model," *American Political Science Review,* 55 (March, 1966), pp. 66-72.

52. A book that demonstrates the hostility felt toward those Algerians who cooperated with the French is Said Benaissa Boualam, *L'Algerie sans la France* (Paris: Editions France Empire, 1963). The author emphasizes the harsh treatment given to the collaborators after independence.

53. It is important to note in the case of Untouchables, that ex-Untouchables have tended to cut themselves off from their community. See "Untouchability: The Test of Fellow Feeling," in Rudolph and Rudolph, *The Modernity of Tradition,* pp. 132-154.

54. An excellent survey of this period, with an emphasis on administrative techniques as well as an overview of political pressures is found in White, *The Republican Era.*

55. Fisher and Rose, *The Politics of Nepal;* Joshi and Rose, *Democratic Innovation in Nepal.*

56. Robins, "Political Elite Formation in Rural India," especially pp. 852 ff.

57. A perceptive essay that emphasizes the psychological correlates of bureaucratic institutionalization is Lucian W. Pye, "Bureaucratic Development and the Psychology of Institutionalization," in Ralph Braibanti (ed.), *Political and Administrative Development* (Durham, N.C.: Duke University Press, 1969), pp. 400-426. Pye emphasizes the role, often creative, of adversary relationships. However, he does (as here) see the end of an entrepreneurial style as a necessity for bureaucratic institutionalization. See the section, "The Spirit of the Adversary Process: The Limits of Structuring Controlled Aggression," pp. 414-422.

58. For discussions on the reaction to exogenous influences on the bureaucracy, whether from within its own general cultural-political ambit or from an exotic source, see Riggs, "Endogenous versus Exogenous Change," in *Administration in Developing Countries,* pp. 38-42; the best single extended essay on this topic is Braibanti, "External Inducement of Political-Administrative Development: An Institutional Strategy."

59. William Starbuck, "Organizational Growth and Development," in James G. March (ed.), *Handbook of Organizations* (Chicago: Rand McNally, 1965) emphasizes the coherence maintenance aspect of organizations, which are more likely to agree to changes in what the organizations do than in who does them and how they are done, pp. 473-475.

60. This is a general point made by Pye, "Bureaucratic Development and the Psychology of Institutionalization." "The prevalence of uninhibited aggression can be paralyzing, but on the other hand creativity seems to depend upon some forms of regulated competition and conflict," p. 424.

61. Toynbee, *A Study of History,* I: pp. 271-299; Moore, *Social Origins* . . . pp. 385-412, though the focus is specifically Indian here.

Chapter 4

INSTITUTIONALIZATION AND ELITE

INTEGRATION IN THE MEDIEVAL CHURCH

Introduction

Up to this point, the examples chosen to illustrate the arguments have tended to be drawn from the modern era. Such an approach is to be expected, given the contemporary orientation of most research in political science. Believing in the essential unity of the political process, not only from country to country (as comparative politics requires) but also from one historical period to another, it is not only appropriate but also important for us to offer an application of the Huntingtonian and elite integration models to a major institution outside the modern period.

Not every pre-modern institution is equally appropriate for these purposes, however. One should be chosen that was broadly significant in its own time period, not that great significance is essential on purely theoretical grounds, for the principles described presumably apply to minor organizations as well as to the great. The reasons for choosing a major institution for discussion are more prosaic. A major institution's operation, functions, etc., will be somewhat familiar to most scholars in political science, and, hence, less time need be spent in introductory description. Even more important, an organization is needed that has elicited a substantial body of high-quality scholarship upon which inferences may be drawn. Such an extensive body of scholarship is essential for this analysis.

No institution is likely to fit these criteria perfectly. However, the Roman Catholic Church in the Middle Ages is organizationally familiar, and a great quantity of academic material is available to the researcher.

In dealing with the appropriateness of the Medieval Church for this discussion, one should turn first to the question of whether the Church was a bureaucracy in Huntington's and this study's terms.

That the Medieval Church was hierarchical can be stated without equivocation. That it also enjoyed most if not all the other aforementioned criteria of bureaucracy[1] can be reasonably demonstrated, as will be seen.

During the period of the early Church (from c. 700 until the rise of the papacy c. 1050), the Church was very largely under state influence and control, though there were strong elements of reciprocity. After that time, major elements of political-bureaucratic elite integration may be discerned, but the situation remained one of secular dominance except in particular geographical areas (most notably the papal states) and during particular events (such as Savanarola's rule of Florence). More time will be given to this subject presently, with special reference to the autonomy (or lack thereof) of the Church in choosing its own officers, appointments to benefices, etc.

One may object that the time period, c. 700-c. 1550, is too long and that consequently this chapter seeks to do more than is possible within its brief length. Certainly a more intensive analysis could have been achieved if limited to a narrower area, dealing with one aspect such as the Dominican Order or perhaps only the great age of papal dominance, c. 1050-c. 1300. On the other hand, a broader overview of the entire period of the Medieval Church gives greater scope and facility for applying the concepts developed in previous chapters. This is particularly the case in the consideration of autonomy and even more so in the criteria of adaptability. Eight centuries and a great deal of a continent permit one to see the operation of various criteria and forms of integration in a way that no other scope of study can.

Inevitably, there are certain areas of concentration that occur in such a survey. The experience of the Church in England looms larger in this discussion than its activity anywhere else.

A few additional words should be given about the material. The principal source for this chapter is R. W. Southern's *Western Society and the Church in the Middle Ages,* published in 1970 for a scholarly and informed, but not specialized audience.[2] Southern will be cited when directly quoted and at certain other key points, but a general debt in terms of information and organization is acknowledged as well. Several other sources for more specific pieces of information and analysis have been used. Heath's *The English Parish Clergy on the Eve of the Reformation*[3] and Jacob's book on the *Fifteenth*

Century[4] are two such works which have proven useful in determining the career history of high episcopal officials. Others will be cited as the chapter progresses.[5]

Ecclesiastical Elite Selection and Recruitment

Earlier, it was indicated that to a very large extent the Medieval Church was the bureaucracy of the state. It would be the worst possible mistake, however, to consider the Church nothing but this. First and foremost, it was an institution that sought to aid its members to achieve everlasting life and to be pleasing to God. Of course, most—certainly very many—people today do not believe it ever did this. Whether it did or did not does not concern us. What does matter is that, though often distracted and corrupted, this was the essential, the primary, mission of the Church.[6] Its success or failure in this mission will not be dwelt upon, because that is outside the direct scope of this inquiry. The concern here is to emphasize the fact that the Church did carry out the type of bureaucratic governmental functions described in the previous chapters. The Church supplied advisory and administrative officials to the crown and local secular powers. It served as a means of information-gathering to the government in a variety of ways, from the keeping of records to the reporting of political information. Some of the religious orders—the Cistercian, most notably—were active agents of what would be called today economic development. In certain periods, the Church[7] organized men for war, especially in conducting campaigns against non-Christians. In effect, it served as a tax collector for the state, since its own system of revenue collection was often taxed. It was also the instrument by which almost all the educated population learned, and of course aided the crown in providing symbolic—legitimating—support.[8]

This impressive list of functions may make it appear that the Church was the government itself, or so much of it that no one is justified in considering it a subordinate portion. But there were two crucial powers it did not have. First, it did not, except in unusual cases, have direct coercive power. As Southern notes,

> It [the Church] had no police. It had no dependable army. Even the inquisition, the most efficient instrument of coercion in the hands of the church, was swallowed up in a melee of local interests. Over most of Europe the worst terrors ordinary people had to face were archdeacons and rural deans. They were seldom men of liberal outlook, but they wanted a quiet life and kept most of their thunder for village lechers, drunkards, and adulterers.

When we speak of a church-state therefore we say too much, for the church was weak in the means of coercion. In the end, the decisive factor in the exercise of coercion was the consent and cooperation of independent secular rulers, who were mainly concerned to safeguard their own inherited interests.[9]

Where such a refusal by the secular authority occurred—except in the papal states or under extraordinary conditions such as Savonarola's rule of Florence—the Church was stymied. Even excommunication often failed to achieve its object.[10] Although it was the bureaucracy in all other things, the Church was not the bureaucracy of force. This was a power that the secular arm reserved to itself, in a separate organization.

Another limitation on the Church should be mentioned. The Church existed within a polity having secular as well as sacred traditions and was, of course, a product of its own traditions and sincerely held beliefs. It operated within those traditions—the power it exercised was authoritarian, not totalitarian. Consequently, the Church was largely limited by social traditions, social pressures, and also by what it itself believed to be right and proper.

Let us turn now to a general outline of institutional elite integration in the Medieval Church. This, of course, changed over time, and was different in, say, the settled areas of Italy from that of the more frontier areas of Eastern Europe. Nevertheless, the general pattern was quite consistent.

Becoming a member of the Church in the sense of becoming a Christian was very rarely a matter of choice. One became a Christian at baptism, and it was an irreversible event. It was an event, moreover, that occurred when one was an infant, and so the Christian acquired the responsibilities of that status with as little choice as most people today acquire the responsibilities of citizenship.

A person wishing to enter the clergy selected such a career partially on the basis of his temperament—whether he felt a vocation—and also partially on the basis of what practical, worldly advantages the Church could offer him.[11] The Church offered employment not only in orders (principally, in this period, the Benedictine) and parishes, but also in chantries, cathedrals, and private households—these latter occupations being less demanding.

Entry into the Church itself, the various ordinations, etc., was at the pleasure of the Church, and certain categories, such as that of bastardy were presumptively excluded, though exceptions were commonly made.

The appointments to certain posts, even the lower parish ones, were by and large effectively within the power of the local lords to grant, or at a minimum, to veto. As Jacob points out:

The country clergy, especially in areas of great lordship, are found taking an important part in the affairs of their patrons and masters.

There is the famous case where the vicar of Paston came into conflict ('the great fray made at the time of Mass') with his parishioners because he carried out the instructions of Agnes Paston. A rector like William Coting of Titchwell was anxious to vindicate his patron's authority "when in the grey morning three men of my lord of Norfolk with long spears carried off three good horses from John Pleyn one of your farmers at Titchwell, telling him to 'treat with my lord of Norfolk', if he desired redress." The parish priest while loyal to his patron could also be a local man of business, or even an advocate acting for his patron or influential friend in cases at a manor court and reporting whether the tenants were to be trusted or not. The parson could help his lord by urging the tenants to pay their farms [i.e., rents], and act very much as a bailiff.[12]

The political sensitivity and rewards of the post varied, of course, and so did the interest of the secular ruler.[13] Appointment to any post, however, was in some degree political, and was never made without some involvement, direct or indirect, of the political arm.

Let us make a general outline of the type of career history characteristic of the pre-modern Church.[14] It is not necessary to go through the eight stages in the progression from lay to priestly status. It was possible, while still in minor orders, for a person to change his mind and revert to lay status, even marrying. Life in minor orders differed little from an ordinary layman's life. Once he received the first of the major or holy orders, the subdeaconate, his status as a member of the clergy was, however, established.

This stage could not be reached until the age of eighteen. A man could not become a priest until twenty-four. In other words, there was a period of apprenticeship and probation. There were also periodic examinations as to learning and morality, which varied considerably in their severity or laxity.[15] Once clerkly status was acquired, it was possible for the clerk to become a parish auxiliary, often a chaplain, though at very low income and with modest responsibilities. Unless the clerk was a graduate or well-connected, this is where he was likely to start.

Indeed, it is at the point where a new clerk begins to seek a benefice that one can begin to speak of a bureaucratic elite. Finding such a benefice was decidedly a political process. In late Medieval England, for example, there were 9,000 parish churches, hardly enough to satisfy the number of competent ordinands.[16] Although there were other ways of securing a remunerative post, being a parish priest was the most common. A good, or even a poor, benefice (ecclesiastical living) was secured through "influence, vigilance, pertinacity,"[17] and often simony (the purchase of office) as well.

Then, as now, the ambitious looked first to family and friends for aid, but in institutional terms the principal source of preferment was the monarch.

The extent of his control, not to mention influence, is illustrated in the following quotation.

> By far the greatest single patron of livings in England was the King. Not only did he possess many advowsons of his own, but those of the tenants in chief so long as they were minors and of deceased bishops during the vacancy of the see also came into his hands. True the Chancellor had the gift of all crown livings valued at less than twenty marks, or during Wolsey's tenure of the office less than £20, but he was not impervious to royal pressure and his chief beneficiaries were the king's clerks in Chancery. When no living was immediately available for one of his clerks, the king made a grant from the Exchequer or from the customs, or, more often, he obliged an abbot—or a bishop-elect to grant a pension until a benefice was vacant.
>
> Royal patronage, therefore, is not to be measured by counting royal livings.
>
> Meanwhile the king did not neglect his own resources, which ranged from bishoprics and prebends down to parish churches. For many royal clerks parish churches were but the beginning of a career, or a trifling, though not contemptible, addition to an already large income.[18]

This situation varied over time; in certain periods, the pope succeeding in his attempts to limit or even abolish the monarch's power. In all but a few periods and all but a few cases, the monarch—the man with the instruments of coercion—eventually won. Another point that should be mentioned is that appointment to a parish or benefice did not necessarily mean that the person appointed would actually carry out the pastoral duties. Frequently livings were held in plurality or in absentia. Lesser clerks carried on the actual parish work, while the holder of the livings worked for the king, or perhaps occupied a high administrative post in the episcopate.

Once a clerk had received a benefice, he sought, if he were ambitious, to improve his position by securing additional ones, if this were possible, or to secure a better one. Advancement was acquired in three ways: by exchange, by simony, and by connection. A clerk's efforts in these regards were, of course, enhanced by his own intelligence, efficiency, and reputation for godliness.

Exchange was practiced at its height in the late fourteenth century, but not limited to that time, and, indeed, did not largely cease until the mid-fifteenth century.[19] Actually, the process was a form of simony because money was almost always involved as part of the exchange "packet."[20] Simony was a common practice, and obviously having friends in high places was also of great use when a new position fell open. The matter will be discussed later in further detail, but suffice it to say that the three methods of advancement described were not supportive of bureaucratic autonomy, though they were consistent with complexity, adaptability, and perhaps with cohesion as well—though this latter criterion is also in doubt.

Promotion to the highest ecclesiastical offices in the realm was little different in procedure.[21] The offices were quasi-political ones—existing like such contemporary offices as the Director of Central Intelligence and the Chief of Staff of the Armed Forces, on the margin of the bureaucratic and political elites—and so the recruitment catchment area was quasi-political as well. High positions in the "national" church fell to the *sublime* (men of high birth) and the *litterati* (lettered clerks) who had distinguished themselves in service to the crown.[22] Younger sons of the noble houses were assuredly proportionally overrepresented, but men such as Chichele, Kempe, and Wolsey were drawn from the ranks of yeomen, traders, and franklins. The situation was different in different areas and countries, but members of the religious orders were underrepresented.

In the fifteenth century, for example, Jacob summarizes the situation thus:

> The personnel of the episcopate that Henry IV found in the southern province on his return falls largely into four groups: *nobiles;* civil servants and king's clerks who had arrived at their position through service to the government; the academics who had made themselves useful to the crown through their legal studies or in an ambassadorial capacity; and (sometimes overlapping with the latter class) the religious.[23]

The situation in England was fairly typical, and it displays a system, excluding perhaps the *nobiles,* that is not all that different from the bureaucracy of, for example, Bismarck's Germany.

It was a bureaucracy enjoying a high degree of internal self-selection and self-rule, but clearly serving and, even at its higher levels, merging with the political elite.[24]

There were three possible ways a bishop could be appointed. Least common and of decreasing importance over time was the election of the diocesan by his chapter and its confirmation by the metropolitan.[25] Next in importance, and, indeed, a good deal more important, was translation of bishops by the pope.

In this procedure, the pope sought to lessen royal influence. A bishop, most especially an old one, would be transferred (translated) to another see. By convention, the pope was empowered to appoint a bishop's successor with much less royal involvement when the bishop was transferred than when the previous bishop died or retired.[26] From about 1300 to 1350, thirteen percent of the episcopal appointments in England were by translation, but in the next half-century, the percentage reached a little over a third (thirty-one translations out of eighty-six appointments).

However, the usual source of appointment was the monarch, as mentioned earlier, who chose men he knew and trusted, especially those who had served him in the past and whom he could expect to serve him in the future. The pope, technically, only provided the monarch's nominee. As Jacob puts it:

> But bishops were too important a factor in the state to be left to the nomination of the Pope. It was a useful expedient, says Dr. Hamilton Thompson, to throw upon the Pope the responsibility for their appointment, but the nominations were none the less those of the government in power, and during the Great Schism the Roman Popes, anxious for English support, were on the whole compliant. The normal practice was for the king, after a discussion in the council, to convey his wishes to the Pope, and unless the council was hesitant or divided, the Pope accepted: if he did, the government offered no opposition to the Pope formally *providing* the royal nominee.[27]

The papacy was in an especially weak position, of course, during the Schism, but the procedure was not unique to that time.

Such is the outline of the elite selection and recruitment during this period. In terms of the topics and historical periods described below, Huntington's criteria of institutionalization, and interpretation of these criteria in light of what has already written about elite integration, will be applied. The theory will be more meaningful applied in this manner, and, perhaps most useful of all, its weaknesses will be exposed. No theory is without defects, and the worst defect is not to know where the weaknesses lie.

In looking at coherence, one notes with Southern that "we have here a grimmer, more earthy church than that of scholastic theology or monastic contemplation."[28] How did elite integration affect this coherence in terms of morale, the setting of functional boundaries, the resolution of disputes? In discussing the Church's organizational complexity, not only the papacy and the episcopate will be examined, but also the monastic and parish levels. Earlier arguments must be examined, not in anything approaching detail, certainly, but elite integration not only accompanies complexity, but is essential for it. In discussing autonomy, as much space will be proportionally given here as earlier was given to autonomy—defined in terms of elite integration—inside the organization as between it and the political elite. Concerning adaptation, the Medieval Church is clearly one of the most adaptable institutions in political history, scoring high, as to be expected, in chronological, generational, and functional age. The role of complexity in achieving this adaptive capacity will be examined.[29]

An Overview of Institutionalization and Elite Integration in the Medieval Church

THE PRIMITIVE AGE, c. 700-c. 1050

Looking at civilized Europe as a whole about the year 700, one observes a society with a very low level of institutionalization. Six hundred years later, one observes a highly organized, complex, and coherent society. The next two and a half centuries see this development challenged, especially the clerical aspect, and in some decline, but still at a high level. This rise and moderate decline will be looked at when an examination is made of the great division of Christianity between the Eastern and Western Churches; the development of the papacy and the major episcopates; and when also the development of the religious orders, the fringe orders, and the anti-orders is noted.

Let us first turn to an overview of the early Church (c. 700-c. 1050). The Roman Empire had, of course, been the great source of European unity and authority. Elite integration was well established, based largely in the latter period on Roman citizenship and family ties. The collapse of this great system took several centuries and was an extremely complicated process. By the year 700 it had been completed and Europe was in a state of political, social, intellectual, military, and spiritual ruin scarcely imaginable five centuries earlier.

Coherence: The first object of any political-religious system of the time was to restore a measure of coherence—the setting of functional boundaries for a variety of moribund and primitive institutions and the establishment of some sort of regular procedure for resolving societal conflicts. This was a process set in motion by the Carolingian Empire and the Roman Catholic Church. Eventually, the Church, especially the papacy, was to replace the Roman Empire as the great pan-European unifying organization.[30]

Parenthetically, it should not be thought that the Church accomplished this work unopposed. Its enemies even in the earliest period were the Eastern Church, the majority of secular rulers at one time or another, and critics within the Church itself. Needless to say, there were the enemies outside—Islam, and the often powerful pagans in the frontier areas (as well as those remaining within). The Church's triumph over these enemies was never complete, though its universal unifying influence was more nearly achieved than the Napoleonic, Nazi, and Communist modern equivalents. The Church, by the end of this period, had become the single most important institution in all Europe.

The Church first sought to re-establish stability and order.[31] This early period was the great era of the Benedictine Order,[32] which was the first great religious order, and indeed nearly the sole religious order in this period. The establishment of this organization permitted a sort of "franchise" arrangement, where one successful organizational program could be duplicated all over Europe. Organizational techniques for the achievement of internal complexity, coherence, and especially autonomy and adaptation could be applied over a wide area in different contexts.

More significant for the present purposes, the Church took a crucial role in defining elite status—the first necessity for elite integration—by limiting it first of all to Christians and also by its anointing of the rulers. Political elites were largely defined—though not exclusively—by lineage. The bureaucratic elite—the Church as an institution—was, however, defined by its rational relationship to a defined and hierarchical secular organization.

In this era, the person himself was of little worldly account; he was what he was because of his position in a bureaucratic hierarchy, because of his family descent, or because of what his community was. Southern suggests that the basic reason for this depersonalization was a dependence on the supernatural.

> The individual was swallowed up in his community or (if he were a great man) in his office. And both community and office drew their strength from the supernatural. The rules of life for monks and laymen alike emphasized the littleness of man, the impersonal majesty of the spiritual world, the dignity of an order which was only attainable in his life in symbolic ritual, and the peace of spirit which could be found only in a rigid discipline. Thus in a paradoxical way it came about that the feebleness of man, his insecurity, his weak grasp of the laws of nature, and his ineffectiveness in government, all combined to impose an extraordinary appearance of strength and stability on the products of this first period of the Middle Ages.[33]

Looking at this depersonalization from the perspective of psychological effects of a reliance on the supernatural (which is what Southern suggests) gives one view. Looking at it from the perspective of political development gives another. In institutional terms, this depersonalization was probably necessary to counter the terrible social forces generated by Rome's decay and the rise of extreme feelings of tribalism, personalism, and communalism. Only an organization that was above these social forces as much as the times permitted could have mediated them.

Coherence, morale, the setting of functional boundaries, and systems of dispute resolution required an organization that would itself be highly stable and dedicated. The Church largely achieved its organizational stability by requiring its officers to take perpetual vows of loyalty, generally enforced with rigor and even severity, and by forbidding these members to have any other personal loyalty—to wife or children—or to hold personal property. Furthermore, the Church profered an escape from the extinction of death, an offer of everlasting life, and the feeling that one had a special relation to God and was doing His work. It should also not be overlooked that the Church offered practical rewards of security, status, and even a degree of worldly eminence. Internal vertical elite integration was assured, for the most part, by reserving the greatest of these rewards to the members of the clergy and the religious orders.

Complexity: Effectiveness demanded not only coherence, but complexity as well. The government—the secular power—was finding it difficult enough to carry out the very basic functions of government, the collection of taxes and the turning aside of direct challenges to its authority, without trying to carry out such "luxury" functions as social regulation and the development of a coherent system of law. To a large degree, these functions were taken over by the Church.

Although several of these functions could be and generally were carried out by one organization, a certain degree of specialization did develop and, with it, complexity. The great source of complexity, however, was not functional specialization—of which there was very little indeed in this early period, but rather hierarchical and geographic elaboration.[34]

There was a great need for the organization to expand into new geographic areas, and also to refill the administrative void left by the Roman Empire's gradual collapse. The Church that developed in this age of primitive communications and often lax loyalty required a high level of internal social knowledge. In other words, complexity—and size—required then as now a large information base to make it work.

Personnel files, elaborate bookkeeping techniques, and other methods help provide such a base today as a supplement to personal knowledge. In the eighth, nineth, tenth, and eleventh centuries, such aids were seldom available, and, where they were available at all, it was only in the most primitive form. Elite integration served—along with other forms of bureaucratic and social intercourse—as part of the process for supplying this social knowledge. An essential part of making this elite integration work—keeping the positions within the Church—was the previously referred to Church rules on celibacy and vows of obedience. In organizational terms, there was no other place for the clerk to go—he could serve a secular master, but he could not leave the ecclesiastical bureaucracy. This organizational flexibility, combined with organizational integration, reached its apogee in this period in the institution of the Benedictine monasteries.[35]

Autonomy: An effective bureaucratic institution must not only have complexity, it must also have a substantial degree of autonomy—vis-à-vis the political elite, vis-à-vis the society at large, and also to some degree a certain amount of internal autonomy, as described earlier. Although its degree of autonomy was not as great in this period as it became later, the Church did manage to establish not only the principle, but also the reality that it was an organization unlike all others, and, indeed, it came to be the only major institution in this period which enjoyed a degree of autonomy from the political elite. It also managed the even more difficult task of working very closely with the common people, yet maintaining a genuine element of separateness. Undoubtedly, the belief that the Church had special supernatural powers was an important element here, but the Church's superior organizational skill was certainly also a factor.

This autonomy was achieved by (1) the vows of obedience made in entering religious orders; (2) the practice of celibacy; (3) the general belief in the Church's unique supernatural powers; (4) the elaborate and redundant organization of the Church; and (5) a very high level of elite integration.

The vows of obedience and chastity and the supernatural aspects of the Church not only permitted the clerks a feeling of separateness but also gave them a moral capacity to resist political and social encroachments. This moral capacity would have been far less if the church had been simply a secular organization among other secular organizations. The very high degree of vertical elite integration particularly set the organization apart. With some less stringent form of elite integration—that is, if it had permitted its members to come and go at will, acquiring property and families, drawing its higher officers from outside the organization—the Medieval Roman Catholic Church would have lacked this essential element of autonomy and could not have carried out its developmental role.

Adaptability: Concerning adaptability, the Church in the year 700 was better equipped—in terms of Huntington's and our analysis—than it would have superficially appeared.[36] The Church's chronological age was not as great, obviously, as it would eventually become, but it could already be measured in hundreds of years. Its generational age was proportionally long, and, most important, its functional age was significant. By 700, the Roman Catholic Church had already made the great transition from an essentially private religious group—hardly an organization—to a unit of social governance. This event predates the period of this study, but, of course, it was a crucial element in the Church's subsequent adaptive success.

Civil administration and social regulation were two areas for which the Church's organizational resources were well suited. The necessity to move into the frontier areas of the North and East was complemented by the ready expansion of the ecclesiastical organizations.

Was the high level of internal elite integration essential to this adaptability? Of course, one cannot reconstruct history—say that if such and such were so, such and such would or would not have occurred. However, the value of different forms of organizational or technical capacity can be evaluated by estimating their contributions. It is not intellectually arrogant, for example, to say that the history of Spain and the Aztec empire in the sixteenth century would have been different if the Europeans had not crossed the ocean.

At each expansion into a new area, geographic or functional, the Church was able to (1) apply political and bureaucratic principles developed in a parallel or similar area and (2) send members trained, formally or informally, in the previous organization. In other words, the very first elites in the new areas were recruited by and large from the elites in older areas (though, of course, local elites were then very rapidly recruited). It could have been otherwise, and it was in empires such as Asoka's in India a few centuries earlier. But certainly the integration of the bureaucratic elites in a single organization, the Church, was a far more efficient, rapid, and orderly way to achieve political integration. It was the way the Roman and later the great European empires were built as well.

THE AGE OF GROWTH, c. 1050-c. 1300

The period from 1050 to 1300 was one of the great ages not only of the Medieval Church, but of European history. After centuries of decay followed by a precarious development, European art, political forms, imagination, and economic well-being flowered. There was a general development of all productive things, and even of more interest to us, it was a great age of corporate development—the institutionalization of society—that aspect of the West that had in the Roman period, then again in the Medieval period, and even today been the major mark of Western organizational genius. There was no institution better able to adapt, and, indeed, lead, this process than the Medieval Church. As will be seen in the following section, this period of organizational advance and development also set in motion disruptive forces.[37] But, during this period, there was a general note of progress and even of optimism.

Coherence: Coherence had been largely achieved, certainly in terms of the hopes of those looking forward in 700. Europe was Christian, and the Catholic Church was an effective regulator of the personal aspects of that society. Not that everyone obeyed the rules of the Church, but the Church was the principal maker of those personal rules that were obeyed. The secular and bureaucratic elites were adequately differentiated. Compared to the earlier period, the rules of the political game were well settled and politics, for most, had lost its terror.

Of course, we know that the growth in strength of the Church, and especially of the papacy, was itself to be a factor in challenging some of these rules. The Church never won a clear-cut and lasting victory over its secular masters. By and large, the relations between the political and bureaucratic elites were elaborated, rather than changed in this period.

Complexity: At the beginning of the Age of Growth, the Church was already a complex organization, and it was to become more complex still. J. Q. Wilson's theory that simpler organizations are more likely to accept innovation, whereas more complex organizations are more likely to suggest, rather than adopt, innovation is relevant here.[38] The reason for this relationship may be explained at least in part by the relative costs of adoption (big organizations simply have more to change) and the need for adoption (simpler organizations are benefitted by increased complexity and so are somewhat more likely to accept it). In any event, the Medieval Catholic Church stands as an excellent illustration of Wilson's theory. At the beginning of this period, relatively few innovations were proposed, but a high proportion were accepted; at the end, many were being proposed, but the Church had become increasingly hostile to innovation.

The past pattern of elite integration was not changed in essential features, but rather developed, strengthening previous patterns. Political elites became more institutionalized, but the bureaucratic elite (the Church), because of the superior rationalization of its organization, was able to develop even faster. Out of this parallel political and bureaucratic development, the Church pulled ahead.

The first area in which the Church expanded was in the unifying and centralizing role of the papacy. As will be seen in a later section of this chapter, the disproportionate growth of the papacy up to about 1300 made it the major source of internal political conflict in these two and a half centuries, and also the major source of opposition to the reconciliation of the Western and Eastern churches.

The other major bureaucratic expansion was in the number of religious orders. Before the twelfth century, the Benedictine Order was the principal organization in religious life, to such an extent that Cardinal Newman designated the period before the twelfth century as the Benedictine Age.[39] Although

> In 1050 the Benedictine monopoly was unchallenged, by 1300, almost every possible variety of religious organization had been established; the Carthusians and numerous Orders of hermits; the Templars and similar profusion of military Orders; the various branches of Canons Regulars; the Cistercians; the four great Orders of friars; hospitals of many different kinds; organizations for the relief of prisoners. All these Orders and organizations had their own constitutions, widely different in type and aim.[40]

The papacy played a large role in fostering and protecting these organizations, which carried out a variety of functions from providing a seemly place for the unmarried daughters of the politically influential to economic development in the frontier areas.

Autonomy: This growth in complexity was accompanied by an increasing autonomy—indeed, even to an occasional challenge of secular rulers by the Church. Furthermore, the Church had gradually become the sole source of supernatural authority. Relics had served to give secular rulers an element of divinity, but in this period, though relics retained their importance in personal worship, their political significance largely disappeared.

The Church's monopoly on education and its near monopoly on all knowledge—scientific, medical, legal, theological, etc.—continued.[41] The merging of the educational and ecclesiastical systems is perhaps the most striking example of the value of elite integration in this period. The theological, scientific, legal, priestly, and administrative elites were all in one large organization, well-defined, coherent, and complex.[42]

The secular ruler, the political elite, remained dominant in this period. His power over coercion and, in the final analysis, over material resources, was superior, but he had to choose most of his important appointees from the Church. The necessity for choice continually limited this power. This period serves as a useful example of the limitations of money and force, and the value of organizational and technical and social skills.

The Church's autonomy came not only from its skill and organizational effectiveness, but also from its traditions (like other guilds) of enjoying certain liberties. These practical attributes, combined with its and the society's belief that it was carrying out a divine mission aided it greatly in maintaining its own internal rule-making authority.

Adaptation: The adaptive capacity of the Church was probably greatest in this period. The secular society was expanding in a variety of ways, as were the powers of the secular rulers—after the weakening, especially in France in the tenth century, of the monarchy. The gradually increasing capacities that the other secular rulers enjoyed, however, encouraged them to challenge the Church, and the Church, within the same general context, responded in kind. It was not a question of the Church or the laity increasing in capacity at the expense of the other, but of each expanding and coming into conflict with the other. In this conflict, the Church enjoyed great adaptive resources: a powerful history of functional adaptation, a high generational age, and a long chronological age.

The new age it was adapting to was not a demoralized stagnant society. It was an expanding one, and the Church's function here was to guide and maintain that expansion.

THE AGE OF UNREST, c. 1300-c. 1550

In this period, as in the others, the emphasis will be principally on the stresses on the elite and organizational structures. Great disputes on theological and other essentially normative matters accompanied these stresses, both reinforcing and reflecting them. St. Thomas was accurate in writing that man is very much a reasoning being, and the relative brief space we give to these matters is not an indication of their lesser general worth, but only a reflection of their lesser particular reference to Huntington's and the present theories on the topic.

Both the ecclesiastical and the political elites—as well as many secular economic ones—had become institutionalized by this period. Here was a developed, though not a modernized, society. The complementarity of the Church elites and other elites, however, had considerably declined. The Church was no longer seen as only an aid to the secular ruling authority (though as will be seen, it continued in that capacity), but also as, at times, a dangerous rival to that authority. Furthermore, the Church was no longer only a spiritual and material aid to the laity, but, at times, it was seen as an exploiter, and even the religious Orders were sometimes viewed as economic competitors to certain guilds.

The Church in its organizational aspects was no longer essential to social well-being; other institutions had arisen to carry out its nonsacred functions. At the same time the Church was demanding a higher price for its services. Serious conflict was to be expected, and occurred. This conflict was for a time moderated by the Church's being so deeply involved in the entire warp of society—and the state being so dependent upon it. Any major challenge was full of danger for all.[43]

Complexity: Concerning complexity, the period was one of conservation, and to a limited degree, simplification. The creation of new Orders, so characteristic of the previous era, largely ceased. This reversal was dramatized in the destruction of the Order of Templars in 1312-1314. Although a variety of considerations entered into the decision to abolish the Templars—scandals within the Order and perhaps a lessened need for their military activities—nevertheless such an action would have been quite unlikely very much earlier.

Institutional innovation was also discouraged—this, in contrast to the Church's earlier receptivity and encouragement of organizational innovation. Again, the first great move in this direction can be dated from the first decades of the fourteenth century, when, in 1323, the Franciscan doctrine of poverty was condemned.[44] This condemnation reflected a growing fear of extremism in the Church, a fear that dynamic movements that once could have been harnessed would now be destructive. In terms of elite integration, it meant that the Church recognized that its control over its officers and its ability to mediate social forces were declining.

The papacy will be discussed in its own right soon, but that institution showed strain in this period by its resort to what Southern refers to as inflationary tactics—the increasing use of its resources for temporary advantage despite their declining marginal utility.

Coherence: Coherence was another aspect that showed a real, though not too apparent, decline. The Church was still the unchallenged spiritual leader and principal judicial authority of the West, and Christianity itself was also unchallenged from within. Ecclesiastical morale had declined, however, and there were various serious challenges by men such as William of Ockham and Marsilius of Padua (as well as by the Franciscan ideal itself) to the way the Church carried out its duties. These challenges were met by repression rather than by redirection. More specifically, in Huntington's terms, the methods of dispute regulation, even among the highest elites, declined in effectiveness. The first great example of this was Pope John XXII's humiliation and the renunciation of his Doctrine of the Beatific Vision early in the fourteenth century.

The designation of functional boundaries within the Church became less clear. The proliferation of the various types of Orders, of course, inevitably brought many of them into conflict. This conflict appeared as early as the twelfth century with the decay of the Benedictine Order, and the appearance of the Augustinian Canons and the Cistercian monks.[45] Early friction grew into conflict with the organization of the more distinctive Dominican and Franciscan friars. After the great development of the religious Orders in the 1050-1300 period, they increasingly came into conflict in the next period, and so the functional boundaries and dispute resolution procedures were increasingly difficult to maintain.

More serious perhaps, in the 1300-1550 period, those without the customary authority in the Church, and even laymen, began to challenge doctrine. Of course, laymen had always been to varying degrees involved in the development of Church doctrine (and very much involved in Church politics), but the extent and vigor of their involvement here presaged a challenge to the hierarchy's very legitimacy. Again, the problem was to some extent that the Church had succeeded too well in helping the society to develop. Challenges were especially severe with regard to the Church's temporal activities. Non-Church organizations, in trade and diplomacy, for example, were seeking a still greater role in social governance. To a large degree, the growth of town life played a part in this development, but there was growth and development throughout the society.

The pope was the great regulator of functional boundaries and resolver of disputes within the Church. He also occupied a unique legitimizing (principally through judicial or quasi-judicial activity) position in all of Western Christendom. This special position rested on a belief that the pope had cer-

tain spiritual—supernatural if you will—attributes that had political consequences. The pope was a prince lile others, but unlike others, as well. Dante
was among the first to challenge in his writings the idea that the pope was
politically unique, but it had also been seen by others.[46]

Autonomy: The autonomy of the Church in this period appears superficially very high, maintaining at least its previous levels. In fact, we know
that the Church had organizationally overextended itself, and its efforts to
retain its customary liberties (effectively expanded in new circumstances)
required it to resort to an inflated provision of its spiritual gifts (such as
indulgences), and living off its past capital of good will and respect. This
process will be seen at work in the case of the papacy.

Adaptability: In short, the Church was not adequately adapting. Its
chronological age was growing, and it continued to master, by and large,
generational renewal. But it was in the area of functional adaptability that
it was at its weakest. It was stated earlier that a belief was growing throughout society that many of the major institutions of the Church, some spiritual
and many temporal, were irrelevant. It was seen that the charge was not
completely ill-founded—the remarkable development of Western society,
which the Church had done so much to foster, made elements of the Church
redundant. Yet organizations have a momentum, and the Church's organizational momentum, metaphorically, collided with that of such secular institutions as trade guilds and royal courts. The situation may be summarized
thus:

> This tendency to view established institutions as irrelevant was all the
> more dangerous because it coincided with a changing attitude [toward]
> politics. Here too the hierarchical structure which had been raised up
> with so much painful effort began to seem impractical and probably
> wrong. Everyone could see the secular governments with no theoretical
> pretensions were growing in strength and independence, and this cast
> doubt on the relevance, and then on the validity, of elaborate theories
> of papal overlordship, universal rule, and sacerdotal supremacy. At the
> same time everyone could see a wide gap between papal actions and
> papal pretensions.[47]

Ideally, the proper adaptation, in the broadest terms, would have been for
the Church to retreat gracefully. But an organization that has been so successful in growth, that has achieved so many great objects, that is still so powerful, that has such a strong sense of mission, and that has so many vested
interests is not likely to commit organizational suicide. The Church's "adaptive" behavior in repressing new ideas and being increasingly lavish in the
distribution of its spiritual favors was perhaps the only procedure open to it.

Looking more directly at elite integration in the Medieval period as a whole, the continuing dynamic element was the organizing capacity of the Church (its complexity, coherence, autonomy, and adaptability), and its complementary enhancement of the rest of the society's organizational capacity. As the Medieval society became stabilized, the Church became less relevant and increasingly redundant in terms of societal organizational utility, while at the same time raising the social cost of its operation.

In the first of the three periods, elite integration within the Church (vertical elite integration) was moderate, and the level of political-bureaucratic elite integration (in the present terms) was low. In the second period, high vertical elite integration was characteristic, with moderate—sporadic—political-bureaucratic elite integration. In the final period, vertical elite integration become in several areas, particularly on the "international" level.

The parallels between levels of institutionalization and forms of elite integration are clear in general terms. The types of elite integration which were described—and of which contemporary examples were given—were associated with institutional political development in our contemporary period. They were similarly associated in the Medieval period we just described. The first period was one of effective, but imperfectly developed, elite integration; the second period fits the model of an effectively integrated elite in almost every respect. The final period serves as an illustration of the disadvantages of overdeveloped vertical elite integration and strong political-bureaucratic elite integration.

Furthermore, the reasons in terms of elite integration and institutionalization for these relationships appear to be consistent in terms of the events and practices of the period. Autonomy was based principally on ecclesiastical self-selection and internal governance. When this procedure became overdeveloped—when the Church was able to make its rules with little moderation by the secular authority—the bureaucratic elite became increasingly parasitic. Coherence was high when it rested on, among other things, social contributions, but when it rested on independent sources of income and authority, esprit de corps became arrogance. Adaptation was based in the most productive stage on a flexibility (especially the ability to shift and draw on a variety of elites) and closeness to the larger society. Later, the ecclesiastical elite lost this creative adaptability and turned principally to various forms of repression. Complexity was the only virtue that remained, and even this one lessened marginally in the final period.

This is a general picture of the period. Greater specificity in the analysis is necessary to refine and further confirm it. The following two sections will, it is hoped, help do this.

The Division of the Western and
Eastern Churches

A useful political date for the division of the Christian Church into Eastern and Western wings may be that of the coronation of Charlemagne in 800. Indeed, this date could have been used as the starting point for the Middle Ages itself. The division of the Church, however, did not in fact begin so abruptly, but was the consequence of policies undertaken (inadvertantly, of course) about half a century earlier,[48] and the product of even earlier trends.

Nevertheless, the breakup of the Church was by and large an event that was not obviously foreshadowed. In fact, it appears to have occurred with what one can only call a remarkable suddenness given the size and age of the united Church. Until the late eighth century, the Church was under the political domination of the Emperor at Constantinople. In fact, as recently as 700, all Christian Europe was one political whole, with the Emperor at Constantinople ruling much of Italy. This realm included Rome itself, where the pope acted as the Emperor's secular deputy in the Roman Duchy.

Elite relations were well developed in this pre-division period. Byzantine officials were a common sight on the streets of Rome, and by 750, when the pressure of Islam was severe indeed, Rome had become very cosmopolitan, filled with all sorts of refugees. At the higher levels of the hierarchy, a remarkable degree of elite contact existed. Nowhere was this integration more evident than in the papacy.

> The nationality of the Popes reflected this state of affairs. From 654 to 752 only five out of seventeen Popes were of Roman origin; five were Syrian, three were Greek, three came from the strongly Greek island of Sicily, and one from some unknown part of Italy. In other words, eleven out of seventeen Popes during this century had mainly Greek, and only six a mainly Latin, background. This was in marked contrast to the century before 654 when thirteen out of fifteen Popes had been Roman or Italian. From this point of view of Christian unity the growth of the Greek element in the Roman church was a hopeful sign: it meant that the two halves of the Christian world could still hold familiar discourse together.[49]

The papal relation with the Emperor was not a hostile one, and when the Greek Emperor visited Rome in 663, he was received as its ruler.[50] Although there were substantial doctrinal disputes between the Eastern and Western wings, it was still possible as late as 680 for the pope to send legates to Constantinople, and for them to agree with their Greek counterparts to condemn as heretical the teachings of a previous pope, and the teachings of four patriarchs.

Though the situation in many respects was a favorable one on the surface—and, indeed' somewhat beneath the surface as well—it is now known that the Church was soon to divide. Theories on elite integration or Huntington's theories on political development and decay may provide clues as to why this was so.

COMPLEXITY

It has already been demonstrated that, though the Church in the West was not as organizationally developed as it was later to become, it had already reached a high level of organizational complexity. The form of complexity in the East differed in several respects, but it too was of a high order. Organizational ties between Rome and Constantinople were well institutionalized in terms of elite exchange, conferences, etc., as previously indicated.

COHERENCE

It was true that by the eighth century "Greek and Roman were already divided by an impenetrable wall of divergent habits, most of them insignificant, but deeply disturbing to orderly minds."[51] This was a serious problem, and perhaps even a growing one. At this time, though, there was still a sharp feeling that both groups were Christian, and that their doctrinal differences, though irksome and worrisome, were not sufficient to create a breech.

Divergent ways were of more concern to the second-ranking, generally northern European, elites. This elite discontinuity (between the European subelites and the higher ecclesiastical officials) will be discussed later, but an idea of the type of conflict is illustrated by the experience of the great papalist, St. Wilfrid.

> He arrived at Rome as a litigant in 704, appealing to the Pope against the archbishop of Canterbury. He made his speech in Latin and was mortified when the Greek Pope turned to talk in a foreign tongue with his advisers, 'who smiled and said many things that we could not understand'. It was a trivial incident, but it has a dramatic significance. Men like Wilfrid were the backbone of papal authority. The countries from which they came—England in the first place, then Germany and France —were the only places where papal influence could be strong because it was strongly desired. This kind of loyalty and the heroic actions which it inspired made the linguistic and cultural unity of the Greco-Latin world seem very thin.[52]

The point here is that, although the intellectual and spiritual tradition remained (and largely continued after the division) as, indeed, did much higher-level elite integration, what was increasingly lacking was the intimate

social, economic, and political base. Time and distance prevent social cohesiveness below the higher level, and this lack of social cohesiveness, and
the hierarchical form of ecclesiastical organization, made institutional elite
integration below the highest level impossible, too.

ADAPTATION

The chronological age of the still united Church was already a very long
one, and the Church, of course, had renewed itself generationally several
times. Functional age was a problem, however. The Church had not the depth
of resources in this area as it perhaps did in others. It may be that the two
wings of the Church were faces with different types of adaptive problems.
There was a more direct and continuing external threat in the East than in
the West, and problems of social organization and development may have
been greater in the West.

On the other hand, both wings managed to deal with their problems fairly
well after the division. It should be recalled that the Eastern church continued to defend itself against one of the greatest expansionary forces of
history for approximately six hundred years after the division.

AUTONOMY

The picture here, too, is mixed, but the general situation is clear enough.
The Church and the secular authorities were reasonably well differentiated—
certainly the period after the split did not show any marked changes. Elite
integration was at its most effective, however, at the very highest bureaucratic-political levels.

Since the unified Church apparently scored high on the Huntingtonian
and elite integration criteria, one should expect it, at a minimum, to maintain
its existence and perhaps even to expand. In fact, it dissolved (though its
component parts did not). One can identify a variety of reasons for the dis-
solution—an organization of such age, scope, and complexity does not break
up for one reason alone. There was the factor of distance, though this
element may easily be exaggerated; there was the influence of the tempera-
ments of the major actions—Charlemagne's passion for uniformity, for
example; there was the fact that the type of external threat each faced was
different in degree and kind.

The interest here is in the effect of elite integration, of course, and examination of this factor is revealing. As indicated in the previous two chapters,
elite integration is a multidimensional phenomenon. It is possible to have
vertical elite integration with horizontal elite integration; it is possible to have
elite integration in the political elite and not in the bureaucratic elite, and
vice versa; it is also possible to have good elite integration at one level and

poor at another. This latter is what occurred in the case of the East-West division. The higher officers of the church before its division were well integrated with each other—earlier we pointed this out with regard to the regional and ethnic origins of the popes, frequency of councils, etc. The second-ranking elites, however, especially in the West, were very poorly integrated—in institutional, social, or any other terms, with what was to be the Eastern church and the Eastern empire.

In other words, what is evident here is a well-integrated bureaucratic elite of elites (and, indeed, the very top elites are quasi-political) but beneath that level, in terms of elite integration, two largely separate organizations. This situation was not new in the eighth century and, indeed, its roots lay several centuries back. The division at about 800 was the culmination of a discontinuity travelling from the bottom up.

Second-ranking elites are very rarely as integrated as top-level elites, even in the most developed societies. The lower levels, however, generally serve as a supply region to higher ones, where there is, as here, adequate vertical elite integration. Attitudes acquired, or not acquired, earlier eventually have consequences at the higher levels. Even in the short run, the higher levels of an organization depend on the lower, and where division and alienation exist, the higher levels become less effective. The agreements, rules, and principles arrived at at the top must be translated at the next level. It is at these levels—especially the episcopal level in this period—that cohesion, autonomy, adaptation, and complexity have practical consequences. Many of the problems of adaptation that senior churchmen had in Germany must have seemed (and probably were) very far indeed from the problems that high churchmen faced in and around Constantinople.

The foregoing is not to say that poor second-level elite integration was the cause of the breakup of the Christian Church. However, it was probably a cause, and itself an indication that, despite surface appearances, the united Church suffered from severe internal stresses. The breakup of the Church did not appear conclusive then. For the next six hundred years, the higher officials of the two churches were in frequent, though sporadic, contact, attempting to work out some sort of reconciliation. There was never in the West much support on the secondary elite level for this reunification, and, of course, the pope was adamant about his own primacy. The problem was a political one at bottom—there could be no religious unity, it was assumed, without political unity. Orderly minds demanded it so, and, more important, the religious sphere required the coercive support of the state.

In a disparate world, an institution that unifies one part must at the same time separate it from the rest. The papacy was such a force in this period, becoming the principal unifier of the West, but also serving as the principal divisive institution to Christian unity. To a significant extent, this desire for

Western ecclesiastical autonomy/supremacy was based on ignorance and conceit.

> In the range of their ideas and experience, the scholars and statesmen of the West with very few exceptions were small men, whose strength lay in not knowing how small they were. They knew just enough about the thoughts of the Greeks to think that they were contemptible, and they knew nothing at all about the thoughts of their contemporaries in Islam. In this ignorance the West was able to develop a measure of confidence, however misplaced it might be.[53]

This ignorance was, of course, nourished by the two churches' separation, and the increasing difficulties of the Eastern church was seen in the West as a sign by God of the wrongness of the Eastern church's ways.

There was a steady drift apart until 1054, which culminated in the excommunication by the pope of the patriarch of Constantinople. This event may appear greater in retrospect than it appeared to the participants, but it was a serious sign that even the top elite ties were continuing to weaken.[54] It was becoming evident that "an ecclesiastical union, arranged for political reasons over the heads of clergy and people, could not succeed."[55] Efforts continued in the direction of reconciliation, however, and it was possible for the Greek Emperor Manual Paleologus to visit Paris and London between 1400 and 1403 seeking financial and other support against the Muslims.[56] Even at this time, mutual advantage would have dictated a reconciliation. More important, the Greeks were weak and ready to compromise, and the pope was relatively secure in his position. Though some support was given (for example, sixty-one loans were raised in England amounting to a little over £14,000),[57] the amount was grossly inadequate to the needs (assuming, as is doubtful, that any amount could have saved Constantinople from the Muslims). Despite the desire of many in the West to save their Christian fellows, the practical material of interaction was missing.

Elite integration, or rather its lack, operated between and within the two wings as a great element of autonomy and division. It contributed to the division, it contributed to the maintenance of the division, and it acted to discourage the establishment of any significant aid to Constantinople.

The Papacy and the Episcopates

Although these two complementary institutions are to be examined in terms of the concepts of political development and decay, and of elite integration, it is useful to follow the same three-part historical division used above.

THE EARLY PERIOD, c. 700-c. 1050

In this period, vertical elite integration with the ecclesiastical bureau-cracy[58] was well established by the papacy over the entire church, and could be called at least moderate in terms of the major sees. Although each see recognised the pope's primacy, each was largely able to direct its own affairs, though under the domination of the secular ruler.

> It [papal unity] was a unity compatible with the very slightest exer-cise of administrative authority. The affairs of the church received little direction from Rome. Monasteries and bishoprics were founded, and bishops and abbots were appointed by lay rulers without hindrance or objection; councils were summoned by kings; kings and bishops legislated for their local churches about tithes, ordeals, Sunday observ-ance, penance; saints were raised to the altars—all without reference to Rome. Each bishop acted as an independent repository of faith and discipline.[59]

The bishops had to look out for their own interests because in this period a bishop could expect very little aid from the pope in most conflicts he might find himself involved in with the monarch or local magnate. In fact, in most cases, the pope was in a very weak position if he came into conflict with one of "his" own bishops. The pope had little authority in their selection and less in controlling them thereafter. Bishops usually occupied the oldest insti-tutions in each of their own areas. Their own resources, and those of the ruler, were generally far greater than any the pope could hope to bring to bear. This situation varied from place to place, but the overall tendency was one of weak central and strong local authority.

Political-bureaucratic elite integration that existed was principally of the type we have characterized as social—based on family ties, particular his-torical experiences, etc. The bishop and his associates were very active in government and extremely influential—however, the bishop was not the directing authority.[60]

In the next two centuries, however, the superior adaptability of the Church in comparison with secular governments became evident. Such superiority pointed up the greater resiliancy and adaptability of an organ-ization that is high in complexity, autonomy, and cohesion over those that rely on some other form of social support. The church was also an organ-ization that enjoyed a high level of vertical elite integration, a characteristic that materially assisted it in making it complex, autonomous, and cohesive. The political system, on the other hand, was far from developing the political parties, the secretariats, and the legislative organs that eventually would permit it to be as effectively developed as even a primitive bureaucracy.

Of all the characteristics of elite integration, the one that probably was most useful was that of providing social information. The episcopal see was the principal institution for this purpose, and even at this relatively early date—before the establishment of papal legates, extensive correspondence, and frequent councils—the pope himself played a significant role in supplying and disseminating the type of who-is-who and who-can-do-what information that any large and complex organization needs.

PERIOD OF PAPAL GROWTH, c. 1050-c. 1300

This was a great age of papal expansion.[61] Principally, the papacy established an effective authority over the episcopates and improved its position in relation to the great secular rulers. The pope's role was also strengthened (and expanded) in relation to the new religious Orders developing in this period. Bishops lost much of their independence, but gained a strong ally in the pope against secular rulers. The secular ruler's power was not, however, greatly decreased in his own realm in terms of his relation to the bishop, though the pope became an increasingly powerful figure on the international level. Still and all, the basic fact of secular political supremacy continued in this period.[62] The rules of the game were more elaborate than before—as they are in any developed polity—and the opposing players were stronger and more skilled, again a general characteristic of developed over less-developed polities.

The Church's greatest contribution, in Huntingtonian terms, in the first period was one of coherence; in this period, the pope built upon strength and contributed still more coherence to the society. Coherence in the first period permitted the Christian polity to survive and then to grow. Growth, even more than decay, is disruptive, and if no new cohesive factors appear, or if the previous ones are not strengthened, growth will destroy its own base and the society will fall into decay.

The papacy's major contribution—and major expansion—here was in the areas of law and diplomacy. There were both specialized areas involving a highly trained and skilled elite. Both diplomacy and law contained certain tendencies toward centralization, which meant increased complexity and thus increased internal elite integration: the Church here selected and, more than at any other time, promoted its members, made its own internal rules, etc. New or expanded and revived institutions and practices became evident. Legates, councils, and vastly increased correspondence were the principal organizational tools that the popes called on to exercise their increased authority.[63] Leo IX, who laid the groundwork for this expansion, fostered it as a means to expand the papacy's temporal power, but it was necessary in any event as support for the Church's enhanced cohesive role in an increasingly complex society. In short, in this period, the Church became a coherent whole, with very few of the loose ends that characterized the early Medieval period. As indicated in Chapter 2, one of the problems with such a successful organization is that it tends to overexpand. This is what happened here.

We will not go through all the principles and examples of bureaucratic and political-bureaucratic elite integration and political development in this period. The most interesting effect is not a specific, but a general one: this great organization fell into decline, not only by violations of Huntington's criteria (though as we have seen, it did so and suffered for it) but also by their exaggerated application. In terms of political development, the Medieval Church suffered not only from its vices but also from an excess of the virtues that earlier established it.

One of the most unfortunate effects of the decreased political differentiation between the Church (especially the papacy) and political elites was that the Church lost what ability it previously had to stand somewhat separate from, and so to mediate, social conflict. In societies where the institutions are open to the direct influence of social forces, major conflicts are often associated with the fortunes of one institution or set of institutions—as illustrated by the English civil war in the seventeenth century and the American one two centuries later. If the Church had been more differentiated from the society, would the birth of the modern world have been fought out so much in religious terms? One does not know, but if one may make the "if" statement, one could say that the price of the Church's attempt in the next period to establish its temporal primacy was its spiritual primacy.

The principal cohesive element, obviously, in this middle period was the rise of the papacy. What we have not stressed was that the pope did not grow in stature over the hierarchy because he forced himself upon it (for he had no power to do so) nor certainly because the secular rulers, except in a few cases, invited him. He rose because he had the support of the other church elites; his rise served their interests. It was therefore also obvious that if the time came that he no longer served their interests, their support would lessen.

THE LATE PERIOD, c. 1300-c. 1550

The statement that the light bulb burns brightest just before it dims and goes out may not be accurate for light bulbs, but it is a useful analogy for some historical periods. Though it seemed so, the age of monarchy was not signalled in the eighteenth century by the rise of powerful kings, but what was foreshadowed was its demise; the age of the proletariat was not about to be ushered in in the first three decades of the twentieth century, but rather, again, the decline of the political influence of the common laborer.

The papacy was about to go into a slow, complicated, and often painful decline after the brilliance it achieved in the thirteenth century. The first two and a half centuries of this decline in terms of the above political development and elite integration models will now be considered.

Autonomy: In a developed state, the bureaucracy, which is the cutting edge of most governmental policies, is shielded from the social forces it deals with not only by its internal rules of procedure, its esprit, its emphasis on internal elite integration, but also by the political elite. The political elite stands as the protector of the bureaucratic elite principally by the political elite's serving to deflect the demands of the social forces in the society on to itself.

As the papacy sought to displace the secular ruler's temporal authority, it found itself (unknowingly) in a contradictory position. Successful or unsuccessful, these efforts alienated the powerful magnates. The damage was possibly the greatest when the challenges appeared to succeed—though the successes were relatively few—for in these cases the Church lost a valuable shield. The increasing conflicts of a developing society came to enter into the very heart of the papacy.

Because the papacy's strategic position was unsound, the tactics that it pursued also had the seeds of contradiction within them. For example, the Church attempted to increase its autonomy by demanding that only its nominees should be appointed to the numerous benefices and livings. However, to preserve its good relations with a variety of local interests and claimants, the Church resorted to an inflation of nominations—that is, it nominated many more for the posts than there were posts to be filled. Consequently, the monarch or local magnate had a very large number of nominees among which to choose—so many, in most cases, that his effective power of choice was not abridged and perhaps was even enhanced. Furthermore, it was easier for the monarch to deal with one pope than with a variety of local influences, and he could ascribe his rejections to the pope. Thus, the position of shield and protector was effectively reversed: the bureaucracy became the political "fall guy," a position it was not equipped to maintain.[64]

It would be the grossest of oversimplifications to say that all the clergy cared about the papacy was how well it could protect them and how well it could enhance their position. On the other hand, it would be unrealistic to ignore the practical origin of the clergy's support. The fact was that the monarch in the final analysis remained in a better position to protect, reward, and punish the clergy and the bishops than did the pope. The support for the pope in this period, as in the earliest, consequently weakened. However, the pope in this period was more demanding of support than in the earlier periods, and so the situation was a more brittle one.

Though the Church and the secular elites were often at odds, they were closely entwined, and any disruption of their sometimes uneasy symbiosis was likely to endanger the interests of both. Their autonomy was consequently a limited one. The destruction of the authority of either was likely not to enhance the other, but to endanger both. The Reformation itself—which of course had a variety of causes—was reflective of the breakdown in this mutual aid and advantage, but it falls outside our study. An earlier example was that involving the papal conflict with first Otto IV and then Frederick II.

> The Pope had been obliged to nominate Frederick II, the candidate whom he had least desired. The way was opened to that long course of destruction which swept away the Hohenstaufen family, the empire, and the whole prospect of effective temporal authority exercised by the papacy into a common political limbo.[65]

Thus, political-bureaucratic elite integration, where it occurred, actually weakened the Church (the "victor") as well as the vanquished.

> In the course of the fourteenth century the papal administration reached a level of activity which would have been unimaginable two hundred years earlier. . . . Every further step towards real power stimulated a more than correspondingly great contrary movement, and created complications within the system that nullified the effectiveness of papal action. Consequently there was a growing disproportion between the growth of papal administration and the effectiveness of papal leadership.[66]

Complexity: The papacy in this period, curiously, managed to sustain both an overelaboration of its activities, while at the same time experiencing a diminution of effective complexity. The correction for an overelaborated organization, to outsiders, is to simplify that organization. Simplifying an organization is a painful and difficult procedure for its members, however, and the "solution" usually undertaken is to attempt to cut through the red tape and vested interests by establishing yet another office, though with special powers. This is what the papacy did in the establishment of the papal legates and vicar-generals. At the same time, the papacy discouraged the development of new religious Orders, and even helped to abolish some older ones as well.[67]

In this period, papal influence and activity appeared to permeate the society. Councils, correspondence, papal agents, an elaborate system of diplomatic activity were all very much in evidence.[68] In a healthy, developed polity, there are more or less built-in brakes to these activities and organizations. The main limitations being the level of social demand (and resistance) for their services and the amount of resources available for their provision. We already indicated that the papacy was not so much responding to a demand, but rather was attempting to extend its jurisdiction regardless of need or demand. Papal resources were great—springing from the Church's large land-holdings and the fact that much of the legal activity was paid for by the litigants.

Diplomatic and judicial activity are necessary services in any complex society,[69] but the problem here was that the Church was duplicating in many cases (though certainly not all) services that could be rendered elsewhere at lower cost.[70] It should be added, however, that although this complexity was unnecessary in terms of the Church's contribution to the larger society, it was often of considerable utility for the Church itself, internally, as, for example, where a bishop was of political but little administrative use. In such cases, other Church officers could be used to administer his see.[71]

Coherence: The pope's cohesive significance was of three types. First, it was symbolic. The pope as leader of the Church occupied a position that symbolized the Christian unity of Europe. Second, it was legal. In many matters, the pope was the point of final appeal. There was less question, however, as to the pope's moral or symbolic authority in a variety of matters, than there was to his effective jurisdiction. Third, the pope was Europe's principal diplomat. This position did not spring so much from his sacral position as from the reality of his wide interests and the great amount of diplomatic and legal talent available to him.

The development of these cohesive capacities was discussed in the previous section. Their subsequent decay was produced by a variety of causes, but the ones stressed here are those that are relevant to the consideration of elite integration and political development. Of course, nearly all institutions and their leaders seek to maximize their own positions, but their self-interest—if it is to be considered functional—must be complementary to some social need. The problem with the Church here is that its capacities were exclusively redirected toward its own advantage. It seems that an institution benefits from its capacities, in the not very long run, only by their reflection from the body politic.

To be specific concerning coherence, the Church's efforts to enhance its temporal power did not serve to maintain and regulate conflict resolution procedures; quite the contrary, by challenging the rules of the game, it disrupted those procedures. Second, these efforts, rather than setting and maintaining functional boundaries, were in fact designed to destroy those functional boundaries. Finally, the effort to establish its temporal primacy damaged rather than enhanced morale, not only within the Church but in the larger society as well.

Adaptability: In this period, the chronological and generational age of the papacy was obviously higher than in the previous one. Its adaptive age also increased, though the fact that a new type of adaptation was called for put the adaptive capacity of the papacy to the test once again. It is well to remember that the Church did indeed adapt to the modern world. The Church and the papacy survived as a major—in some areas, a dominant—social force in Europe and, indeed, spread with Western civilization throughout the world.

Given the difficulties just described under coherence, complexity, and autonomy, the Church's adaptation was outstanding. So the question is not why the Church did not adapt—it did—but why it did not adapt so well and why it lost much of its influence.

As indicated above, the Church did not fully adapt because what it had to offer—and what it had given in the past—was being adequately supplied from secular sources. The church in the period 700-1050 acquired many temporal responsibilities because only the Church had the bureaucratic capacity for carrying them out. In the middle period, these capacities, enhanced and complemented by spiritual claims, grew even more. At the same time secular institutions increased in their capacities. For several centuries, the Church reacted to these secular challenges to its bureaucratic role by challenging the secular power's temporal dominance.

Summary and Overview of Political Development, Elite Integration, and the Medieval Church

The first task that the Church faced around 700 was to fill the administrative and moral vacuum left by the fall of the Roman Empire. The Church did this—not unaided, of course—and helped institutionalize what was to become a stable and productive society. After 1100 or thereabouts, the stability and cohesion that the Church had such a role in developing produced first a complementary and then increasingly a competing organizational development in the society. The Church, too, in this period further institutionalized itself, growing now not so much to fill a vacuum, but rather on the basis of its own momentum—supported by large landholdings, profitable judicial activity, and a captive clientele of all Christians. The organization of the Church, however, came increasingly into conflict with secular organs that had become better and cheaper servants of the crown and of local groups.

Several centuries earlier, the Church had divided into two branches, due in large measure to the drift apart of the Eastern and Western second-ranking elites. At the end of the Middle Ages, another great division of Christendom was to take place, again in large part due to the alienation of second-ranking elites from their superiors.

In discussing the Church's development, adaptation, and limited decay in this period, it was first noted that even in an organization as bureaucratic as the Church was in the high Middle Ages (1050-1300), there was a clear—though not invariable—differentiation between the political authorities and the bureaucratic (largely the clerical) elites. This differentiation was largely maintained in terms of vertical elite integration of the clergy which we described in Chapter 2. Though the papacy sought (c. 1300-c. 1550) to eliminate this distinction by establishing itself in a dominant temporal position, this challenge to the secular power failed.

Throughout this period—and for that matter for some time before it and continuing to this day—the Church was a highly complex organization. Elite integration played a large part in creating this complexity—by supplying experienced members to the new organizations as they developed out of the old. Moreover, and probably more important, the fact of vertical elite integration permitted the leadership to have the technical and social knowledge essential to such a large organization.

In the 1300-1550 period, the Church probably became larger than societal needs required. Its efforts to absorb the political elite into itself (political-bureaucratic elite integration as we described in Chapter 3) also put strains on the elite structure—here damaging the differentiation of the organization. The Church was increasingly in need of reform, and up to 1550 there was little effective capacity for internal reform.

Given its size and complexity, the Church was a very coherent institution indeed, and among its major contributions to Western civilization was its cohesive significance to the larger society.

There were many elements in the Church making for coherence—its long history, its supernatural aspect, its elaborate ritual. The most outstanding, of course, was the fact that it had a level of elite integration almost unmatched in any other organization. Promotion was almost exclusively from within, and entry, usually in young manhood, was for almost all an irrevocable step. An elaborate protege-mentor and key institution system existed to articulate the rise and distribution of elites.

Like any complex system, this one never worked smoothly at all places and at all times. It did work well until papal efforts to achieve temporal dominance damaged its conflict resolution procedures, disrupted internal functional boundaries, and eventually damaged morale—thus undercutting the papacy's own base of support.

It was as an autonomous—or perhaps better said, semi-autonomous—organization that the Church excelled. It had an independent source of income from its landholdings, a captive clientele in the Christian community, and a very well-integrated, differentiated organization. Here again, the Church's very high level of internal vertical elite integration made it possible for it to maintain its identity while deeply involved in temporal matters and also enabled it to resist constant secular pressures, though at the same time being under general temporal domination. The effort of the Church to absorb the temporal power damaged the traditional aspects of the Church's autonomy, as efforts to change the rules of the game always do. And, where successful, the Church was damaged. The secular power then no longer acted as a shield, no longer protecting the Church by bearing the brunt of the more extreme social pressures.

In the final analysis, though, it is the Church's adaptive capacity that is of most interest throughout the period. For the eight and a half centuries which we have briefly surveyed, the Church persevered, elected and maintained new generations of leaders, and met new challenges of many sorts. At the end of this period, the Church was to face the growth of the modern world, which released pressures that destroyed or basically changed nearly every institution in Europe.

The modern period lies outside this survey, but looking at the very considerable time period we do survey, it is evident that the Church not only survived, but on the whole prospered. Of course, the Church changed—that is what adaptation is all about. Errors were made, damaging trends were permitted to develop, and its contribution and authority declined in many instances and areas, but it was not destroyed.

The Medieval Church disappeared (for that matter, the primitive and high Medieval Church had earlier also disappeared with the ages they had lived and grown in), but then so did the Middle Ages. The point here is that the continuity of the institution—the Church itself—was not destroyed, but remained as a major social force not only in Europe, but throughout the world.

The reasons for this persistance have been discussed at length and have been summarized: the Church's cohesion, complexity, autonomy, and adaptive capacities in Huntingtonian terms and in terms of elite integration. It would be difficult, if not conceptually impossible, to conceive of this institution achieving the success it did in any terms which ignored Huntington's criteria and that of elite integration.

NOTES

1. See note 15 and the accompanying text in Chapter 2. Also see Joseph R. Strayer, *On the Medieval Origins of the Modern State* (Princeton: Princeton University Press, 1970).

2. Richard William Southern, *Western Society and the Church in the Middle Ages* (Harmondsworth, England: Penguin Books, 1970).

3. Peter Heath, *The English Parish Clergy on the Eve of the Reformation* (Toronto: University of Toronto Press, 1969).

4. E. F. Jacob, *The Fifteenth Century, 1399-1485* (London: Oxford University Press, 1961).

5. The principal theoretical work in political science dealing with the topic of religion and political development is Smith, *Religion and Political Development.* In his section on the Roman Catholic Church, Smith principally analyzes the Church from the late Medieval and in the modern period. Though the period of time he covers only partially overlaps with this one, his conceptualization of the role of religion in political development is complementary.

Other works which have been consulted and which also form the theoretical context in which we have written this chapter are Arendt van Leeuwen, *Christianity in World History* (London: Edinburgh House Press, 1965); Eisenstadt, "Religious Organizations and Political Process in Centralized Empires"; Peter L. Berger, *The Sacred Canopy: Elements of a Sociological Theory of Religion* (Garden City, N.Y.: Doubleday, 1967); Singer, *The Scientific Study of Religion;* and two other books by Donald Smith, both having a more contemporary but less general orientation: *India as a Secular State* (Princeton: Princeton University Press, 1963), and *Religion and Politics in Burma* (Princeton: Princeton University Press, 1965).

For an appreciation of Weber's work, which nearly all writings on religion as a social and political institution are indebted to, see Reinhard Bendix, *Max Weber: An Intellectual Portrait* (Garden City, N.Y.: Doubleday, 1962).

6. Smith well sums up the Church's simultaneous spiritual separateness and practical unity when he comments that, especially after Aquinas, "Medieval Catholicism thus developed strong organic tendencies toward identification of religion with society. But there are two important qualifications to this statement. First, whatever the church's political pretensions or success in securing political power, it remained structurally and organizationally completely separate from the state. Second, no matter how extensive the church's regulatory powers over society became, these could be cut off completely without destroying, or even causing major damage to, the church's essential structure" *Religion and Political Development,* pp. 273-274. Smith does note later that, in fact, such a separation has only become a practical possibility in the modern period.

7. See, for a discussion of the Cistercians, with special reference to their developmental contribution, Southern, *Western Society and the Church in the Middle Ages,* pp. 250-272, especially "Religion and Capitalism," pp. 259-261.

8. Note that this summary of functions coincides with Braibanti's description of the role of bureaucracy in terms of "the maintenance of compatibility between the spirit and substance of statutory law and administrative discretion"; "the role of the bureaucracy as an institution with the capability of converting political and social demands into programs and action"; and "the bureaucracy as a social institution for a large segment of the employed population." "Introduction," in Braibanti (ed.), *Asian Bureaucratic Systems . . . ,* pp. 5, 6. These points will be somewhat elaborated upon presently. As the next few paragraphs will indicate, however, the definition diverges somewhat from that of Fainsod, who takes an approach emphasizing the bureaucracy's role in coercion. "Bureaucracy and Modernization," in LaPalombara (ed.), *Bureaucracy and Political Development,* pp. 233-267.

9. Southern, *Western Society and the Church in the Middle Ages,* p. 19.

10. Ibid., pp. 134-135, for the relative lack of effectiveness of this sanction in the thirteenth century.

11. Heath, *The English Parish Clergy on the Eve of the Reformation,* pp. 1 ff. Also see W. A. Pantin, *The English Church in the Fourteenth Century* (Cambridge: Cambridge University Press, 1955), pp. 195-205, 213-214.

12. Jacob, *The Fifteenth Century,* pp. 288, 289.

13. Heath, *The English Parish Clergy on the Eve of the Reformation,* p. 19.

14. This description taken from ibid., pp. 12 ff.

15. Ibid., pp. 16 ff.

16. Ibid., p. 27.

17. Ibid., p. 28.

18. Ibid., pp. 28, 29.

19. Ibid., p. 44.

20. Ibid., p. 45.

21. Thompson, *The English Clergy,* pp. 13, 38. Thompson's broader narrative does not differ substantially from Heath's.

22. Ibid., p. 38.

23. Jacob, *The Fifteenth Century,* p. 271.

24. It is important to note that this discussion concerns a bureaucracy in a feudal, not in a bureaucratic state. See Gaetano Mosca, *The Ruling Class* (New York: McGraw-Hill, 1939) on this point. As Huntington comments, following Mosca, "The essence of the bureaucratic state is the one-way flow of authority from superior to subordinate; the essence of the feudal state is the two-way system of reciprocal rights and obligations between those at different levels in the social-political-military structure" *Political Order in Changing Societies,* p. 149.

25. Thompson, *The English Clergy,* p. 16.

26. Ibid., p. 13.

27. Jacob, *The Fifteenth Century,* p. 268.

28. Southern, *Western Society and the Church in the Middle Ages,* p. 5.

29. Ibid., pp. 16, 18, 22. Smith comments, "It is widely, and correctly, assumed that religion is in general an obstacle to modernization, and a major part of this analysis is concerned with the complex phenomenon of secularization. However, different religious systems present obstacles at different points" *Religion and Political Development,* p. xi. There is no argument here with Smith's contention that Catholicism in the Medieval period presented barriers to the reorganization of society's structure and values. Rather, his discussion concerns how certain relations involving institutionalization and elite integration operated in this pre-modern period in the same fashion that we have noted they operated in the modern world, both in developed and less-developed societies.

30. To note the parallels between the establishment of the Church bureaucracy in this primitive era with the establishment of the still developing colonial bureaucracies in new colonies, see Pye, "Bureaucratic Development and the Psychology of Institutionalization," in Braibanti (ed.), *Political and Administrative Development,* pp. 408 ff.

31. Southern, *Western Society and the Church in the Middle Ages,* pp. 28, 31.

32. On the Benedictines, see ibid., pp. 217-240.

33. Ibid., p. 33.

34. A point that is implicit in our description of this pre-modern bureaucracy but would not be in a parallel description of the modern bureaucracy of a contemporary developing country, such as Thailand, is that the changes being described were self-generated. They were not generated in response to any external model. In Riggs' terms, the Medieval society is "endo-prismatic." See his *Administration in Developing Countries,* pp. 38-42.

35. Southern, *Western Society and the Church in the Middle Ages,* p. 28.

36. The Church was in a favored position for adapting in part because it was one of the major, if not the major, legitimizers in its period. See Smith, *Religion and Political Development,* in his chapter, "The Religious Legitimization of Change," pp. 201-245.

37. The Church, of course, was not unique in producing disruption by engendering progress and change. The best discussion of this relationship is still that of Alexis de Tocqueville, *The Old Regime and the French Revolution* (Garden City, N.Y.: Doubleday, 1955). A more recent work which notes the same processes is Brinton, *Anatomy of Revolution.* The same general perception underlies Huntington's *Political Order in Changing Societies.*

38. James Q. Wilson, "Innovation in Organization: Notes Toward a Theory," in James D. Thompson (ed.), *Approaches to Organizational Design* (Pittsburgh: University of Pittsburgh Press, 1966), pp. 193-218.

39. Southern, *Western Society and the Church in the Middle Ages,* p. 28.

40. Ibid., pp. 42, 43.

41. The case was the same with the Chinese bureaucracy, without the dynamism and expansionism that occurred in Europe in the late Medieval and early modern period. See Balazs, *Chinese Civilization and Bureaucracy,* especially note pp. 23 and 35 for a discussion of the economic influence of the scholar-gentry in China.

42. St. Thomas offered a strong theoretical underpinning for this state of affairs: the more self-sufficient a community is, the more nearly perfect it is. *De Regno,* ii, c. 3 as quoted in Southern, *Western Society and the Church in the Middle Ages,* p. 47.

43. Southern, *Western Society and the Church in the Middle Ages,* p. 51.

44. Ibid., p. 44.

45. Ibid., see section on "The New Order," pp. 240-272. As Southern comments, "The collapse of the Benedictine monopoly in the late eleventh century coincided with the beginning of the period of rapid expansion in western society. It was an inevitable result of the new diversity of life and opportunity which this expansion made possible. For the first time for several centuries, there was room for many different kinds of organized life in the single area" pp. 240-241.

46. Ibid., p. 49.

47. Ibid., p. 48.

48. Ibid., p. 60.

49. Ibid., p. 54.

50. Ibid., p. 55.

51. Ibid., p. 56.

52. Ibid., p. 58.

53. Ibid., p. 66.

54. Ibid., p. 67.

55. Ibid., p. 78.

56. Jacob, *The Fifteenth Century,* p. 76; and Southern, *Western Society and the Church in the Middle Ages,* p. 84.

57. Jacob, *The Fifteenth Century,* p. 76.

58. It is important to bear in mind that political-bureaucratic elite integration (and disintegration) was being referred to here, not merely bureaucratic elite integration. The division to be analyzed was of a political as well as a bureaucratic elite, and, indeed, the two overlapped considerably.

59. Southern, *Western Society and the Church in the Middle Ages,* p. 96.

60. During the Carolingian Reconstruction of the Ninth Century, the bishop was "a man endlessly exercised in the care of temporal and spiritual things, a chief agent in the royal government of the kingdom," ibid., p. 175. Consequently, his loyalty to pope and king was a very mixed one.

61. Smith identifies this period as one of the key ones in the eventual modernization of the West. He notes that "(1) modernization in the West proceeded from a medieval

synthesis of church integralism; and (2) the integralist medieval society was shattered by revolutionary pluralism in the religious and intellectual spheres," *Religion and Political Development*, p. 27. It was the first point that occurred in this period. See the entire section on "Religious and Political Development in the West," pp. 26-32.

62. Southern, *Western Society and the Church in the Middle Ages*, p. 130.

63. Ibid., p. 100. This new activity and authority were, as is so often the case in new movements, perceived as a revival of an authority that the papacy once had, but had lost.

64. Huntington notes this protection by political elites of bureaucratic organizations, though he limits his example to that of the influence of partisanship. He comments, "The parties which at first are the leeches on the bureaucracy in the end become the bark protecting it from more destructive locusts of clique and family," *Political Order in Changing Societies*, p. 71. In the final analysis, the political elite is the protector and endangerer of all. This point applies equally to the relation between the secular/political and the religious/bureaucratic elites in the Medieval period.

65. Southern, *Western Society and the Church in the Middle Ages*, p. 145.

66. Ibid., p. 168.

67. This was a reversal of the general medieval practice of keeping the differentiation of functions within and among institutions to a minimum. This practice tended to keep power more or less equal among institutions. See Huntington, *Political Order in Changing Societies*, p. 109, for a discussion of this point.

68. Southern, *Western Society and the Church in the Middle Ages*, p. 134.

69. To a substantial extent, the rise of papal judicial activity may be a reflection of a decline in consensus in the Medieval world. See Huntington, *Political Order in Changing Societies*, p. 125, where the subject of the translation of political into judicial conflicts is discussed. Huntington relies on two books by Louis Hartz in this area: *The Founding of New Societies* (New York: Harcourt, Brace & World, 1964); and *The Liberal Tradition in America* (New York: Harcourt, Brace & World, 1955).

70. Southern, *Western Society and the Church in the Middle Ages*, p. 168.

71. Ibid., pp. 201-202.

Chapter 5

POLITICAL INSTITUTIONALIZATION

AND ELITE INTEGRATION

Introduction

In Chapter 2, it was indicated that it was most useful to define political elites as those working through or against the government who have significantly more than their statistical share of the capacity to affect the probability of social decisions. The form of the search for power by "political" elites, however, is distinguishable from that of bureaucratic ones. Political elites operate in an entrepreneurial fashion, seeking power in a political marketplace commonly structured by elections, the use of money to buy influence, or the use or threat of force.[1] The bureaucratic elite, on the other hand, characteristically operates to seek power in a well-defined hierarchical structure where emphasis is on seniority and demonstrable expertise.

Of greater substantive importance, the decisions of the political elite are of a policy nature and are conclusive for the period and level at which they are made. That is, this group is dominant over the bureaucratic elite. The term "political" is somewhat of an awkward one here, because all governmental elites are political in the broader sense. But the term "political" is that one which is generally used to describe this policy-making elite, and so it will be used rather than inventing a new term.[2]

This usage of the term is suggestive of an operational aid in identifying the political elite. The political elite is that group, in the positions it occupies, which is generally acknowledged throughout the society as being dominant. Here for guidance one must turn to the Braibanti configurational approach,[3] which requires the interpretation of any model in terms of specific societies and institutions. This is not merely a crutch to aid a model to fit a reality, but a consideration that always must be made when applying any model. The dominant governmental groups and institutions in a society are well known. A close observer of any political system will (except for details) be in little doubt as to what groups—particularly what groups of institutions—are dominant in a society. This was seen clearly in the preceding chapter when the Roman Catholic Church in Medieval society was examined. Even in such a structured—though frequently undifferentiated—society, where the Church bureaucracy was so pervasive, it was still clear that the political elite was identified with the secular powers, local and monarchical. This is quite a different process from developing a universalistic and deductively applicable concept of what an elite is.

In line with Huntington's and the approach described in the first chapters, the political elite will be operationally defined in institutional terms, focusing on formal governmental institutions. As a frame of reference, the presumptive elites will be identified as the following:

(1) *Indirectly or directly elected position holders.* Officers such as city councillors, most cabinet members, mayors, etc., all qualify here, though at different levels. There are apparent exceptions of course, such as the national legislatures in pre-Weimar Germany,[4] perhaps the legislatures of Communist states,[5] and certain "show" or captive legislatures in certain monarchical or one-party states.[6] These are exceptions, however, and will be evaluated in terms of the configurative criteria previously mentioned.

(2) *Hereditary rulers in traditional and in certain transitional polities.*[7]

(3) *Holders of power who have achieved their position by the use or the threat of force.* In practice, the successful user of force requires that he or his appointee be put in a position that is dominant. Once force becomes part of the rules of the game, it is apt to be used again, and those in power demand the highest level of security possible.[8]

(4) *Holders of party positions in one-party states are presumptive political elites.* As Huntington remarks, one-party states where the party has arisen from a praetorian, corrupt, or mass society must find their legitimacy in the party.[9] Consequently the holding of a post in the party—and in some cases membership itself—is presumptive of membership in the political elite.

At each level, the bureaucratic and political elites commonly work together very closely and are intimately involved in the processes of policy development and social mediation. Their contributions, however, are not of the same type. In India, for example, the principal divisions are at the village, the *tehsil* or block in a few areas, the district, the state, and the national levels. Though bureaucratic officials are active at each, from the district level up, the position of the bureaucrat is subordinate from the standpoint of final decision-making.[10] The bureaucrat is subordinate; the politician, dominant. Though the bureaucrat and the politician share the creation of policy alternatives, it is the politician who makes the final policy decision for that level.

Political Horizontal Elite Integration and Political Institutionalization

This unit of analysis refers to the movement of elites from one position (at the same level) to another. If big-city mayors could and did move from one city to another, or a governor in one state became a governor in another, or if chief executives of one nation became chief executives of another, horizontal elite integration would exist. There would be conceptual problems, of course, such as whether a move from the prime ministership of Upper Volta to the prime ministership of the United Kingdom would be a horizontal or a vertical case of elite integration. The construct in these terms, though theoretically possible, is empirically fanciful. Even within a polity, the nature of recruitment to political elites is such that horizontal elite integration in political terms (bureaucratic terms is another case, as indicated in Chapters 2 and 3) is very rare.

The resources for becoming a political elite—social skills and connections, ascriptive characteristics demanded by the particular polity—are such that they are not readily transferrable horizontally. Furthermore, and perhaps more important, there is little individual reward in such horizontal movement. Consequently, horizontal elite integration is virtually unknown in any polity, developed or not.[11]

There is a need for some type of integration on a horizontal level, however, and developed (and many less-developed) polities have created alternatives. The principal one—and a very old one—is the majoritarian or consensual council or legislature, which serves as a substitute for horizontal elite integration. In a council, each member (say, the representatives of city wards, states, or even nations) effectively loses part of his authority to the other members. Each member becomes an elite of parallel polities. For example, in the U.S. Senate, each senator gains legislative power over the affairs of each state in the union. A senator from Pennsylvania becomes a member of the elite of all the other forty-nine states. Of course, the system is modified by various sub-institutions such as the committee system and senatorial courtesy, but it effectively operates to distribute talent and power.

Another institutional substitute for horizontal elite integration is the constitutional structure which delegates authority, particularly in federal or confederal systems. Of course, it should also be noted that the need for horizontal integration may be less, say, for mayors between their cities than for mayors in wards within cities. In the former circumstances, all forms of horizontal integration will be weaker, horizontal elite integration among them.

The method of horizontal integration has been best rationalized in the parliamentary systems, in the United Kingdom especially. Here, the constituency that a Member of Parliament represents is less relevant to his representative functions than is the case in the presidential-congressional system of the United States. This arrangement is in part due to the federal nature of the U.S. political system, and in part due to the retention in the United States of certain late Medieval (Tudor) political patterns that have atrophied in Britain.[12]

But a discussion of the different substitutes for horizontal elite integration falls outside this study. Suffice it to say that political horizontal elite integration—the moving of elites from one post to another at an equivalent level—is extremely rare, and its relevance to a study of political institutionalization is consequently marginal.

Vertical Elite Integration

Political actors in almost all polities hold a variety of positions throughout their careers. There is a clear tendency for these positions to increase in prestige and influence, though often declining at the career's end. Political positions, of course, are ranked in influence and value by various complementary factors—such as the degree of discretion granted the incumbent, and his or her financial reward. Generally the size of a constituency or other unit of representation or governance is relevant to its ranking—the bigger, the more prestigious. For example, U.S. senators enjoy, on the average, higher prestige than representatives because there are fewer of the senators representing the same area; national ministers have more prestige than provincial ministers. These are obvious distinctions. Other considerations are also relevant in identifying various levels such as those of policy and the amount of resources (especially financial) that may be expended. Furthermore, the degree of discretion enjoyed by the elite, the form of power exercised (directly coercive, persuasive, etc.), and the personal attributes, ascriptive or not, of the leader generally associated with the position also influence the ranking of a position.[13]

The analysis could be limited to the exercise of specific functions (controlling the organs of education, etc.), and not attempt to describe a multidimensional elite structure. In institutional terms, however, the elite described will in most cases be a composite of several elites (of coercion, of mass communication, etc.), recognizing that individual actors may be more specialized in their capacities.[14]

A simplifying assumption will be used, that the government positions are elite positions, and that their generally acknowledged ranking is accurate, recognizing, of course, that individual and particular circumstances can change rankings. Such considerations are, however, exceptions and do not change the general pattern.

Vertical elite integration occurs where political actors start at a lower position and move to a higher one, and where this movement is systematic and stable. Each of these positions is not merely a place on a continuum, but rather is a discrete elite, having its own powers, mores, and expectations. The higher elites in such a circumstance are characteristically composed of former members of lower elites. Lower elites strive to enter the higher elites. Such a circumstance can be discerned in polities such as the Soviet Union, where a Khrushchev can start at or near the bottom of the party and rise to the top along a well-defined route—and where such a rise is not considered particularly unusual.[15] The same situation can be discerned in a democratic polity, where an Abraham Lincoln can start at a low elective post and become president. One major characteristic of developed polities is a high level of elite integration encompassing the middle and perhaps the lower political levels as well.

The lack of vertical elite integration would be seen in a polity that was highly ascriptive, where positions at certain levels were easily open to certain groups and absolutely closed to others.[16] Hereditary systems are often this way. Other polities which excluded designated racial or regional groups from certain levels of office would to that extent have poor vertical elite integration. Probably, no polity is completely open in these regards, though some are much more so than others. The developed and democratic polities are much more open than the less-developed. Some of the reasons for developed and democratic polities having this more open elite structure will become evident as we discuss each of the institutionalization criterion in turn.

Aside from the extent key positions are open to those holding inferior positions, there is also the matter of which positions are open and how these positions are related to their inferior ones—i.e., the *form* of elite integration. There are what may be called efficient and inefficient paths of advancement. For example, a typical aspiring politician in the United States would involve himself first in some sort of charitable activity, such as the Community Chest, and eventually run for some state office, such as state representative, and then run for a national office, such as to the U.S. House of Representatives. He will in most cases avoid associating himself too closely with labor union activity and will also avoid municipal office. In India, however, the aspiring politician would not be so sedulous in associating himself with charitable organizations, and also would not avoid municipal office. In other societies, active membership in a political party may be the first step in a political career and in others entry into the armed forces may be an ambitious politician's first move.[17]

Comparing the structures of elite integration in several polities, even where the political systems do not differ a great deal, may tell us much about the level and type of institutionalization and the key groups in those societies. It is worthwhile to note that, whereas in England membership and office in a labor union may be a great aid in political advancement (in the Labour Party), such strong involvement would be a strongly negative factor in all but a few areas of the United States. More could be said about this difference —its causes and consequences—but at a minimum it demonstrates that organized labor in England is more politicized (in the dimension of its elite structure) than in the United States.

Variety in the forms of elite integration is necessarily more restricted at the top than at the lower levels of a polity. Although a large country (and even many small countries) shows considerable variety in forms of elite integration at the lower levels, inevitably the paths decrease in number as the top of even the most flattened pyramid is approached.[18]

Great and significant differences exist among countries in terms of the form of vertical elite integration they have. An even more important distinction, however, is that one between political systems whose elite recruitment systems though weak, do function, and those that have little or no institutionalized paths of elite recruitment. For example, in discussing land reform, Huntington notes that "in the absence of effective parties, peasant unions, or other political organizations, the crucial resources are economic wealth and social status and the traditional elites capitalize upon their possession of these to secure election to the parliament in overwhelming numbers.[19]

In such cases, where there are few institutions capable of recruiting new elites, the capacity of the political system to coopt new groups and mediate their demands is greatly lessened. In less-developed states, vertical elite integration is less institutionalized, and, hence, social forces operate much more directly on the political system.

Complexity

The complexity of the political elite system refers principally to its differentiation and specialization. Are the elites alike in terms of race, age, region, wealth, etc.? In institutional terms, is there a variety of institutional paths through which an aspiring elite can enter and rise, and are these institutional paths specialized and differentiated enough to attract all or nearly all the extragovernmental (prospective, oppositional) elites in the society? A complex political system would be one, from the standpoint of elite recruitment, that would provide for a variety of paths to political power. There would consequently be a greater variety of opportunities for decreasing the level of social tension and encouraging reform.[20]

It may not always be sufficient to say that an elite structure has no overt bars to membership of certain groups. Particular groups—such as tribal minorities who are physically isolated or who speak a different language—may be effectively excluded unless special provision is made for them.[21] Likewise, if in practice entrance to politics is predicated upon a high access to financial resources, the elite structure is effectively less complex because it offers no paths to those who lack such financial resources.

On the other hand, it should be noted that prospective elites generally have among their skills the talents associated with money-making. This being the case, it is reasonable and probably functional as well that money be over-represented in any elite structures.[22] It is also politically unwise to ignore the intellectual skills that polemicists often have, or the social skills such as regional, tribal, or ethnic leaders are likely to enjoy. In an effectively functioning system, none of these talents is excluded. Politicians have a variety of skills and a variety of resources. Only a complex elite recruitment system is capable of converting these leaders into effective and integrated political actors.

The same variability of resources applies to groups as to their leaders. Certain groups may be small in number, but rich in money or intellectual influence or in some other skill that is politically exchangeable. Jews in America would fit this description. Other groups may be large in numbers, but relatively poor in other resources. Unskilled and semi-skilled laborers fit this description in most polities. A simple, undifferentiated elite system would be likely to leave such groups unrepresented. Where the elite system—such as through political parties or local elective institutions—makes provision for such groups, the system is consequently strengthened and the prospect for stable and effective government improved.

The alternative—a system that only rewards one or a few types of political ability—has several defects. First of all, it wastes talent, not only within the political system but in the larger society as well. It is rarely possible to discriminate against a group politically while at the same time giving that group the opportunity to develop its capacities in other respects. The most notable example of a polity which attempted such an arrangement was that of the former Belgian Congo.[23] A second consequence of low complexity and elite integration is that those excluded, if not severely repressed, are apt to be a source of political instability in the state. The best-known example of this was the exclusion of certain elements of the new bourgeousie from policy decisions in the last decades of the *ancien regime*.[24]

Specific instances may be open to question as to how much and how long a group has been excluded, but there is little question that a group whose financial and perhaps social standing has risen will be a source of instability and opposition until its political status is brought into line with its social and economic status.

Some societies are manifestly better developed in this regard than in others. The political system of Canada, for example, provides a variety of paths to political power, accommodating at some level nearly every major social group and type of elite. No ethnic or racial group is specifically excluded, though, as in most countries, individuals tend to base their power on the support of a public with the same sort of background. It is also possible in Canada for money to be converted, in an institutionalized fashion, into legitimate political power.[25] In another mature country—Spain, for example—certain groups (such as Basques and Catalans) are not only politically restricted to their area of origin, but are also largely effectively excluded from higher office. Furthermore, a semi-aristocratic "old money" class acts as a severe damper on the conversion of new money into political power.

Complexity has certain specific uses in elite integration, in addition to the general ones just described. A continuing elite must from time to time co-opt new members. One of the most efficient ways for a ruling group to defuse an extremist opposition is to deprive that group of its leadership. Such co-optation is very rarely a matter of conscious choice by the established elite, still less a matter of conspiracy. Co-optation takes place when the excluded leaders are pushing to get in and where there is a variety of institutions and paths of advancement suitable for absorbing them.

The posts of a political system act both as a magnet and as a net to the prospective political elite. The sheer numbers of posts are an advantage—and, hence, the advantage of federal systems—because they offer the possibility of giving places to a variety of elites and groups. One of the reasons for the U.S. success in integrating new elites is that it has enjoyed a very large number of elected (and also appointed) positions to distribute to the more demanding of the newer groups.

Of course, the pre-eminent institution for elite recruitment is the political party, particularly one that has branches over a large geographic area. National parties in democratic systems, such as the Indian National Congress, and cadre parties in one-party states, such as the Communist Party of the Soviet Union, fulfill this requirement. Where there is no single party encompassing the polity, several parties, each covering a certain area, may be as efficient in elite recruitment,[26] at least on the regional level. In fact, in a diverse state, close analysis indicates that the national party (such as the Democratic Party in the United States in the 1940s or the Congress Party in India in the 1950s) is actually effectively composed of several regional organizations more or less articulated into one "holding company"-like institution. The essential point here relative to elite integration is that every part of the country be "covered" by a party with national links.

Regionalism is one of the most powerful sources of political action[27] and, consequently, if any region is not served by a political party—in a state where political parties serve to recruit and advance elites—the elite of that section is likely to be excluded, to that region's own and probably eventually to the larger polity's detriment.

Another characteristic of a complex party system—aside from its geographic complexity, just discussed—is the variety of opportunities it affords to aspirants with different types of skills. This is a specific application to political parties of the advantages of complexity discussed a few paragraphs earlier. Political parties perhaps even more than governmental institutions are able to make use of a variety of skills, often on a temporary basis. This is particularly the case with relation to fiscal and persuasive skills. Where political parties exclude certain skills—such as a doctrinaire left party might exclude those with exceptional ability to amass wealth, or a doctrinaire right party might exclude individuals who lack this ability—the elite recruitment and integration system is weakened by narrowing its range of available resources.

There is a reciprocal relationship between the complexity of a political system and elite integration. An elaborate governmental system is an aid to elite recruitment in terms of the number of positions—in simple terms, more people can be involved if there are more places to put them. Furthermore, a complex system is apt to be hierarchical, and, consequently, not only make for the recruitment of elites but for their internal integration.

All government systems have formal positions, to a greater or lesser extent. However, all government systems are not assisted in their recruitment to these posts by a political party system. Therefore, in terms of their government structure, polities will vary in degree of complexity. In terms of the political party system, they may vary in the kind of complexity.

As Huntington notes, it is not necessary to have political parties for elite recruitment and integration.[28] Before the development of political parties—and still in many areas today such as Burma and Sierra Leone—elites are promoted and recruited into the political system more or less directly (that is, a person is appointed to a post or is elected by a private following). This recruiting process is generally articulated with certain ascriptive groups, such as leading families, hereditary craft guilds, ethnic-oriented religious groups, etc. Such a system is highly retentive of the existing power structure, and so is favored by conservative groups.[29] Indeed, such a recruitment system continues to be a major distinction between conservative and liberal polities in developing as well as in developed states.

It is possible for a party system to decline, and perhaps disappear, and to be replaced by such an ascriptive system. This may be the case with new nations and anti-colonial political parties. Vigorous political parties (such as the CPP of Ghana[30] and perhaps the Basutoland Congress Party of Lesotho) which grew up in opposition to an external power often decay soon after independence. As Huntington points out, in such cases, the members frequently shift their loyalties (and practical interests) to the government, leaving the party increasingly weakened.[31]

The reasons for such a shift of political energy from the revolutionary or nationalist party to formal government institutions are several, among which is the natural desire to benefit financially from independence (more likely in a governmental than in a party position) and the elimination of the previous principal issue (e.g., colonialism). Another reason—of more interest here—is one relating to elite integration. In many new states, whether they be Burma in the late 1940s, or the government of South Vietnam in the early 1950s, there is a very small elite group available for governmental and party positions.[32] In the first place, a less-developed society, and particularly one where the previous government was not only skeletal but also dominated by foreign rulers, has a relatively low number of people with the necessary social and administrative skills to carry on the more demanding administrative and political tasks. Political skills, like other skills, are for the most part acquired and not inborn, and the same may be said for a stable clientele basis.[33] Furthermore—and probably more important—the establishment of the new state has made large numbers of normal prospective elite members politically unacceptable due to their former association with the losing side. The victorious nationalist or revolutionary party excludes these groups, and they attempt to exert their influence in other ways, thus weakening the dominant party.

Another reason for the decline of the political party after independence or a revolution also concerns elite integration. Although a revolutionary party may continue on a leftward course concerning property rights, it is apt to become somewhat conservative concerning its own scope and action and its relation to opposition groups. The ability of the political party to bring in new groups is consequently not so attractive to the new ruling group. It does not want additional groups admitted with whom it will have to share power and whom it may not trust. For the admission of new members, the new regime, like older conservative ones, is likely to turn to restrictive screening alternatives such as personal relations or regional ties.[34]

On the other hand, a continuing advantage of a political party over other methods of elite recruitment and integration has to do with what may be called its low level of immediate consequence. A political party—even a political party in a one-party-dominant state—is able to recruit and use and even reward a variety of elites without necessarily giving many of them what would be considered a dangerous or disruptive amount of influence in the state. Where a government—such as that of the former King Mahendra of Nepal[35]—attempts to eliminate political parties but to carry on a somewhat democratic system, more and more groups fall into opposition. In the final analysis, however, a party system which is deceptive in its distribution of posts—which is to say, a party system that for certain elites recruits without real prospects for advancement—is not likely to retain the support of these groups. This is to say, in another way, that a political party system which is not part of a system of elite integration will not be successful in integrating new groups.

It was mentioned earlier that political parties may be many or few, so long as, as a whole, they effectively cover the entire polity. What must be stressed before going further is that the role of political parties is supplementary in any polity. It is an important supplement, and sometimes an essential one, but, in the final analysis, the effectiveness of a polity relies upon the effectiveness of the government institutions in distributing the values and meeting the needs and demands of the society. Political parties must be evaluated not in their own terms, but in terms of how well they support the institutions of government.

Not necessarily the most important, but probably the most dramatic instance of political party support of the institutions of government occurs in transitional states, soon after a new elite has acceded to power. This may occur after a political revolution or after the transfer of power from a colonial regime to an indigenous one. In these circumstances, all the institutions of the previous system are in question, and those of the new group have not yet been established in the new context. In such a circumstance, the new elite is unsure of its supporters and of its own power.[36] The leadership at the top must establish and maintain a high degree of control of the many new people in the government. Commonly used methods are those of the secret police (as in the case of the Soviet Union up to at least the late 1950s) or the encouragement of a high degree of public criticism and accusation of purported "public enemies" (this was the case after the French Revolution). The secret police may be institutionalized and may last a long time; the public accusation phase usually ceases fairly soon.[37]

The revolutionary/nationalist party plays an important role in establishing organizational complexity, and complexity in elite recruitment and elite distribution in the new government. If, however, there was no independence or revolutionary struggle, there will consequently be no such political organization, and so the new countries—such as those of French Africa which (except for Guinea) were given rather than won their revolution/independence—will lack a key aid in establishing themselves.[38] Where the new rulers find themselves in power and have a tested organization, this organization may be a substitute (though more often a supplement) for a secret police, as it can also supply the necessary evaluation and winnowing services.[39] On the other hand, a party can only carry out this function where it has a special relation to the government and is dominant in the society. The need for an official dominant party—that is, the need for a political party that has a monopoly or near monopoly of elite recruitment and distribution—is even greater if the new government promises and must provide an increased level of popular involvement in the government. This participation may be through elective means (as in India) or by an expansion of the bureaucracy (as in Burma).[40]

Especially in transitional societies, political institutions are enhanced when strong political parties make their contribution to political stability by establishing elite integration. It has been seen that strong parties make for strong elite integration in the political system as a whole. The focus shifts now to whether elite integration enhances political parties themselves. This question will be evaluated in terms of Huntington's three criteria for political party strength.

(1) "A party . . . is strong to the extent that it has mass support."[41] Mass support is not necessarily the same as mass participation. A government may have mass support and mass participation—in terms of popular demonstrations, for example—but this support may only have significant political consequences where it is adequately institutionalized. The more the mass participates, the greater must be the institutionalization of this participation, else the political system becomes incapable of ruling—turning into, in Huntington's terms, a praetorian society.[42]

A party secures mass support by obtaining the support of elites who are capable of manipulating the masses. For such elites, in return for their support, the party must have an essential—perhaps *the* essential—capacity to serve as a step in political advancement. A party may serve other societal functions as well: it may, for example, be the means by which values are distributed from the top down. That is, it may not be part of the process of elite recruitment, but only part of the process of the distribution of values such as security or honor. In fact, of course, successful parties tend to distribute both power and other values.

Two outstanding examples in this century of masses being manipulated (probably to their advantage) by a new elite using newly acquired social skills are those of the Congress Party of India since the Rowlett Satyagraha of 1919[43] and that of the U.S. civil rights movement since the early 1950s, especially the Southern Christian Leadership Council.[44] In both cases, a new (actually a second-generation) middle class rose to prominence by creating an organization that could control large numbers of people for the purpose of bringing social pressure to bear on an authoritarian but not a totalitarian government. It is instructive to note that, though both systems of mass mobilization were institutionalized, only the Congress Party continued and developed, whereas the SCLC (and other similar organizations such as the Congress of Racial Equality) declined. There were, of course, a variety of reasons for the development of one organization and the decay of the other, but it is worth noting that the Congress Party permitted a high degree of vertical elite integration, whereas the SCLC was much more closed in its own leadership, and the organization as a whole lacked the explicit orientation to the regular political system that the Indian National Congress had.

(2) In a second aspect of "party strength is organizational complexity and depth,"[45] Huntington discusses organizational complexity and depth partly in terms of the linkages of the party with other institutionalized social forces, such as labor unions and farmers' organizations. These linkages will not be discussed in any detail here—the analysis is being generally linked to explicitly governmental and political organizations. From the standpoint of a political party, however, such contacts are facilitated where the political party is part of a system of elite integration. In other words, party/institutional social forces links are a matter of mutual effort, and the leaders of organizations such as farmers' bureaus and labor unions are more likely to establish links with a party in which they can become members and rise than in a party which does not give them the opportunity for advancement. Where the party is an instrument of elite advancement, it may serve—especially in modernizing countries—as a means of integrating rural and urban elites.[46] Illustrative of a party serving to integrate rural and urban elites is the Turkish Republican People's Party.[47]

A successful party is also one which enjoys links to a variety of social groups without being the creature of any one group. In the short run, a political party in power and closely tied to one social group—for example, to the rural poor or the industrial rich—may have a greater flexibility of action than one with a variety of clientele to satisfy. One of the reasons that revolutionary parties can accomplish so much in the way of establishing new social and political patterns is that their narrow and relatively uninstitutionalized clientele base permits the party to act with little restriction. Over the longer run, however, a government or a political party seeking adequate social support usually acquires a more various social base. This enlarged base—this variety of membership—is generally achieved in party terms by making the party a means of upward advancement for the elites of clientele organizations. Obviously, these organizations must themselves be somewhat institutionalized if they have elites to supply.

Turning to the contribution of elite integration to party complexity (and leaving the topic of the contribution of party complexity to elite integration), the same arguments discussed in Chapter 2 are found again. Any organization that is complex, and also has depth in terms of the variety of social groups it encompasses, requires a high level of internal technical and social knowledge. Furthermore, its leaders must be trained at each level in appropriate techniques, and also their personal characteristics must be known to their superiors.

These principles of complexity, which were discussed at length regarding the formal institutions of government, apply equally to political parties. The techniques of political organization are learned in political organizations, usually in an apprentice capacity. Untrained leaders—especially in democratic systems—are occasionally brought in at high levels precisely because they have not committed themselves to any group (Eisenhower in 1952 was such a case). Nevertheless, the party at all levels, including in most cases the highest, requires a substantial number of officers who are skilled in all the techniques of politics from creating a mass propaganda campaign to seeing that the right voters have transportation on election day.

A complex organization—and perhaps especially a political party more than any other—requires a high degree of internal social knowledge. It is essential that lower-level elites seeking mentors and higher-level elites seeking proteges know about their prospective allies. The same applies to peers seeking political allies. This type of knowledge—who is politically reliable, who is politically compatible, who is politically effective—is necessary for any well-run complex organization. A complex organization can only acquire the bulk of this information by internal recruitment, though a certain significant amount can be acquired by recruitment from closely associated clientele organizations. For the most part, a large and complex organization—whether it be General Motors, the Communist Party of the Soviet Union, or the Neo-Destour Party—must recruit internally to maintain its essential political equilibrium.

(3) "A third aspect of party strength concerns the extent to which political activists and power seekers identify with the party and the extent to which they simply view the party as a means to other ends."[48] This is essentially a question about the symbolic value of the party and its effect on esprit

and morale. Many of the earlier comments of Huntington and myself on coherence apply equally here. There are various reasons for people acquiring an emotional tie to an institution—pre-eminent among these reasons is a history of the institution fulfilling (or holding out the prospect of fulfilling) strongly felt social needs. There are other reasons as well—perhaps including an emotion-satisfying ritual—but the ones that are relevant here are those relating to the systematic shift of elites upward from position to position.

Individuals who have risen within an organization are likely to have affection toward that organization. They may not only feel a measure of gratitude ("the party's been good to me") but, perhaps even more important, they will admire the political wisdom of an organization that has rewarded them. There will also be a social dimension to such an attachment, because if they have, with others, risen in that organization—shared their past and intend to share their futures—the constituent elites will owe that organization a greater loyalty than one they see merely as a tool for political advancement. Indeed, one of the great advantages of depth in a political party—the existence of a variety of organizations such as ladies' auxiliaries or social clubs—is to create this type of attachment. Again, complexity alone is no guarantee of elite integration, but elite integration can seldom exist without complexity.

One other aspect of elite integration and emotional attachment to a political party should be mentioned. A political party with high levels of elite integration perceives its lower-level elites as prospective upper-level elites. Those not at the top are consequently favored with a special degree of influence and information in contrast to other prestigeful groups in the society—or at least a self-perception in this regard. They are insiders and consequently consider the party theirs. This perception increases their loyalty to the party, and consequently the strength of the party.

In summarizing what was said about complexity and the political party, it must be noted, with Huntington, that a political party system is a major element of any developed, complex system. There are notably different types of political parties, but a greater distinction than among types of party systems is a distinction between party and non-party systems. Even among political systems, however, major distinguishing factors can be discerned in the degree of vertical elite integration which the party enjoys. No broad, deep, or emotive system can exist without elite integration, because the process of elite integration supplies the technical and social knowledge that all elaborate organizations require for effective performance, and also because a system where elites are integrated is apt to have a higher effective level than a system where elites are unintegrated.

One final point before the argument on complexity and elite integration as a whole is summarized. Huntington demonstrates[49] that complex states enjoying a wide distribution of power are more stable than centralized regimes. Major types of political disruption—revolutions in particular—are more likely in centralized regimes than in any other, though obviously centralization is only one variable affecting proneness to revolution. Vertical elite integration is compatible with both a centralized and an uncentralized political system. A centralized system—such as that of the contemporary German Democratic Republic[50]—may have a high level of upward mobility for its lower elites, and its higher elites may be composed of those who rose through the ranks. On the other hand, a centralized regime may not be characterized by such integration, as is generally the case with such rightist authoritarian regimes as Trujillo's in the Dominican Republic[51] and that of Hassan[52] of Morocco.

Where there is a distribution of power and where this distribution is articulated and integrated by a central authority—as is the case in India and the United States—a system of vertical elite integration is necessary for the reasons outlined at length above, and so is invariably found in stable, complex, political systems.

In this section, it was noted that political elite complexity could be evaluated in terms of the complexity of the formal institutions of government—the village council, the state legislature, the national chief executive, for example —and it could also, complementarily, be evaluated in terms of the quasi-political "feeding" organization such as prominent families, farmers' bureaus, and, most important, the political party. The argument was made that, though there are different types of political parties, the most important distinction is not among the types of political parties, but rather whether there is or is not a party system at all.

The relation between political parties and elite integration was twofold. In the first place, elite integration was seen to enhance a political party system, and perhaps in certain cases it would be essential to such a system's continuation. This was due to the fact that parties were much more effective in securing and retaining membership where the party is a vigorous institution for upward mobility. Aspirant elites would in this circumstance seek out the political party, as well as the party seeking them. Not only would they be more likely to join the party, they would be more likely to remain in it, for their prospects for upward mobility would be enhanced by their seniority. Furthermore, long membership, advancement, and the social interaction of the members will give them affective ties to that party.

Not only does elite integration enhance a political party system, so a complex political party system enhances elite integration. The value of elite integration for socializing, identifying, and distributing political talent was discussed in several contexts. Political parties, because of their flexibility in receiving members (and quietly letting the less useful drift off), are an excellent means of testing and evaluating new elites. Finally, it was argued, along with Huntington, that complexity—especially in terms of a distribution of power—is a deterrent to revolution and an aid to stability. Elite integration is compatible with a centralized system, but centralized systems are also in many cases characterized by a lack of such integration. However, complex and decentralized systems that are articulated and integrated by a central authority require and invariably have a vigorous system of vertical elite integration.

AUTONOMY

The autonomy of the political system and its components refers to how well the political system is differentiated from other social institutions and how independent the political system is in mediating social forces. This differentiation and modified independence are accomplished by the institution's self-selection of its leadership and its determination of the principles used for the distribution of values within the organization. The political universe here is defined in terms of institutions—principally, the formal organs of government, and those institutions (pre-eminently the political parties) which are very closely related to the formal governmental structure.

Let us first look at political autonomy and elite integration in terms of the governmental structure. To a large extent, democratic norms—and, to some extent, democratic reality—argues against self-selection of the political elite in terms of formal government offices. That is, former mayors may not appoint their successors; U.S. presidents may not formally choose senators. Indeed, the U.S. Senate may be the most exclusive club in the world, but it is a very curious club in that its incumbent members may not choose new ones. The choice is made by an outside agency—in the final analysis, by the electorate. In fact, of course, the influence of the incumbents may be considerable. Though it is seldom exercised jointly and overtly, incumbent elite influence is often employed individually and directly through the political party and other ancilliary organizations and processes. Indeed, to a large extent, this is how elite self-selection operates.

In regard to the choice of their own leaders within the government structure, the incumbents are very little restricted. Here, the leadership choice is principally affected by internal variables.[53] In most parliamentary systems, explicit rules require the cabinet and the prime minister to be drawn from the parliament. In fact, most parliaments provide for an elaborate system of apprentice positions such as membership or chairmanship of key committees, under-secretaryships, etc. These positions are first organized by party, but after that broad distinction, it is the principle of political reliability and effectiveness—moderated in many cases formally or informally by seniority—that dominates.[54] The institution of the U.S. cabinet, where members are frequently drawn directly from outside the government or political party hierarchy is an exception, reflecting as it does the "regal" aspects of the presidency.[55]

The capacity to choose its own leaders is undoubtedly one of the greatest sources of autonomy any institution may have. It is one of the major explanations why—for the good or ill—many old, stable, and powerful elective organizations are peculiarly unresponsive to popular pressure. Thus, political autonomy and political responsiveness may be in conflict. This is particularly illustrated by institutions that are elected, but resistant to public pressure, such as the U.S. Senate, which has very high levels of vertical elite integration concerning its own leaders.[56]

Political vertical elite integration and government autonomy in electoral states have just been discussed. Let us turn to the same topic in authoritarian systems. It is a notable distinction between left and right political groups (democratic or not) that the left tends, more than is the case with the right, to rely on its own organization for recruitment. This is due in large measure to leftist organizations desiring to weaken existing social groups (such as prominent families or business associations). Thus, such groups hardly constitute an appropriate supplier *in institutional terms* of left political leadership.[57] The Mexican PRI is a good example of this tendency to rely on internal means for elite renewal (avoiding other institutions such as the Church or alliances of influential families) in a semi-electoral context. It is notable, however, that the PRI retains societal links through its emphasis on sectoral organization.[58]

The right—especially the authoritarian right—on the other hand, tends to rely much more on external, especially traditional, social institutions for its supply of new leaders. These groups—families, ethnic or racial associations, economic associations—are well organized and carry out the function of vertical elite integration better than a relatively new organization, such as a party. The associations organize, socialize, winnow, and in some cases, such as the economic ones, test the prospective members. Furthermore, since it is the position of these traditional organizations that conservative parties, more or less, want to maintain, there is no political contradiction in using them as an aid in elite integration. An example here is the Spanish political system under Franco. Even so captive and loyal an organization as the Falange Party has decreased in importance, being displaced increasingly by the direct influence of such organizations as the Church, the military, and certain prominent families.

Here, in terms of elite integration, reasons for the different behavior and capacities of left and right political organizations may be discerned. The left tends to be more autonomous in terms of elite recruitment than does the right. This autonomy also permits it to be more active in policy implementation, and, not being beholden to external organizations, better enables the leadership to take strong action against its own members when it serves its purposes. Purges are more likely to be a left-wing than a right-wing phenomenon. On the other hand, the left parties lack the social resources of the right. The right's resources tend not only to be deeper, but, for a variety of reasons associated with the age of these relations, more institutionalized and especially more valued.

There is thus a contradiction (moderated by the political party) between autonomy and access to social resources. In these terms, "He travels fastest who travels alone" applies to social change. Thus, the left can progress rapidly, though it has difficulty in consolidating gains.

After self-selection, the next criterion for autonomy is the level of freedom the government organization has in its own rule-making concerning internal procedures, especially those involving the resolution of conflict and the distribution of internal values.

Effective rule-making rests upon the assumption that rules will be applied and enforced. It is not possible to develop a set of rules in a context where they are not tested in experience and especially where their effective application is uncertain. A system that largely depends on external organizations for supplying its elites will have less authority over those members than one that selects internally. In the first case, members will enter with key attitudes and obligations acquired elsewhere and will look to those external organizations for continuing guidance and support. Consequently, these external organizations will have substantial influence over the political organization.

It is instructive to note when the autonomy of a political organization is at its greatest, and to see to what extent it then has control over its own elites and rule-making. Two occasions where such absolute governmental autonomy is evident are in the case of a military government, such as that Germany experienced after World War II, and where a group rules another along some rigidly ascriptive principle. This may exist in a strict aristocracy, or is more likely to be seen in this century by one coherent minority racial group ruling over a larger, less cohesive one. In these cases, the political system is as autonomous as possible, given the inevitable real limits that exist in any governing situation. The rules are made by the governing group, and they select their own members.[59]

Yet, such a static elite structure in what eventually becomes a changing society is inherently unstable. A stable polity requires consultation with and the cooperation of those ruled, and this interaction between rulers and ruled must be institutionalized in order to be effective. Consequently, the tendency of any stable system of government is to create elites of some sort among the ruled and admit them—albeit in very limited terms—into the ruling process.

The political party is the usual modern means, especially in left regimes, of resolving elite autonomy with effectiveness. The party does this principally by maintaining links between the government and the relevant social forces through elite integration. For our purposes, there are two general types of parties, though with some overlap. First there is what might be called the governing party. That is, a party which seeks to impose policy decisions and personal choice on the formal government apparatus. These parties are, of course, characteristic of an extreme form of Communist states, though curiously they are even more characteristic of "party-machine" democratic polities. Examples here are many, including the Democratic Party machine in Pittsburgh under David Lawrence. In the more extreme cases, there is a constant conflict and tension. The party/ministerial conflict in the states of the Indian Congress Party in the 1950s and early 1960s is the classic example.[60]

In this context, the level of governmental autonomy is inversely related to the level of party dominance. But if the government structure suffers in terms of restriction of policy alternatives, it gains in terms of access to wider social forces, for which the party serves both as buffer and converter of demands.

Although the dominant party system (dominant in its relation to the government) has been widely written upon, it should be noted that it is probably not the most characteristic form of government-party relationship. A more common type of political party—in both authoritarian and nonauthoritarian states—is the subordinate type whose major function is acquiring support by recruiting elites for the government structure. The party has little policy control over the government, but it does require a clear loyalty from those who hope to become government officials. The U.S. party system is an example of such a case, as was the Indian Congress Party under Nehru, and the British Conservative Party.

In summary of autonomy and political elite integration, we noted that the autonomy of a political system is achieved principally by the setting of its own internal rules (primarily for the distribution of values and the resolution of disputes) and the selection of its own leaders. Both these processes may be facilitated by vertical elite integration, though it is possible for the level of autonomy achieved by a severe restriction of the elite pool to result in a decline of effectiveness through that organization's isolation from a wider polity.

Internal rule development and application are greatly facilitated when the subjects of the rules must look to the rule-making authority for their advancement, and where their entry was also dependent on that authority. If other institutions have authority or are in a near monopoly position for supplying such elites, it is to be expected that they will have a proportional influence over the rule-making authority of the receiving body. Furthermore, rules are made and applied in a context that is reflective of previous socialization.

Members politically socialized outside the political organization—and carrying the effective attitudes engendered by that exotic socialization—will bring those attitudes into the political organization.

Second, vertical elite integration is an effective way for an organization to maintain control over its selection of its own members. We noted, however, that the selection of new elites by old ones in electoral states is indirect, usually being mediated in the more developed states by the political party.

COHERENCE

Coherence in a political system refers to the agreement within the organization as to its functional boundaries and to its conflict resolution procedure. Organizations that score high in these respects are also those that are characterized by high morale and high discipline.

There is a distinction between the type of coherence that is associated with political organizations on the left and on the right, particularly with regard to functional boundaries. In this century at least, left political organizations—organizations that seek to make major innovational changes in the society—tend to have less definite functional boundaries than the right. That is, the area of policy-making and action is wider for left organizations. This follows on the greater desire of left parties to create changes.

Functional limits in left organizations, consequently, are not as well defined as in right organizations. Indeed, most of the internal conflict of a left policy concerns the setting of functional limits. To a large extent, Brinton's natural history of revolution can be understood in terms of the shifting definition of functional limits in the ruling group. Innovation is a far more open-ended process than is conservation. There is even less anchor on this process due to the left's tendency to recruit directly from its own organization (high vertical elite integration) or externally on the basis of ideological commitment.

The conservative polities have lower vertical elite integration and better-defined aims. It is much easier to identify what is, than what is desired. The conservative parties have their functional limits more or less given to them. Furthermore, their reliance on external agencies—families, churches, etc.— for recruitment and often for policy direction also simplifies, albeit by limiting—their choices.

Thus, right organizations—or any organizations that choose to preserve what is and to be influenced in their choice of leaders and policy by closely associated organizations—are likely to have better functional limits than those on the left. The role of elite integration here is not a simple one. High internal vertical elite integration tends to create disciplinary and affective commitment—two aids for agreements on functional limits. But it was also noted that the innovative orientation of left organizations and the relative lack of external organizations limiting their options by control over their elites, makes agreement on functional limits more difficult.

Agreement on methods of conflict resolution is Huntington's second aspect of coherence, which we will examine in terms of political elite integration. There are three general types of conflict resolution procedures. At the most primitive level are those relying more or less directly on the use of violence and coercion. Haiti, especially under "Papa Doc" Duvalier, and to a lesser extent, Jordan, fit this category.[61] Second, there is a very wide range of polities that depends on a variety of nondemocratic but institutionalized consensual processes. The outstanding example here is that of the Soviet Union. Finally, there are, of course, various types of electoral majoritarian systems, such as in Denmark or in Australia.

It is beyond the scope of this work to analyze each of these conflict resolution systems in detail, but each will be looked at in terms of the effectiveness of the system and elite integration.

Conflict resolution by violence and coercion may seem a contradiction in terms—that is, the purpose of conflict resolution may be seen to be the elimination of violence and so a system characterized by high levels of violence is consequently necessarily failing in this function. This would appear an unduly limited—and somewhat unrealistic—definition to us. Political conflict is most usefully defined as when two groups seek contradictory objectives, involving in some way the structure of the polity. This type of conflict is in fact frequently resolved by the use of violence and coercion.[62]

Such a means of conflict resolution is characteristic of polities having a low level of institutionalization, with or without major popular participation. Elite integration could exist in a violence-resolution context, if the elites of higher violence were drawn from those of lesser violence. To some degree, this is the case, because no polity is completely unstructured. In fact, the structure that generally applies in this type of state is a military or paramilitary one, often including the secret police. These organizations, have, of course, a great capacity for institutionalization.

The second type of conflict resolution polity is a nondemocratic consensual one, such as exists in Yugoslavia[63] (where the political party is important) or as existed in Salazar's Portugal[64] (where it was relatively less important). These polities may be structured along a more or less all-encompassing party, as in the Soviet model, or perhaps along long-established lines of certain leading families enjoying certain special relations to the government organizations. The more bureaucratized and rationalized the polity is, the greater is the scope for a regular movement of elites from one position to another. This was discussed in detail with examples in Chapter 2. The relation between rationality and hierarchy and vertical elite integration is a complementary one: complex organizations require elite integration for the provision of information and technical skills and socialization, and elite integration only can operate within a complex organization. Less highly organized institutions, however, rely on methods for their integration other than the movement of elites—such as a share ideology or family traditions. Thus, elite integration enhances the effectiveness of bureaucratized nondemocratic polities more than is the case with the more traditional nondemocratic ones.

The third method of dispute resolution is that found in majoritarian states. It was noted that elite integration serves to aggregate and socialize elites—common histories, the prospect of shared futures, the effective ties developed during a long and successful association, all operate to permit conflict to be resolved with greater facility than where backgrounds and attitudes are different.

As was also noted, conflict resolution in a complex majoritarian state requires a political party. The political party not only serves as a buffer to and as a converter of external social forces and their associated demands, but also is a means of recruiting, socializing, and distributing elites. These functions are all enhanced by the party's serving as a means for elite advancement.

In short, elite integration is not only a useful but an essential process for the resolution of conflicts in any developed polity—majoritarian or not. It can take somewhat different forms, and certainly exist to different degrees, but there must be some institutionalized movement of elites from lower to higher institutions of government in any institutionalized state.

The third major factor that Huntington notes as being relevant to coherence is the rather abstract but essential one encompassing morale, discipline, esprit—the general self-perception of the leaders of an organization that the organization is worthwhile and that personal values should be (and are) subordinated to organizational needs. This self-subordination is to some extent a product of the two previous variables—clear functional boundaries and effective means for internal dispute resolution. It is also a product of much more, such as a strong history of high self-regard, a clear and well-articulated organization, a high level of social support, and a history of success.

It would be a mistake to overemphasize the role of elite integration in producing this discipline and morale. The general social milieu and past accomplishments are most important. On the other hand, morale, esprit, and discipline are reflections of what in other contexts is called community. Through its socializing function, elite integration aids in the development of esprit as well as giving the organization the political effectiveness that well-founded pride requires. This coherence—the identification of boundaries, the provision of dispute resolution procedures, the existence of esprit and morale —is provided at different levels by different structures. The nation-state itself is one such level of coherence, the political party is another, and a local system of family alliances would be yet a third. Elite integration may play a role in all these systems—it certainly does in the more-developed—but it is seldom the major factor.

A final word on coherence. In Chapter 3, it was pointed out that in bureaucratic terms it is possible to have at least the first two criteria of coherence—those concerning functional boundaries and dispute resolution—imposed from the outside. Though unsatisfactory in many ways, an external organization—a dominant political elite—can impose such limitations on a bureaucratic elite, though with negative effect on that elite's capacity. However, there can be no external authority on a dominant political elite. It is possible that a polity can for a time be made coherent by a strongly emotional tie to an overarching ideal—such as a religious or an ideological one. We know of no case, however, where this ideal has proven successful for more than a few years. Coherence, it appears, must not only be institutionalized, it must be self-generating as well.

In summary of coherence and elite integration, it can be said that elite integration plays an often important but seldom crucial role in generating a high level of coherence. It aids by its socializing and recruiting functions, but unquestionably there is a variety of other considerations—past success, social support—that go into making a political elite coherent.

ADAPTABILITY

The final general criterion of institutionalization to be discussed in terms of political elite integration is that of adaptability. Adaptability is measured in terms of the institution's chronological age, generational age (how many times it has made a generational transition), and functional age (how many times it has made a transition from one set of functions to another).

In Chapter 2, it was noted that old political systems are more adaptable than new ones and that old institutions, by and large, are associated with old elites.[65] This relationship is not invariable by any means, but it is a characteristic one because (1) old institutions tend to have some developed system of elite integration, such integration being an aid to effectiveness and, hence, longevity, and (2) in any system of elite integration, time is required for a member to rise. Consequently, leaders in elite integration systems will tend to be at least in their late middle years. Also, it was suggested that older members may enjoy a higher level of political skill—perhaps including flexibility as well—and so make for a more effective institutional elite.

It is thus principally in indirect ways that elite integration aids in establishing (rather than simply reflecting) chronological age. There is one other effect, however, that is often overlooked. Lower level elites entering an organization that has a tradition of drawing its higher members from within have, after even a fairly limited tenure, a vested interest in that organization's continuation. They are consequently resistant to changes that lessen the degree of elite integration in that organization. This "young fogey" effect serves as a nonadaptive influence.

Generational age is the second criterion for evaluating an institution's adaptive capacity. The process of generational renewal is accomplished in most political systems by the protege and key institution system, described above. In many polities, generational renewal is accomplished by means of heredity, purchase, or some form of coercion. Less often and only in simple organizations, chance may play a direct role, as it did in certain electoral practices in ancient Greece. Sometimes all methods exist at different places within one polity. There may simultaneously be a hereditary monarch, an elective parliament, and local terrorism in some areas.[66]

In more developed polities, generational renewal—which is to say elite renewal—is accomplished in large part by the key institution process. In nearly all highly organized polities, there is a more or less generally noted set of institutions—or steps—to power.[67] In ascriptively dominated polities, it may be necessary to be of a certain race or family to be considered eligible to occupy specific posts. In most modern polities, the ascriptive considerations, though present, are broad enough to open the competition for elite status to a very large number of individuals.

The key positions vary from polity to polity. In the United States, there are strong institutional elite ties between state legislatures and the Congress.[68] In the United Kingdom, there are obviously strong links between certain subcabinet positions and the office of the prime minister.[69] The military itself—and especially the positions leading to the chief of staff—are important links to national political power in Turkey.[70] The same situation can be observed on the local level in any political system, where the path to county councils or mayor may require certain intermediary positions such as alderman or justice of the peace.[71]

There is a great variety of elite integration patterns, though those in elected polities tend very strongly to include elected positions from the early stages of a member's career. The key institution method—which describes a high level of vertical elite integration among institutions—is one of the most common and also one of the most effective methods of generational transition in existence. It assumes continuity of policy and a trained and compatible elite. Its defect is that it may become so distinct from the rest of the polity that, as in fourteenth-century China, the elite becomes estranged from the larger society.

Another method of generational renewal—though not necessarily separate in practice from that of elite integration—is the protege-mentor system. This system, wherein members of the old elite individually choose followers and favorites, training and smoothing the way for them, is most characteristic of ascriptive societies, where the basis of the mentor-protege relation is family, caste, tribe, etc.[72] It does, however, exist in all societies, and may have some basis other than ascription. A similar scholastic background (the school tie) or merely a strong temperamental affinity is quite sufficient to establish such a relationship.

This is a rather effective method of generational renewal except in periods when the nature of the elite must undergo rapid change. Even here, the process has the advantage of flexibility, given its decentralized nature. Furthermore, this process is not antithetical to the key institution system described above. In fact, the two often go along together, with the protege following in the mentor's footsteps. It is difficult in such circumstances to discern whether elite integration is operating as a passive or active force in generational renewal. Loyalty does tend in these circumstances to be centered on the personal relationship, rather than on the institutional one. However, the protege does not advance in a vacuum. In most systems, he must perform at a minimum level regardless of his mentor's assistance, and, of course, receive training and socialization in this institutional context.

The protege and the key institution systems are the two most common means of generational renewal, but they are not the only means. There are methods of generational renewal that involve coercion and violence as dominant themes. Institutions can indeed survive by such methods—as the history of Haiti in the nineteenth and twentieth centuries illustrates—and also sections of a larger polity may be subjected to this form of generational renewal, though higher or lower levels may not.[73]

Even under such circumstances, a degree of elite integration and institutionalization generally applies. The most effective wielders of violence and coercion are individuals who have a special relation to institutions of violence (the armed forces, the police) or of coercion (banks, courts of law). In such circumstances, there will be a degree of elite integration involving violence/ coercion institutions and their hierarchical superior institutions.

In summary of the relation of adaptation to elite integration, it has been indicated that the general effect among political elites, as among bureaucratic elites earlier examined, has been positive. The positive relation exists moderately for chronological and functional renewal, and is of greater utility for generational renewal.

Summary

It was noted in this chapter that the relation between political elite integration and institutionalization is in almost all cases a positive one. The uniform positive relation is in some contrast with that between bureaucratic elite integration and institutionalization which was discussed in Chapter 2. In the latter case, the relationship was seen to be a mixed one: positive at points, negative at others.

The reason for this difference probably has to do with the fact that political elite structures are less rationalized than are bureaucratic elite structures. Consequently, the less-rationalized political structure is more likely to benefit from any additional means of integration. This is especially the case with left political organizations—whether polities or subordinate political groups—because these organizations frequently are deficient in the integrative aids of ascriptive forces (such as family, tribe, religious institutions, and secular traditions).

In the next chapter, political elite integration will be examined in a more specific context, looking at the case of India.

NOTES

1. For a full-scale analysis of political elites and power distribution using economic and quasi-economic models, see Anthony Downs, *An Economic Theory of Democracy* (New York: Harper, 1957). Stein Rokkan uses such an analysis in his "Norway: Numerical Democracy and Corporate Pluralism," in Robert A. Dahl (ed.), *Political Oppositions in Western Democracies* (New Haven: Yale University Press, 1966), pp. 70-115.

2. Riggs makes this distinction in his *Administration in Developing Countries,* pp. 54-57. Also see note 1, Chapter 3.

3. Braibanti, "Political Analytics Reconsidered."

4. See Stein Rokkan, "The Comparative Study of Political Participation: Notes Toward a Perspective on Current Research," in Austin Ranney (ed.), *Essays on the Behavioral Study of Politics* (Urbana: University of Illinois Press, 1962), pp. 73-76.

5. See Meyer, "Historical Development of the Communist Theory of Leadership," and Friedrich, "The Theory of Political Leadership and the Issue of Totalitarianism," both in Farrell (ed.), *Political Leadership in Eastern Europe and the Soviet Union,* for a theoretical perspective on how one should evaluate "representative" forms in Communist states.

6. See Rupert Emerson, *Representative Government in Southeast Asia* (Cambridge, Mass.: Harvard University Press, 1955). Emerson argues that one of the reasons for the weakness of these institutions was that they were "basically modelled on well-established Western patterns, rather than seeking inspiration from their own remoter past or that of other Asian people," pp. 5, 6.

7. It may be objected that this grouping apparently violates the procedural definition of a political elite. Medieval dukes and modern monarchs in states such as Iran are not engaged in seeking (though perhaps in expanding or retaining) power. This group is, however, appropriate to the substantive criterion; these are the people who are dominant in terms of policy decisions and who are generally acknowledged as being dominant.

8. A book that takes a careful analytical view of the role of violence as an ongoing rather than an occasional phenomenon is N. C. Leites and C. Wolf, Jr., *Rebellion and Authority* (Chicago: Markham, 1970).

9. "In the absence of traditional sources of legitimacy, legitimacy is sought in ideology, charisma, popular sovereignty. To be lasting, each of these principles of legitimacy must be embodied in a party. Instead of the party reflecting the state, the state becomes the creation of the party and the instrument of the party," Huntington, *Political Order in Changing Societies*, p. 91.

10. Taub, *Bureaucrats Under Stress*, for a excellent analysis of this situation in the Indian state of Orissa.

11. Horizontal elite integration would perhaps be useful if it did exist, but in fact it does not.

12. See the chapter, "Political Modernization: America vs. Europe," in Huntington, *Political Order in Changing Societies*, pp. 93-139.

13. For a general discussion of the question of elite ranking, with specific reference to elite integration, see Robins, "Elite Career Patterns as a Differential in Regional Analysis: A Use of Correlational Techniques and the Construction of Uniform Strata." See also T. Fox and S. M. Miller, "Occupational Stratification and Mobility," in S. Rokkan and R. Merritt (eds.), *Comparing Nations* (New Haven: Yale University Press, 1966), pp. 217-237.

14. Hayward Alker, Jr., "Regionalism vs. Universalism in Comparing Nations," in Bruce Russett et al., *World Handbook of Political and Social Indicators* (New Haven: Yale University Press, 1964) discusses this additive approach of indices of selected factors.

15. For two fairly brief analyses of the Soviet elite, emphasizing institutional forces, see Gehlen, "The Soviet Apparatchiki," in Farrell (ed.), *Political Leadership in Eastern Europe and the Soviet Union*, pp. 140-156; and Michael Gehlen and Michael McBride, "The Soviet Central Committee: An Elite Analysis," *American Political Science Review*, 62 (December, 1968), pp. 1232-1241. For analyses of the patron-client model see Armstrong, *Soviet Bureaucratic Elite;* Barghoorn, *Politics in the USSR*, pp. 184-185; for evaluation of this thesis, Stewart et al., "Political Mobility and the Soviet Political Process."

16. An excellent study of such a polity in miniature is found in Edward Banfield, *Moral Basis of a Backward Society* (Glencoe, Ill.: Free Press, 1958).

17. See Chapter 6 for a specific discussion of the role of efficient and inefficient paths on the nature of an elite.

18. Such relative lack of differentiation and specialization is one of the reasons for upper level elites being less stable in personnel and policies than the "mass" of elites below them.

19. Huntington, *Political Order in Changing Societies*, p. 390.

20. Huntington notes the key place of new elites in reform: "In each case, reform is made possible by the intrusion of new elites and new masses into the formerly restricted political arena," *Political Order in Changing Societies*, p. 386. See his entire chapter on "Reform and Political Change," pp. 344-396.

21. However, if these groups are truly isolated, whether geographically or socially, there would be no political need for their inclusion. An interesting study that describes how socially isolated groups may attain elite status is Joseph P.L. Jiang, "Towards a Theory of Pariah Entrepreneurship," in Gehan Wijayewardene (ed.), *Leadership and Authority* (Singapore: University of Malaya Press, 1968), pp. 147-162.

22. A Marxist interpretation of politics would consider such a statement naive or gratuitous, and, of course, it is not necessary to subscribe to a Marxist view to note the continuing importance of wealth in politics. It is simply being observed here that political and elite systems vary in their responsiveness to financial influence, and that a lack

of such responsiveness produces social strains. For a study of how money operates in a developing Western polity, see William Gwyn, *Democracy and the Cost of Politics in Britain* (London: Athlone Press, 1962). See the chapter, "The Cost of Elections: 1832-1918," pp. 21-60.

23. Ernest Lefever, *Crisis in the Congo* (Washington, D.C.: Brookings Institution, 1965). Especially note "The Belgian Colonial Legacy," pp. 6-10.

24. Brinton, *Anatomy of Revolution.* "Classes and Class Antogonisms" and "The Eternal Figaro," pp. 54-73.

25. For a discussion of the various forms of political influence that wealth may take, see Gwyn, *Democracy and the Cost of Politics;* Robert R. Alford, *Party and Society* (Chicago: Rand McNally, 1963). Of special note is James S. Coleman, "Political Money," *American Political Science Review,* 64 (December, 1970), pp. 1074-1087; see especially "The Negotiability of Money and Political Power," p. 1078.

26. See the section by Huntington called "Strong Parties and Political Stability," in *Political Order in Changing Societies,* p. 408. We will be referring to this section in more detail later in this chapter.

27. An excellent theoretical study of the influence of regionalism is E. Allardt, "Implications of Within-Nation Variations for Cross-National Research," in Rokkan and Merritt (eds.), *Comparing Nations,* pp. 337-372.

28. Huntington, *Political Order in Changing Societies,* p. 411.

29. Huntington, *Political Order in Changing Societies,* pp. 404 ff., comments on the distinction in levels of institutionalization and type of elite recruitment between conservative and left political groups.

30. Martin Kilson, "Authoritarian and Single-Party Tendencies in African Politics," *World Politics,* 15 (January, 1963), pp. 262-294. Kilson stresses the anti-democratic aspects of the CPP.

31. Huntington, *Political Order in Changing Societies,* p. 411. This results in a more general decline because "a marked dispersion of resources means a decline in the overall level of political institutionalization," ibid.

32. See Wilson, "Nation-Building and Revolutionary War," in Deutsch and Folz (eds.), *Nation-Building.*

33. Ibid.

34. The problem is resolved, where it is resolved, by retaining a one-party dominance. Huntington, *Political Order in Changing Societies,* pp. 422 ff., suggests some persuasive reasons for the success of one-party systems in modernizing states, emphasizing the historical origins of the one-party state.

35. Rose, *Democratic Innovation in Nepal,* especially pp. 475-477.

36. See Wilson, "Nation-Building and Revolutionary War"; the FLN legitimized the government of revolutionary Algeria, not the reverse. See, however, Hannah Arendt, *Origins of Totalitarianism* (London: Allen & Unwin, revised edition, 1967) for the importance of coercion in achieving a legitimizing function.

37. See Huntington, *Political Order in Changing Societies,* p. 400; also note the quotation from Leonard Schapiro, *The Communist Party of the Soviet Union* (New York: Random House, 1960), on the same page.

38. Ghana may be contrasted with its French neighbors. The existence of the CPP gave Ghana a head start in institutionalization. However, Nkrumah's dissipation of his own and his nation's energies eventually created a situation where the army and the civil bureaucracy were the only institutions capable of maintaining stability. Sri Lanka and Pakistan are two other countries, neatly contrasted here with their neighbor and fellow imperial subject India, where the lack of a pre-independence political party movement damaged them after independence.

39. The decline of the secret police under Khrushchev and the rise of the party were probably not simply functions of the personal power vacuum created by Stalin's death. A society with a strong, highly institutionalized party does not require a strong secret police.

40. Note, however, that the one-party system is inherently less complex than the multiparty system and consequently more restrictive in the number and variety of elites it permits into the system. For a discussion of the role of party and elite recruitment in a multiparty system, see Huntington, *Political Order in Changing Societies,* p. 430; and concerning a one-party system, see ibid., p. 425.

41. Ibid., p. 408.

42. Huntington borrows this term from David C. Rapport, where it first appears in his "Praetorianism: Government Without Consensus," Ph.D. dissertation, University of California, Berkeley, 1960.

43. An excellent study of this movement, principally along historical lines, is that of R. Kumar (ed.), *Essays on Gandhian Politics: The Rowlett Satyagraha of 1919* (London: Oxford University Press, 1971).

44. See Hanes Walton, Jr., *The Political Philosophy of Martin Luther King, Jr.* (Westport, Conn.: Negro Universities Press, 1971).

45. Huntington, *Political Order in Changing Societies,* p. 410.

46. Ibid., pp. 434-438.

47. For most of the period since 1923, the Republican People's Party was the only legal political party in Turkey. The Democratic Party ruled from 1950 to 1960. The best analysis, emphasizing elite characteristics, is Frey's *The Turkish Political Elite.*

48. Huntington, *Political Order in Changing Societies,* p. 410.

49. Ibid., p. 367.

50. Heinz Lippman, *The Changing Party Elite in East Germany* (Cambridge, Mass.: MIT Press, 1973).

51. The Dominican Republic under Trujillo, though centralized, also had many praetorian characteristics. See the quotation from Abraham Lowenthal in Huntington, *Political Order in Changing Societies,* pp. 215-216.

52. A book that emphasizes the modernizing aspect of recent Moroccan history is William Zartman, *Destiny of a Dynasty: The Search for Institutions in Morocco's Developing Society* (Columbia, S.C.: University of South Carolina Press, 1964).

53. Matthews, *U.S. Senators and Their World.*

54. Guttsman, *The British Political Elite,* pp. 200-221; Buck, *Amateurs and Professionals in British Politics, 1918-1959.*

55. Huntington, *Political Order in Changing Societies,* p. 114. Huntington relies on A. F. Pollard, *Factors in American History* (New York: Macmillan, 1925), pp. 72-73.

56. Obviously, the Senate has sources of autonomy in addition to its capacity to choose its own leaders.

57. We must distinguish here between the social and the personnel base of recruitment. Revolutionary leaders, of course, very often come from dominant and conservative groups. The point here is that these revolutionary recruits have no institutional relation to their groups of origin. Children of bankers may become revolutionaries, but bankers very seldom will be and those selected to represent bankers probably never will be.

58. It should also be noted that the PRI, though having strong links with traditional groups, has made its strongest electoral gains between 1952-1967 in the most developed areas of Mexico. Barry Ames, "Bases of Support for Mexico's Dominant Party," *American Political Science Review,* 64 (March, 1970), pp. 153-167.

59. For a detailed examination of occupation in one area, see John Gimbel, *A German Community Under American Occupation: Marburg 1945-1952* (Stanford: Stanford University Press, 1961). For an analysis of the creation of supporting elites, note Chapter II, "American Democratization Efforts" pp. 167-184. Also see Seymour Bolton, "Military Government and the German Political Parties," *The Annals,* 267 (January, 1950), pp. 55-67; Edward H. Litchfield and associates, *Governing Post-War Germany* (Ithaca, N.Y.: Cornell University Press, 1953).

60. See Chapter 6.

61. Violence is not, of course, an independent variable, but is rather a consequence of, among other things, an imbalance between participation and institutionalization. Note that in the examples just given, one, Haiti, has a low level of institutionalization and also a low level of participation; on the other hand, Jordan has long had a low level of institutionalization and a relatively high level of participation, due to the activity of the Palestinian refugees. One would expect in the case of Jordan that with the continuation of the monarchy and the elimination of the Palestinians as an active group, the level of violence would decrease. In the case of Haiti, there are apparently reasons other than simply those concerned with participation and institutionalization that account for the continuingly high level of governmental violence.

62. See Leites and Wolf, *Rebellion and Authority.*

63. A study of Yugoslav Communism in the 1950s, principally in historical terms, is Charles McVicker, *Titoism* (New York: St. Martins Press, 1957). A book that is more analytical and emphasizes practice is Fred W. Neal, *Titoism in Practice* (Berkeley: University of California Press, 1958).

64. D. L. Wheeler, "Thaw in Portugal," *Foreign Affairs,* 48 (July, 1970), pp. 769-781, which emphasizes the Caetano reforms.

65. See note 39, Chapter 2.

66. A striking case of such variability in a state where there was a notable lack of any type of elite integration, social or institutional, is that of Ruanda in 1963-1964. Indeed, the decay in this area was so rapid that the previous society was destroyed. See Huntington, *Political Order in Changing Societies,* p. 172.

67. Robins, "Institutional Linkages with an Elite Body."

68. A highly analytic volume that treats this subject is Thomas R. Dye, *Politics, Economics, and the Public* (Chicago: Rand McNally, 1966). A volume that takes a variety of approaches is Herbert Jacob and Kenneth Vines (eds.), *Politics in the American States: A Comparative Analysis* (New York: Little, Brown, 1965); especially see Robert S. Friedman's essay in that volume, "State Politics and Highways," which emphasizes federal-state relations.

69. Guttsman, *The British Political Elite.* See the section on "Milestones on the Road to Office," pp. 200-221.

70. This is not to say, however, that the Turkish military does not have a strong tradition of non-interference and support for democratic norms. See Frederick Frey, "Arms and the Man in Turkish Politics" *Land Reborn,* 11 (August, 1960), pp. 3-14; Daniel Lerner and Richard D. Robinson, "Swords and Ploughshares: The Turkish Army as a Modernizing Force," *World Politics,* 13 (October, 1960), p. 19-44.

71. There is, of course, an extensive literature on community politics. This literature, aside from serving as a pool for study of various instances of elite integration, is particularly useful because it, like the present work, emphasizes the role of elites and their interconnection in politics. The community politics studies do not, by and large, emphasize institutionalization. Among the more useful works are Dahl, *Who Governs?;* Agger, *The Rulers and the Ruled;* William H. Form and Warren L. Sauer, *Community*

Influentials in a Middle-Sized City (East Lansing: Michigan State University, Institute for Community Development, 1960); Floyd Hunter, *Community Power Structure* (Chapel Hill, N.C.: University of North Carolina Press, 1953); Robert Presthus, *Men at the Top* (New York: Oxford University Press, 1964); Aaron Wildavsky, *Leadership in a Small Town* (Totowa, N.J.: Bedminster Press, 1964); A. H. Hawley, "Community Power and Urban Renewal Success," *American Journal of Sociology,* 68 (January, 1963), pp. 422-431; J. M. Beshers, *Urban Social Structure* (Glencoe: Free Press, 1962).

72. All societies, except perhaps the most primitive and isolated, are mixed traditional and modern. The mixture varies, however, and the degree and form of the variation is very important. T. B. Bottomore, "Cohesion and Division in Indian Elites," in Philip Mason (ed.), *India and Ceylon: Unity and Diversity* (New York: Oxford University Press, 1967), pp. 244-259. F. X. Sutton, "Social Theory and Comparative Politics," in Harry Eckstein and David E. Apter (eds.), *Comparative Politics* (New York: Free Press, 1963), pp. 67-81, contends that perfect integration is impossible due to historical residues. That is, social groupings, social patterns, laws and customary procedures, etc., continue after the time in which they developed and were integrated. Only ahistorical societies could be perfectly integrated.

73. This type of coercion is still very common on the international level, of course. There is virtually no mechanism of elite distribution or integration on the international level. Institutions such as parliaments, which carry out a horizontal elite integration function, are relatively weak.

Chapter 6

INSTITUTIONALIZATION AND ELITE

INTEGRATION IN INDIA, 1952-1962

Definition of the Political Elite and the
Time Period Chosen

In rather general theoretical terms, we have in the previous chapters been
defining political elites institutionally—identifying the elite with the holders
of formal office. As we indicated in Chapter 1, there are sound conceptual
reasons for our doing so: it is the functioning of the institutions of government in relation to political stability and effectiveness that figures most
prominently in the theories of Huntington, as well as those of Braibanti and
Riggs.[1] There can be no symbiosis among these theories and in theories of
elite integration without their definitional components being compatible. In
dealing with a specific and very dynamic polity, however, it is necessary to
review once again the practical utility of such a definition.

AUTHOR'S NOTE: I have special acknowledgements to make concerning this chapter,
in additional to the general ones I made in the acknowledgements at the beginning of
this book. Many of the ideas for this chapter were acquired while I lived and carried on
research in India. I owe a special debt to Professor R. B. Das of the Institute of Public
Administration, Lucknow University. The Fulbright Foundation and Duke University's
Travel Fund jointly supported that research.

There are several substantial advantages to defining elites in institutional terms, quite aside from such a definition's conceptual convenience.

First, such an approach largely resolves the problem of political boundaries. In a state such as India, where a great variety of groups and institutions affects the political process (and a variety is left outside it), defining the elites in institutional terms assures us that they are indeed integral to the political process. That is, the definition guarantees that the area of inquiry is within the political boundaries. Surveying in this chapter a political system as a whole, this approach is likely to include the great bulk of effective decision makers and exclude only a relatively few behind-the-scenes influentials. In effect, the approach is to start at the center of the political process and work out, rather than starting at the margins and working in.

A second advantage of this approach, particularly as certain statistical and mathematical techniques will be used, is that the data are likely to be sound. Who occupied what position at what time is almost invariably a matter of public record. Basic information on the incumbents (especially matters such as birth dates, previous offices held, region of origin, etc.) is not only likely to be available (in public biographies), but is also very likely to be reliable. An office holder is not likely to say he was mayor of a city in 1956 if he was not, nor is he likely to claim to be born in Tamilnad if he was born in Kerala. Such information is much more reliable and accessible than information on opinions, income, etc., and so can be more intensively and precisely applied to the questions under discussion.

Third, this institutional orientation guarantees a substantial continuity in the functions of the elite being studied. Individual elite members may change their positions and functions, but institutions are likely to be far more stable. This continuity is especially important in light of the necessity, which will next be discussed, of evaluating the theory of elite integration in terms of a discrete and conceptually relevant time span.

Thus, the elites studied will be those who actually hold positions of influence. At times others will be included—such as those who seek office and fail, and voting patterns will also be looked at, but such topics will only have a supplementary role in our analysis.

After who will be studied, the next question is in what country and time period. Guidance in the choice of country and period will be from the same principles followed in Chapter 4 in selecting the Medieval Church for the example of bureaucratic-political elite integration.

The country chosen is India. This country has the advantage of providing the investigator with a wealth of scholarly material, much of it of a very high standard. Furthermore, it offers the opportunity—due to its size and variety—to make within-country comparative evaluations. It is far more convenient, and at least as satisfactory, to compare variables within a country as among several, such as was done in Chapter 5. There is no other non-Western, less-developed country that boasts such variability in its forms of political life.[2]

The time period should have a conceptual relevance to the phenomena examined (institutionalization and elites). The longest or the most recent period is not necessarily the most useful. The time period selected is c. 1952 to c. 1962, but not extending before 1947 or after 1967.

The beginning date, 1952, is an obvious one since it was in that year that the present constitution and its associated institutions began operation, though there was a strong institutional continuity extending before this date.[3] It could also be argued that 1947, the year independence was granted, would have been a more appropriate date. The first five years of independence, however, were to a large degree a period of transition.[4] There are, of course, strong reasons against going back beyond 1947, due not only to the fact that India was not yet independent, but also to the constricted political situation that existed during the war.

The point of starting is, however, clearer than the point of stopping. In purely political terms, 1956—the year of the states' reorganization—might be chosen as a termination date. However, this period of only four years would have been too bried to permit an adequate amount of statistical data to be gathered or scholarly analyses to be made. Furthermore, it is evident that, despite the major geographic reorganization that occurred in many areas, there was only limited political consequences. If, however, it is evident that the analysis cannot stop so soon as 1956, it is also clear that it should not continue past 1967. In the elections of that year, the old Congress Party was damaged to such an extent that it was evident that its demise would probably soon occur in one form or another.[5]

The cutoff date, 1962, was chosen for two reasons, one political and one extrapolitical.

To take the extrapolitical factors first, certain basic changes occurred outside the domestic political scene in the early 1960s that were to change the nature of the political milieu. The first and most important was the increasingly severe economic situation, particularly in terms of agricultural production, that began to be felt in India. It is evident now that the 1950s was a period of economic expansion and improvement in India.[6] Perhaps it is too strong to say that the period 1952 to the Chinese punitive expedition of 1962 was something of a Golden Age in India politics, but then again people living in Golden Ages probably never recognise them as such. The fact is that during this period, India enjoyed a steadily increasing level of living, substantial international prestige, and all within a democratic framework. Linguistic disruption was contained by the states' reorganization and the threat of a legal Communist victory was also weathered. From the beginning of the 1960s, however, economic stagnation became increasingly evident and with it, per-haps—and this we cannot measure—came a more general malaise.

The economic and international environment, thus, had changed after about 1962. Without suggesting any simplistic interrelationship between these extrapolitical factors and the domestic political system, we can nevertheless note that the 1952-1962 period had an economic integrity. Politically, the period is nearly equally distinct. In this period, one may observe a stability of the Congress' popular support, as well as its ability to convert this support into seats in the legislatures. After 1962, both the level of popular support and the capacity to turn this support into legislative influence declined.[7]

Hence, 1952-1962 is a period of political and extrapolitical conceptual integrity. It is an era: a largely successful and stable one, though we know that problems were growing that would be more evident later. The period is also long enough, and distant enough in time, to offer us a substantial body of scholarly material that can be looked at with some perspective. It may be objected that the period is atypical. This criticism is difficult to answer briefly. All historical periods, like all individuals, are unique, and, hence, not essentially typical. Yet the variability for this period is not evidently greater than for any other. It has an integrity, and yet is well connected to what came before and what came after. That is all that can be asked of a historical unit of analysis.

Summary of Level and Form of Institutional Political Elite Integration in India, 1952-1962

Before the direct analysis of elite integration in India is begun in terms of Huntington's four criteria, a brief evaluation of the extent and form of elite integration in the period will be offered. Elite integration may be seen to exist on two levels in India: the national and the provincial. Concerning the national level, the interest here is in how elites reach that level. The key national government institution is the Council of Ministers;[8] the key party position is the Working Committee of the Congress or its equivalent in other parties.[9] The provincial-level system of elite integration involves the recruit-ment of elites to the state legislature and cabinet though, as will be seen, recruitment at lower levels is very important. Here again the focus will be on two types of institutions: the state legislature and cabinet, and the Pradesh Congress Committee (the state-level governing organ of the Congress Party) or its equivalent.

On the state level, the concern is what degree of experience the members of the legislative assemblies (MLAs) and the state cabinet have in lower-level government, and to a lesser extent, in party posts. The interest is not only in the extent of the experience, but also in the pattern of relationship among different levels and institutions. It is not suggested, however, that individuals necessarily pass through all, or even many, levels below the highest they achieve—though this may occur. In many cases, individuals enter at one level, move up to another, and then stay there the remainder of their careers. There would be as strong a linkage, in elite terms, between these two levels as where the career paths of the elites had involved several levels. Indeed, due to the relative narrowness of the members' experience, the institutional link between the levels at which the members did serve might be even stronger.

There is a variety of general statements concerning the MLA's close relation to his district or origin in this period.[10] It is necessary, however, to examine this relationship in closer detail. The analysis will be based on two studies, one by Duncan Forester[11] which looked at all MLAs in the Madras legislature in 1962 (the end of our period) and the other by Myron Weiner,[12] which was somewhat broader, but also focused on MLAs, in this case in West Bengal in the late 1950s. Weiner's is the more detailed study, but both are in substantial agreement that the MLAs—especially the Congress MLAs and especially those from rural districts—had strong personal institutional links (in terms of service) to their districts.

Forester suggests that the key positions on the district level are party posts. That is, the route to state office is principally through organizational work. Weiner's analysis is not contradictory to Forester's, but refines it further at some places and generalizes it at others. In particular, Weiner emphasizes the importance of all local institutional ties for all those legislators, Congress and non-Congress, representing rural constituencies: "Even opposition legislators in rural areas must build themselves through local government and civic action."[13]

There is a difference, however, in both the degree and the form of institutional elite integration between rural and urban—especially left-wing—legislators. As indicated in the previous chapter, the more left organizations—which in this period tended to be urban—are inclined to rely principally on their own party apparatus (and closely affiliated "mass" organizations) for institutionalized elite integration. As Weiner points out,

> Few of the 168 rural MLAs have not had some record of activity in local government and 62 in local civic associations. . . . In contrast many of the 38 urban MLAs (19 of whom are members of the Communist or Marxist left parties) have no group affiliation other than the party to which they belong and the trade unions, peace fronts and other associations dominated by their party.[14]

An important point here is not only that institutionalized vertical elite integration is well established and that it includes party as well as government position, but that such vertical elite integration is functionally integral to this particular political process. Vertical elite integration, as indicated in earlier chapters, is an aid to political institutionalization and political development. It was also an aid to getting elected in India in this period. This complementarity of private and partisan advantage with general political development was, and probably still is, one of the strengths of the Indian political system.[15]

At the beginning of the discussion of the MLAs and elite integration, the role of the political party—especially the Congress, in this case—was referred to in the integration of various government institutions. There is, of course, in every area only one government, but there are frequently several political parties. In the 1952-1962 period, the principal parties in India were the Congress, the Communist Party, the Jan Sangh, and the Dravida Munnhetra Kazhagram. The Congress was the only national party in terms of organization, power, and popular following. In certain areas, of course, other parties were often a close second and, in a few cases, overshadowed it.[16]

India is a polity where political parties were with only random exceptions necessary tools for advancement. Furthermore, the major parties were sufficiently institutionalized to prevent advancement being gained by frequent (or even occasional) shifting from one party to another. This has meant that the leaders of a party have tended to be drawn from its most loyal members.[17]

It is appropriate to turn now to an analysis of one state political party, that of Rajasthan in this period. The sources in this section are principally Lawrence Shrader's essay, "Rajasthan,"[18] and Richard Sisson's *The Congress Party in Rajasthan.*[19] Principal emphasis is given to Sisson's work, which is more detailed and most directly applicable.

Unlike West Bengal, which has a long and complex history in political party and popular terms, Rajasthan has a relatively less-developed political history before 1949.[20] Before that date, it consisted of twenty-one distinct polities.[21] The state, established in 1948-1949, was largely unaffected by the states' reorganization of 1956. Consequently, in terms of time and geography, it offers a good unit of analysis. In terms of the maturity of its political party apparatus, if offers a useful contrast to such states as Madras and West Bengal.

In the 1952-1962 period, the major challenge to the Congress came from the Rajasthani aristocracy, though Congress, too, had major elements of the aristocracy in its own ranks. The principal parties in this period were, as Table 1 indicates, the Congress, the Ram Rajya Parishad, and the Swatantra. The Congress will be examined because it was the best developed and most influential one in this period.

The Congress Party institutional elite may be said to have begun in 1948 with the election of the first PCC (Pradesh Congress Committee).[22] The fact

Table 6.1: Results of Three General Elections

Party	Assembly Seats Won		
	1952	1957	1962
Congress	82	119	88
Ram Rajya Parishad	24	16	3
Jan Sangh	8	6	15
Socialists	1	0	5
Praja Socialist Party	0	1	2
Krisak Lok Party	7	0	0
Communist Party	0	1	6
Swatantra	0	0	6
Hindu Mahasabha	2	0	0
Kisan Mazdoor Praja Party (Kripalani)	1	0	0
Independents	35	33	21

SOURCE: Shrader, "Rajasthan," p. 330.

that over half (62%) of the members had not been members of the Rajputana Prantiya Sabha of 1946 (a federation of Praja Mandals and closest thing to a party organizational elite before independence), indicates that the Congress was not simply continuing with the previous elite. This is not to say, however, that the members of the PCC had not previously been active politicians, only that they were not part of a previously institutionalized elite.[23] The tendency away from incumbancy, however, continued even after independence, as Table 2 demonstrates.

The table indicates a low level of institutional elite stability in terms of the PCC. As Sisson states:

The proportion of those who served on the *Prantiya Sabha* in 1946, for example, has progressively declined until in 1963 those who served in 1946 constituted only 8 percent of the total membership. A similar pattern of decline has characterized each of the other Pradesh Congress Committees.

The dispersion of old and new members of successive Pradesh Congress Committees described [in Table 2] indicates the high degree of circulation of personnel at the state level in the Rajasthan Congress. Not only have new members constituted a majority in each successive PCC, but the old members have not constituted a self perpetuating organizational elite. Although between 130 and 159 seats (an average of 146) have been filled on the PCC for the years under consideration, 424 different persons have been incumbents during that time. Only a few have been members consistently. These few, however, are important Congress leaders and will attract our attention later.[24]

Table 6.2: Members Previously on the Pradesh Congress Committee,
1948-1965 (in percentages)

Previous Year	1948-1950	1954-1956	1956-1958	1958-1960	1963-1965
1946	38	19	16	12	8
1948		25	21	19	12
1954			46	28	23
1956				38	33
1958					35
N =	147	134	147	157	159

SOURCE: Sisson, The Congress Party in Rajasthan, p. 190.

Although there is a higher level of top elite incumbancy than these aggregate figures indicate, nevertheless it is important to note where the bulk of the other members came from. A high level of party institutional elite integration would require that these PCC members came from the District Congress Committee (the Congress governing body on the district level, abbreviated DCC), and indeed, this was the case. In 1946 and 1948, nearly all (ninety-five percent) the PCC members in Udaipur and Jaipur were simultaneously DCC members. This was a form of integration, but because it was not always sequential, it does not quite fit our model of elite integration. This relation decreased steadily, until in 1966 sixty-eight percent of the PCC (still a high percentage) held simultaneous DCC and PCC offices.

More important for the purposes of this analysis, a strong element of vertical elite integration was introduced in the mid-1950s when (1) presidents of the DCCs were made ex officio members of the PCC, (2) the leaders of various mass organizations were increasingly brought into PCC posts, and (3) factional forces on the state and national levels used PCC posts as balancing aids.[25] With the limited exception of point 3 (and even here elements of elite integration frequently came into play) the PCC was very strongly integrated in institutional elite terms with the lower-level institutions, especially the DCCs. After 1954, seventy-seven percent of the PCC had previously been members of the DCC, and over fifty-six percent had been DCC officers.

In sum, the Congress Party organization of Rajasthan not only was characterized by high levels of elite integration, but, more important, the extent of this integration steadily increased.[26] Elite integration is thus seen again to be related to political institutionalization. It was seen on the state level—in both general and specific terms—that there was a substantial level of elite integration within the party and the government. It is important to note that this integration increased over time and was not simple in form.

Turning now to the national level, the same question applies: from what government institutions are the leaders on the national level drawn and how strong and in what form is this integration? It might seem most appropriate to examine the Members of Parliament, as the MLAs were examined earlier. This approach would have distinct advantages, including affording a large number of cases and also a methodological parallelism.

The problem with such an approach is that the MP is not such a key figure in influencing policy—and especially in distributing patronage—as is his state counterpart. This tendency is clearest when one notes how much more eagerly state and district posts are sought by local influentials compared to parliamentary seats.[27] Consequently, although the Lok Sabha or Rajya Sabha are not being dismissed as elite institutions, the emphasis will be on the members of the Council of Ministers, 1952-1960 where the level of real influence is clear.[28] A simple percentage analysis of institutional origins of the thirty-five members[29] indicates a substantially similar pattern to that described in the previous section on MLAs in West Bengal and Madras. However, because more detailed data were collected, it was possible to use more precise statistical techniques. The method and a fuller discussion have been published elsewhere,[30] so the discussion will largely be confined to those conclusions which bear most directly on vertical elite integration to the national level.

A method using a procedure similar to causal path analysis was employed and produced Table 3, which described the degree and form of institutional linkage among the indicated government institutions, from the district level to the Council of Ministers.

The institutional linkage among the bodies studied varies considerably. As the note to Table 3 indicates, there is very little institutional linkage between the district/municipal level and the Council of Ministers. Of course, some members of the Council of Ministers have served at the district/municipal level, but their membership is not part of an institutional pattern. The situation is quite different when we look at the relation between the state institutions and the Council of Ministers. Several paths indicate a regular relationship, the highest (state legislature→Lok Sabha→Council of Ministers) explains fifty-nine percent of the variation in the institutional composition of the Council.

This evidence, based on all the members of the Council of Ministers, 1952-1960, is consistent with other studies[31] that indicate that the effective path to central power begins at the state level. Eventual national elites enter national governmental politics at the state level, though with strong local party connections, and then move up. There was no case of a central minister moving directly into national office without first establishing himself in a state office.

If the state, though not the local, level was so important in terms of integration among governmental institutional elites, can the same be said about political party institutional elites? Since the Congress Party was the dominant

Table 6.3: Correlation Products for Various Paths Leading to the Council of Ministers

First Position	Intermediate Position (if any)	Final Position	Correlation Product
Pre-1952 National Assembly and back bench state legislatures (combined category)	.85 ──────────→	Council of Ministers	.85
Pre-1952 National Assembly and state legislatures (combined category)	.82 ──────────→	Council of Ministers	.82
Pre-1952 National Assembly and back bench state legislatures (combined category)	.92 ──→ Lok Sabha .89 ──→	Council of Ministers	.82
State legislatures	.87 ──→ Lok Sabha .89 ──→	Council of Ministers	.77
State legislatures and pre-1952 National Assembly (combined category)	.87 ──→ Lok Sabha .87 ──→	Council of Ministers	.76
State legislatures and pre-1952 National Assembly (combined category)	.76 ──────────→	Council of Ministers	.76
Pre-1952 National Assembly and state cabinet (combined category)	.86 ──→ Lok Sabha .89 ──→	Council of Ministers	.76
State legislature	.77 ──→ Lok Sabha .89 ──→	Council of Ministers	.68
State legislature	.66 ──────────→	Council of Ministers	.66
Back bench state legislature	.60 ──────────→	Council of Ministers	.60

NOTE: No path from the district/municipal level to the Council had a correlation product as high as 60.
SOURCE: Robins, "Institutional Linkages with an Elite Body: A Correlational Analysis of the Institutional Representation in the Indian Council of Ministers, 1952-60," p. 114.

political party—and, indeed, the only party at the national level which had a direct relationship with the governmental elites—it will be examined.

The principal source for this period will be the work of Stanley Kochanek, especially his *The Congress Party of India.*[32] Kochanek works within a time span that is very close to this one. The 1951-1963 period (substantially the same as our 1952-1962 period) he designates the Period of Centralization and Convergence, which was followed by the Period of Divergence, 1963-1967. Our analysis is based on his study of the 1951-1963 period.[33]

The key party institution here is the Working Committee of the Congress, which is (1) the chief policy-making body of the Congress, (2) the chief executive body of the Congress, with power to frame rules, superintend those rules, etc., and (3) the chief coordinator of party-government relations, especially through its subcommittee, the Central Election Committee, which was often very influential in the selection of candidates.[34]

For perspective, it should be noted that the form and degree of vertical elite integration in the Working Committee has changed since independence.[35] Before 1952, when P. D. Tandon was influential in the party, there was a strong element of ministerial-organizational conflict at the national level, and there were a large number of PCC presidents on the Working Committee. Until 1952, the pattern of elite integration on the national level was substantially similar to what it was on the state level, with the higher-level body being recruited to a significant extent from the level below.

With the resignation of P. D. Tandon as Congress president in 1951 and the subsequent acquisition by Nehru of clear dominance in the Congress Party, the role of the Working Committee became weaker; with (and undoubtedly, in part, due to) this weakening, institutional elite movement from the lower-level party elites declined.[36] The Congress president was given complete freedom to choose members of the Working Committee, and the tradition of inviting non-members to sit in on the deliberations was revived. Very rapidly, the key members were no longer drawn from the party hierarchy, but rather were chief ministers of various states and central cabinet members. Kochanek offers[37] a variety of statistics and extensive analysis on this point. Suffice it to say, in this period, eighty-one percent of the long-term members were principally chief ministers or central cabinet members. As Kochanek remarks "in terms of formal membership, the Working Committee came to be dominated by the leaders of the parliamentary wing at the center and in the states."[38]

This arrangement afforded a degree of unity to party and government, though damaging party organizational integrity. The power of the government officials was not total, however. The All-India Congress Committee has exercised indirect influence and since 1960[39] it has elected one-third of the Working Committee, though from an official list which reflected the parlia-

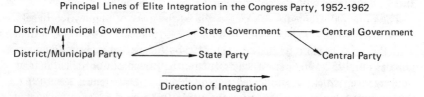

Principal Lines of Elite Integration in the Congress Party, 1952-1962

NOTE: The direction of elite movement is overwhelmingly from lower to higher levels, hence the direction of the bottom arrow. There are of course other forms of integration running down the government/party hierarchy.

Figure 6.1

mentary wing's approval. Thus, the Congress Party was characterized by moderate to strong vertical elite integration up to the state level, but weak institutional integration from the state to the national level.

Figure 1 is, of course, a simplified representation of what must be a far more complex reality. It is not intended to offer a schematic representation of influence, but only the upward pattern of major movement of members. The absence of arrows between state party and central levels is not to say that individuals do not move from state party positions to national government positions, only that this is not the principal linkage. (Furthermore, the figure does not indicate the strength of relationship, only its existence and dominance over any alternate.)

In sum, one can say that the governmental elite of the period—and here the principal concern is with the Congress Party—was well integrated above the state level, and was also the effective link in party integration. At and below the state level, the level of institutional integration (especially for urban constituencies) was weaker, though still significant, and the political party played a larger role.

COMPLEXITY

Complexity refers to the number and types of differentiation of subunits. In terms of elite integration, when it is asked if the Indian political system is complex, this is the same as asking whether there is a variety of institutions through which various elites can rise at various levels.

The fact that the Indian political system is quasi-federal in form permits substantial scope for a variety of elite paths. This well-defined institutional structure largely reflects equally well-defined elite structures at every level and in nearly every region. Even at the village level, leaders are almost invariably drawn from the village itself, and seldom are merely influentials from the general area.[40] Both at the district level (which though once an artificial administrative division has now acquired a distinct political integrity) and at the municipal level, elite members are locally recruited, as Weiner and Rosenthal demonstrated.[41]

It may be objected that such a point is documenting the universal. In fact, this is not the case, as has been noted in this study in other countries, such as Turkey,[42] or in other historical eras, such as the Middle Ages.[43] The congruence of elite and administrative boundaries, though common, is far from universal. India, 1952-1962, enjoyed a notably high level of such congruence, due in large measure to the fact that administrative boundaries, especially at the state level, approximated various caste-communal ascriptive boundaries. It can be argued, of course, that the various units and their specificity to certain geographic regions and hence to local ascriptive groups served to decrease the possibilities for a prospective elite's advancement. That is, when an aspirant found he could not achieve prominence in his own area he was stymied. This was true, of course, and is the other side of the advantage of community. For those with strong ascriptive connections—which included the great bulk of Indian aspirants—the discreteness and distinctiveness of the various elite constituencies was not, however, a disadvantage. For those relatively few who were outside the ascriptive power structure—the Muslim in a Hindu district, the person belonging to a very minor and uninfluential caste—they were for the most part excluded from elective government office.[44]

Political parties, especially at the local level, are very much subject to the same sort of exclusions as we just described in relation to elective offices. Some parties, such as the Congress, have a broader base than others, such as the Jana Sangh, but again for those aspirants without strong ascriptive ties, the variety of political parties is an illusory source of upward mobility. The Congress may, as a whole, have had a broad base, but in any specific area it was likely to rely on a fairly narrow range of ascriptive groups.

Politically oriented pressure groups, whether "mass" organizations such as Kisan Sabhas and urban labor parties[45] or more ascriptively based groups, such as the caste associations that the Rudolphs[46] describe, were fairly weak in most areas. Obviously, caste and communal associations provide a very powerful aid to upward mobility to those eligible and those who belong to such organizations. The associative organizations, however, are in most cases weak, where they exist at all, and they, too, are usually heavily influenced by ascriptive groups.

Of course, despite the variety of political parties and pressure groups, it was difficult for a politician to rise above the district level without being a member of the Congress. Fortunately, this party had a very wide national base—though often quite a narrow one in particular areas—and thus few groups were totally excluded. Another moderating factor was that most aspirant elites sought local posts, up to the district level, and here a wider variety of parties held power.[47]

By and large, it can be seen that the Indian political system in this period was a complex one, especially in terms of governmental and political party posts, less so in terms of interest groups.

It should also be added that political power may also be acquired through financial influence in India as in other democratic capitalist countries. Adequate statistics to evaluate this path to political influence are not available. It is however, one of the more effective paths for minorities. Circumstantial evidence and informed opinion indicate that wealth was a means of permitting an otherwise excluded individual to achieve elite status.[48]

What, then, is the consequence of this type of complexity—strong in terms of governmental institutions, moderate concerning political party and wealth, and weak in organized ascriptive and associative groups. As indicated earlier, the basic contribution of elite integration to complexity is that the process of elite integration supplies a group of trained and informed elites that would otherwise be largely excluded. Higher levels gradually acquire information on individuals (who is effective, who is reliable) and on groups (again, which are reliable, which are effective). Such complexity is only possible where the elites enjoy long service in the system, and such long service is only likely when it complements the private ambitions of the aspirant elites.

Donald Rosenthal in his analysis of politics in Poona[49] in the early 1950s emphasizes the importance of political longevity. He particularly shows this to be the case with the candidacy and victory of the veteran N. V. Gadgil.[50] Gadgil, a Brahmin running for M.P. in Poona in 1952, did not have the ascriptive qualifications that would have made him per se a popular candidate. The support he received from the local elite—based on his holding local office for a decade, and later at the state and central levels, as well as his strong political connections to Nehru—was the crucial ingredient not only in his nomination, but also in his election. He was known to be effective and reliable. The point here is not that the existence of elite integration in this case and many like it helped Congress win the election—Congress would have probably won with a Maratha candidate as well—but that the practice of drawing candidates from a pool of those who have already served permitted the political system to make use of a person who brought valuable skills and experience, but whose ascriptive qualifications were marginal. A complex system requires men like Gadgil to be elected, but an ascriptively dominated society such as India's, that does not enjoy elite integration, is not likely to keep such people in the government.[51]

Not only does elite integration provide the higher elites with information on individuals who would not otherwise receive their support, it also serves the same function for groups that would otherwise find their path upward far more difficult. This has been documented at some length in the work of Robert Hardgrave on the Nadars of Madras and the somewhat broader analyses by the Rudolphs. In these studies,[52] it was shown how a low-status ascriptive group, by reorganizing (and further organizing), itself mobilized resources of caste solidarity, directed them systematically at the immediate society and the government, and rose politically.

Although the case of the Nadars is the best documented and is a somewhat exceptional case, the similar history of the Vanniyars of northern Madras and of the Iravas of Kerala and the even longer history of the Kayasthas of the Gangetic Plain make the same point.[53] Establishing themselves at the local level first—certainly not an unusual procedure—a crucial aspect in their political advancement was that they worked in a system where higher-level elites were characteristically drawn from levels below. Thus, the Indian political system had a built-in mechanism for lessening the natural "repressing" influence of incumbent elite groups on aspirant elites.[54]

In the Indian context, the only way other than by elite integration to achieve such integration between ruling elites and newly rising groups might have been in deflecting the rising elite into bureaucratic positions.[55] To some extent, this can be done, and to some extent was done, especially on the state level.[56] The problem of achieving a broad social integration by bureaucratic means was discussed in Chapter 2, and it need only be noted here that, among other problems, bureaucracies have relatively few elite positions to dispose of. Furthermore, as Ralph Braibanti has pointed out, in most societies—and especially in societies where the traditional duties owed one's caste fellows, family, etc. are very strong—it is necessary for the bureaucrat to erect a barrier of sorts between himself and those he serves to maintain a degree of probity. Such a barrier lessens the ability of a bureaucrat to transmit demands and other sorts of information both up and down the hierarchy.

Another advantage to the Indian political system of elite integration and complexity is that integration assures that the elite at every level is experienced in the process of government and politics and has the social skills such as aggregation and articulation which are associated with successful politicians. It may very well be that these social skills are the greatest contribution that elite integration makes to complexity and hence to institutionalization and political development.

Turning from the government structure to the political parties, a higher level of complexity is observed. On the state, and especially on the district/municipal level, there are a variety of political parties which recruit elites to government positions. The value of these minority parties in recruiting leaders to state and especially to national posts was relatively weak in this period due to Congress dominance. Political parties played a role in some elections in the village and *tehsil* governments, but by and large they were of limited influence at these levels.

Although it would be accurate to see the central and to a lesser extent the state elites as being virtually all Congress, it would be incorrect to make the statement about the district and municipal levels. Elites were drawn into this level by a variety of political parties,[57] and to most aspiring politicians local politics matters most.

Why did aspirant elites on the local level enter political parties that clearly had, compared to Congress, inferior access to higher levels? The principal reason was that in most cases the local Congress Party was already dominated by established groups that were reluctant to share their power with the newly aspiring elites. For new groups not seeking or being refused entry, there were sometimes ideological or programmatic reasons as well. Factionalism (which will be discussed under *adaptability*) within the local Congress often presented opportunities for the admission of new groups, but it was principally the fact of key positions in the Congress being already firmly occupied that served to deflect new elites to other parties. In competitive political environments, this situation is a common one, particularly on the local level.[58]

For the greater part of our period, however, Congress was dominant and the principal source of political party complexity. The reasons for Congress' hegemony have been analyzed in numerous works, from various perspectives. Here Congress' success will be briefly evaluated in the terms Huntington offers.

Huntington notes that the first source of strength of a political party is that of mass support.[59] The Congress Party was the largest party in India in this period, with an active membership of 134,000 in 1958.[60] Its mass electoral support, as measured by the average percentage of the vote in the state elections of 1952, 1957, and 1962 was 44%, 45.2%, and 44.8% respectively. That is, the Congress received nearly half the popular vote, more than any other party. The Congress' success in electing legislators was greater (Congress elected 67, 71, and 62% of the legislators in the three elections mentioned above) due not only to the predominance of single-member districts, but also to superior elite skills of electoral aggregation. Both the level of mass support and Congress' greater experience in waging electoral contests remained fairly stable in this period, though both these advantages declined relatively in the 1960s. That is, the level of the support was stable, but the elites' capacity to convert it to legislative power relatively declined after the period.[61]

The second criterion of a successful party is that of organizational complexity.[62] Not only is a party itself an element of a larger system complexity, but a complex party is even that much more valuable.

It is difficult to say whether factionalism is a source of strength through complexity, or a weakness. The question is not that simple, and the careful student must go to the relevant literature.[63] Certainly, as Brass demonstrated in the case of Uttar Pradesh, it may very well be a source of strength, as well as a source of weakness.[64] The Congress' complexity in relation to extra-party groups such as labor unions and caste organizations was not particularly strong in this period, and probably decreased in relation to other parties as the decade wore on.

The third criterion that Huntington offers in evaluating a party concerns the party's abstract appeal—is it a source of ideals, etc., or is it merely a means for personal advancement?[65] In this period, there was perhaps a higher level of idealism in the Congress than later, though even here the Congress was primarily a vehicle for personal advancement. Parties such as the Jana Sangh, the Communist Party, and the Akali Dal were apparently more attractive as idealistic organizations.[66]

In summary, the Indian political system is a very complex and various one, both in government and political party terms. Elite integration has served in modern India, as it did in Medieval Europe, to aid this system function by supplying it with information on leaders and groups, and in giving it experienced politicians. The party system in this period was particularly effective up to the state level, whereas elite integration above this level was carried on principally by movement of elites from one institution of government to another. The Congress was the major party in this period, but at the district/municipal level other parties were about equally important.

COHERENCE

Coherence refers to the institutionalization of methods of conflict resolution, the establishment of functional boundaries, and the development of morale and esprit. The principal interest here is in determining how the process of elite integration in India affected these aspects of institutionalization. One approach to the problem would be that of Herbert Matthews in *United States Senators' and Their World,* containing a detailed "clinical" study of how intra-elite disputes were settled. Unfortunately, no such study exists for India. Another approach, conceptually more difficult but practically simpler, is to observe the development of coherence in part of the political system (e.g., the establishment of an aggregating political party), and note what role elite integration took in that development.

It will be useful to look at the development of the Swatantra Party as an institutionalized elite of coherence and see how the practice of elite integration affected the formation and success of the party. The principal source used here will be Howard Erdman's work on the Swatantra, especially his *The Swatrantra Party and Indian Conservatism.*[67]

Until the last years of the 1950s, the only significant foci for democratic secular conservative support in India were certain factions of the Congress

Party.[68] These factions were apparently inadequate to arrest what was seen by many to be a drift toward economic "statism" by the Congress. Personal and factional disputes combined with this programmatic concern to lead several prominent politicians to establish the Swatantra Party, a democratic secular party, in mid-1959.

The first thing that is evident in examining the origin of the party was that its leaders were products of previous organizations. It was a new party but composed of established institutions and experienced elites.[69] The Forum of Free Enterprise and the All-India Agricultural Federation, though not old organizations (both were founded only a few years earlier), were quasi-political, with strong ties in their respective areas of Bombay and South India. Neither organization had a mass following per se, but both had an experienced leadership with wide financial and political resources.[70] This still slight organization soon received new recruits due to the Congress' Nagpur Resolution of 1959, which was interpreted in many areas as advocating Soviet-model collective farming. The party's appeal here, as later, was never to the masses as such, but rather to elites with such followings.

It is difficult to imagine how an effective party could have been formed so rapidly in any way other than through the integration of lower-level elites, especially at the district/municipal level where we have noted that the party structure is especially important in political recruitment.

As Erdman demonstrates in his chapter, "The Swatantra Coalition: Growth and Scope,"[71] the process of recruitment was very largely institutionally oriented, as well as elite oriented. For example, the leadership of the Indian National Democratic Congress of Madras was recruited to the Swatantra almost as a single unit. This organization had experience in fighting the Congress, previously contesting forty-six seats and holding twenty-three. Also in Madras, the Tamilnad Toilers Party and the Forward Bloc joined the Congress, ad did the Janata Party and the Jan Congress of Bihar. In Uttar Pradesh, the Paliwal faction of the Congress became Swatantra. The same occurred with the Nagoke Congress faction in the Punjab. Many similar examples could also be given.[72]

Although the Swatantra did not live up to the greatest hopes of its founders, its early achievements were quite substantial indeed. By 1962, it had acquired a variety of support, both North and South, becoming the principal opposition group in Bihar, Rajasthan, Bujarat, and Orissa. It was influential in other states as well and in certain districts it was the dominant power. Note that the Swatantra achieved this influence in only three years, and did so not by grass-roots organization, but rather by rationalizing (making more coherent) an institutional and an elite structure that was already in existence. The Swatantra's organizing success was an indication not only of the effectiveness of elite integration as a mechanism for establishing coherence, but also as a demonstration that it was a process that existed among and could be used by political parties other than the Congress.

Those elites who founded the Swatantra did not do so for the purpose of making the Indian political system more coherent, though that was the effect. They made the sacrifices that unity requires in order to, in most cases, enhance their own political influence. Thus, self-interest was the cohering principle in the formation of the Swatantra. Earlier, another source of institutional coherence was referred to—a commitment to some principal that transcends individual advantage. In India, as in most other areas, the major transcendent appeals have historically been those of religion, nationalism, and communalism. Of course, no principle that unites one section of an elite can do so without separating it from the rest. Even nationalism effectively excludes groups within any society. That there are strong religious, communal, and probably to a somewhat lesser extent, nationalist values binding (and dividing) various sections of the Indian elite is well established. The most relevant set of values for political elite formation is, however, those associated with caste/communalism.[73]

To a substantial extent, the pattern of Indian politics in the 1950s was not only a product of various communal conflicts, but also a product of a more general conflict of new groups with established, less parochial elites. The states reorganization was a major event in this conflict, resolved in the favor of the more parochial elites. The establishment of the "Syndicate" after Nehru's death was the national culmination of this conflict, with a modified victory going to the communally oriented elites. The reader should consult the Rudolphs' comments in "Marx, Modernity, and Mobilization" and "Paracommunities," both in *The Modernity of Tradition*[74] for a demonstration and analysis of the persistance and especially the continuing relevance of traditional patterns of behavior throughout this period, on various levels.

Probably the most detailed study of the importance of communal ties and the relevance of elite integration to resolving the conflicts arising out of ascriptive and achievemental demands can be obtained from Rameshray Roy's impressive five-part study, "Selection of Congress Candidates."[75] In this extensive study of the selection of Congress candidates in Bihar and Rajasthan in 1957 and 1962, Ray demonstrates that, despite frequent counter-pressures, Congress candidates were selected principally on the basis of their representation of parochial loyalties, and that the mechanism of selection was principally that of the candidates' first achieving some sort of institutional elite status at a lower level than that to which he was being selected.[76]

With the achievement by these communal-oriented elites of political power, the political system became legitimated to them and their followers. That is, since their loyalties to caste and community were dominant, the accession to power by caste/communal leaders made the authority of government legitimate, not vice versa. Previously established governmental and party procedures of dispute resolution could then partake of this legitimacy in the eyes of the new elites.[77] Given the nature of Indian society, there could be no other legitimacy without this ascriptive base, and such a base could not have been established without the mechanism of elite integration.

There are two remaining aspects of coherence—functional boundaries and esprit. As discussed at some length in Chapter 5, how well-defined the functional limits of an organization are is principally a consequence of the other aspects of coherence (the development of methods of dispute resolution, and loyalty to some transcendent principle) and the orientation of the political organization toward change. As Huntington notes, organizations in favor of change, especially innovative change, tend to have weaker functional boundaries than do institutions oriented toward conservatism. The reader is referred back to Chapter 5 for the arguments on this point.

It is notable that the Congress, which acted principally as a consolidating institution, especially on the local level, followed the conservative model of elite integration. Its elite ties to external organizations (especially to ascriptive groups) were very strong, and the Congress depended on these organizations to a large extent for its supplies to elites. Left organizations, as Weiner illustrated in the case of West Bengal, were much more organizationally ingrown. The functional limits of the government itself were fairly stable in this period, though perhaps demonstrating a slow leftward movement.[78]

A governmental apparatus of high esprit and morale is one that not only has well-established methods of dispute resolution and clear functional boundaries, but, more important, has a socially supported self-perception of success. Elite integration per se is not a very important variable in this process, and it is difficult to identify it as such in India.

AUTONOMY

In the previous two sections, the Indian political system was examined principally in terms of its capacity to mediate and integrate into political institutions social forces such as wealth and caste. Here the topic turns to the equally important capacity of the system to resist these pressures, to be more than their creatures. Such autonomy is a product of the institution's capacity to make its own rules for the distribution of values (especially those connected with policy-making) and its selection of its own leaders.

Turning to the independence of the system in choosing its own leaders, it must first be recognized that such power must be mediated in a diverse democracy such as India by extragovernmental organizations, especially the political parties. There would be several ways to evaluate the extent of autonomy and the role elite integration plays in it. To a large extent the task here is simplified by referring to earlier arguments and examples. The elements that make for complexity and coherence must also be related to autonomy: a complex and coherent political system must be somewhat insulated from shifting popular pressures. The same distinctions between conservative and innovative political parties apply, for example. Conservative parties by virtue of their strong extraparty ties are less autonomous in leadership selection and rule-making than are the more ingrown innovative (generally left) parties.

Although it would be possible to find numerous examples of the Congress and other parties choosing leaders and making rules in resistance to and also in response to such pressure,[79] the best way of looking at the operation of this process in India is by a careful analysis of two works: Michael Brecher's *Succession in India: A Study in Decision Making*[80] and also his *Political Leadership in India: An Analysis of the Elite Attitudes.* Both deal with the question of the interaction of elite attitudes and public pressure at a high enough level and in a systematic enough fashion to enable us to use them for our purpose.

Succession in India deals principally with the struggle to succeed Nehru in 1964 (and more briefly with the succession of 1966), and *Political Leadership in India* deals with the political elites' (principally Congress Party Leaders') perception of the causes and results of Congress' electoral setback in 1967, the quality and ranking of Congress leaders, and the succession contest of 1966. *Succession in India* will be used in its entirety, but the latter volume will be used only to deal with the perceived reasons for Congress' 1967 reverses.[81]

It is not possible or necessary to summarize Brecher's study of the succession to Nehru. Those who want a detailed analysis are referred to Chapter IV of *Succession in India.*[82] Brecher analyzes the personalities involved—Nanda, Shastri, Indira Gandhi, etc. But at greater length and of more use here, he analyzes certain general themes. It is evident that the decision of who should be Prime Minister was made by a very small number of individuals, with little reference in their deliberation to the desire of the wider Congress Party and virtually no reference to any wider public. The leaders of the relevant institution were clearly dominant and autonomous. To the extent that any external considerations entered, they entered through the composition of the Caucus in its representation of regional forces.[83] These forces were principally reflected in the influence of the Chief Ministers in the deliberation of the Grand Council of the Republic.[84]

Factionalism, of course, played a significant role in the selection of the Prime Minister. There is no evidence to suggest, however, that factional links served to make the caucus the prisoner of external forces. One must assume, however, that external influences did operate through these links.[85]

The succession was a product of elite agreement with little or no involvement of the wider political society. Such a situation was possible only because of the professionalism of the Congress elite—their previous socialization into their roles and the institutionalization of those roles. Only a group of experienced and well-integrated politicians could have achieved such a consensus in such an essentially unique event.

So much for behavior in selecting a leader. In terms of policy-making, to what extent has this same general group in the Congress been responsive in its policy-making to social pressures? Several cases of independent behavior may be cited such as the Hindu Marriage Act, and several accessions to public demand may also be found—for example, the states reorganization. An argument from example here could not be very persuasive due to its inevitable overselectivity. Something more systematic is called for.

In a series of interviews soon after the 1967 elections, Brecher attempted, among other things, to determine the elite perception of the relation between mass preferences and elite behavior.[86] For our purpose, the most important conclusion he reached is that "a substantial proportion of elite respondents did not perceive any link between specific acts—of government or party—and the election results."[87] Rather, the reason for the extensive Congress losses in 1967 was seen as due to a general situation (the unsatisfactory state of the economy), and organizational problems (Congress factionalism and a more united opposition).[88]

This is not to say that the Indian political system, including the Congress, is not responsive to public desires and demands. We have seen that it very frequently is—and it is especially responsive to those demands at lower levels and in its selection of elites.

What is not seen here is that the Indian political system mediates popular demands principally through a process of elite recruitment from lower to higher levels. There is no functional (and, some may argue, no normative) reason for the elite to have in its internal selection of leaders and policy a direct concern for mass opinion. Thus, the political system may remain autonomous from the direct pressure of the larger society because these pressures have already been mediated through a process of elite integration.

ADAPTABILITY

Adaptability refers to the capacity of the Indian political system to overcome the crises of generational renewal, and the passage of time itself. Let us look at each of these factors in turn.

In terms of chronological age, the Indian political system, and especially the Congress Party, obviously rank high: the administrative structure enjoys a continuity from the first half of the nineteenth century, the electoral structure from the 1920s, and the dominant political party, the Congress, from the late nineteenth century. Within a decade, which is the focus of our study, difficulties of a strictly chronological nature did not appear.

Earlier in this study it was argued that an element in the relationship between the chronological age of an institution or a set of institutions, and elite integration is reflected in the age of the members. Older members are likely to be aasociated with older institutions, and the fact that institutional elite integration (individuals going from one institution to another) takes time means that where elite integration exists, it must be associated with an older elite. It was also suggested that an older and more experienced elite would offer advantages in terms of temperamental flexibility within the given institutional structure.

The Congress in this period continued to recruit members, and the age distribution of the active membership of 134,000 in 1958 (the immediate group out of which the elite was recruited) was distributed as shown in Table 4.[89]

This distribution reflects a broad base in terms of age. As would be expected in an old and hierarchical institution, this distribution is not directly reflected at the elite level. Whereas, for example, forty-five percent of the active members were over forty, sixty-nine percent of the All-India Congress Committee (AICC) were over forty.[90] Furthermore, this distribution in the A.I.C.C. is not peculiar to the Congress, but is also characteristic of the entire lower house sitting at that time.[91]

The same dominance of older members may be noted in Roy's study of the selection of Congress candidates for the state legislature in Bihar in 1961.

As would be expected in a mature system with a high level of elite integration, the elite structure is dominated by older members, with a broad subelite base. It is not being suggested that the practice of elite integration is the sole factor responsible for this differentiation—older people in India, as in most other areas, are apt to be selected for a wide variety of reasons. What is suggested is that the practice of elite integration is one of the factors that is associated with such an elite age structure in India, and that the elite struc-

Table 6.4: Age Distribution of Active Congress Membership, 1958 (based on sample)

Age	Percentage
20-30	20
31-40	35.3
41-50	28.6
51-60	12.7
Over 60	3.5

SOURCE: Kochanek, **Congress Party of India,** p. 353.

Table 6.5: Age Distribution of Applicants for Congress Nomination and of Congress Candidates, Bihar, 1961 (state legislature)

Age	Percentage Applicants (N = 2051)	Percentage Candidates (N = 318)
25-30	12.2	4.4
31-40	34.4	30.8
41-50	33.2	32.7
51-60	14.4	17.3
Over 60	3.8	7.3
Unknown	1.9	7.5

SOURCE: Roy, "Selection of Congress Candidates—IV," II (February 11, 1967), p. 372.

ture described is consistent with our model of an institutionalized polity with a high level of elite integration.

The next factor to be considered in relation to adaptation is the Indian political system's capacity to surmount the crisis of generational renewal. In this period—1952-1962—there was no such crisis on the national level, and only occasionally on the local. The problem of generational renewal stands principally outside the limits of this study in the mid- and late 1960s.[92]

Nevertheless, there was some generational renewal in this period, operating through a system of proteges and mentors, and among a set of key institutions. Factionalism—a principal characteristic of Indian, and especially Congress, politics in the period—was the principal mechanism for the generational renewal that did occur.[93] Protege-mentor relationships were made in terms of factional groupings,[94] which were principally characterized by the strong bond that exists between the factional leader and his followers.[95] It was this bond, combined with the faction's key role in political recruitment[96] that played a large role in institutionalizing the process of elite recruitment and, parenthetically, broadened the base of participation in the Congress.[97] India had little need for generational renewal in this period, but to the extent it did, the protege-mentor aspect of the faction played a role in facilitating it. In the next era of Indian politics, it was to play a much larger role.

The other method of elite renewal is that of key institutions, which was discussed earlier in this chapter. It was indicated that one's party position was the most important variable in political advancement up to the state level, and that official government position was dominant after that. The pattern was not a rigid one, though well defined. Given the marginality of the phenomenon in this period, further analysis of generational renewal is unnecessary.

In terms of the third aspect of adaptability, functional age, ways in which the pattern of elite integration is related to the Indian political system's capacity to adjust to new functions will be discussed. As noted earlier, functional age may be evaluated in two ways: how social forces are mediated (institutional adaptation), and whose interests are mediated (clientele adaptation).

In this period, there were no major changes in the institutional pattern of mediating social pressures. The major institutional shifts were (1) the promulgation of the system of *panchayati raj* (directed toward the shifting of responsibility at the local level from bureaucracy to popularly elected bodies) and (2) a wide variety of other policies made to lessen the political influence of the bureaucracy.

Had the panchayati raj system succeeded in generating a major degree of popular enthusiasm and involvement, it would have been a significant force in adaptation. The system, however, did not develop so within this period.[98] The role of the civil service did change somewhat between 1952-1962. Bureaucratic development, however, lies outside the focus of this chapter, and the reader is directed to the relevant literature, especially Taub's study of the Orissa bureaucracy.[99] The principal institutions involved in mediating social forces were the popularly elected ones from the district to the national level. Change and development existed here, but no major discontinuities or innovation.

The same sorts of comments may be made about adaptation in terms of new clientele groups. Earlier we pointed out that in this period there was a steady expansion of the scope of elite involvement, especially of the middle and some of the lower castes.[100] Although this was an important process, there was no major discontinuity (as, for example, there was after independence when the elite base changed radically). To the extent that there was a need for functional adaptation here, the process of elite integration was one of the major factors in its resolution.

Summary

Elite integration has deep historical roots in India. In the 1952-1962 period, elite integration was most evident in party terms up to the state level and in governmental institutional terms above that level. The Congress Party and the formal structure of government were the two major institutions of elite integration, but a wide variety of other institutions—both ascriptive and associative—were also involved, though somewhat less so. At the district level, non-Congress parties were probably at least as important as the Congress for moving aspirant elites into positions of influence.

In relation to political institutionalization, elite integration was of most utility in aiding complexity, of moderate use in aiding autonomy and coherence, and of lesser direct use in this brief period in aiding adaptation. The overall importance of the practice of elite integration was quite considerable.

New groups were brought into politics, and a variety of demands was mediated. These groups and their demands were not mediated by the direct influence of public pressure, nor by the direct and rapid inclusion of their leaders into key governmental posts. Such a procedure would have disrupted and perhaps destroyed the continuity of the political system in India, as it did, for example, in Burma and Indonesia. Rather, the practice has been to recruit higher-level elites from among those who have first acquired a substantial institutional position at a lower level. Requiring prospective higher-level leaders to have first served in lower-level elite posts not only socialized and trained these new leaders, it also made their personal and political capacities familiar to established leaders.

This process of choosing higher elites from those who have well-established institutional links was a major factor in the capacity of the Indian political system to function effectively. Indeed, the methods by which governmental and party elites were chosen in this period must figure in any evaluation of the relative success of the Indian political system in what was—and remains—a very difficult social environment.

NOTES

1. See note 1, Chapter 1, and the associated text for a discussion of the definition of "elite." We may define elites, or any other term, according to considerations of utility. For other approaches, note Weiner's "India: Two Political Cultures," and the section in Fred R. von der Medhen, *Politics of the Developing Nations* (Englewood Cliffs, N.J.: Prentice-Hall, 1964) on "Political Elites of the Developing Nations," in which von der Mehden divides the elites into the traditional elite, the new elite, and the foreign economic elite. Pye, *Politics, Personality, and Nation-Building,* follows a tradition-modernity continuum.

2. Huntington notes the fact that India is a country of very high institutionalization when he writes, "In terms of political institutionalization, India was far from backward. Indeed, it ranked high not only in comparison with other modernizing countries in Asia, Africa, and Latin America, but also in comparison with many much more modern European countries," *Political Order in Changing Societies,* p. 84. Every country is unique, but the aspect of India's uniqueness acts as a bridge for our understanding of other nations that are either economically *or* politically developed.

3. This continuity extends at least to the government of India's Act of 1935 which was implemented in India in 1937, and on which the present constitution is based.

4. It has been said that a period of transition is a period that connects two other periods of transition. Nevertheless, the period between the end of British rule and the institution of the present constitution deserves the characterization of transitional more than does any other period in modern Indian history.

5. See the very useful overview of party politics in India, stressing the effects of the 1967 elections in the November 1970 issue of *Asian Survey.*

6. Gunnar Myrdal, *Asian Drama* (New York: Twentieth Century Fund, 1968) Pantheon edition, II: 1241-1384. See especially Table 26-1 on p. 1247. With certain

variations, this table demonstrates that the gross availability of food-grains per head climbed during the 1950s, but in 1966 (the last date on the table) was at a slightly lower level than in 1950.

7.   Relation of Seats and Vote for Indian State
             Assemblies Elected During the Four General Elections

	Average % Vote Congress	Factor of Congress Advantage
1952	44.0	1.5
1957	45.2	1.4
1962	44.8	1.4
1967	41.0	1.1

Note: Data from S. V. Kogekar and Richard L. Park (eds.), *Reports on the Indian General Elections, 1951-1952* (Bombay: Popular Book Depot, 1956), Appendix; Weiner, State Politics in the Indian States," in Weiner (ed.), *State Politics in India,* pp. 3-58, offers two tables where percent seats and votes are presented. According to Weiner's method of calculation, there has only been a two percent, rather than (as we calculated) a four percent drop in the average percentage of the Congress vote in the state assemblies. For a fuller discussion of this topic, see Robert Robins, "Political Development and Party Disintegration: The Old Congress Party, 1952-1967," unpublished paper read at the Salt Lake Meeting of the Rocky Mountain Political Science Association, March, 1972.

8. The list of members of the Council of Ministers would include all ministers of cabinet rank (even if not members of the cabinet) and all deputy ministers. It is consequently a somewhat larger group than the cabinet.

9. See Stanley Kochanek, *The Congress Party of India* (Princeton: Princeton University Press, 1968), "The Working Committee," pp. 111-316, especially, pp. 111-112, 299-316.

10. The three major approaches to elite analysis in Indian politics—Bailey's "link men" *(Politics and Social Change),* the Rudolphs' caste associations *(Modernity of Tradition),* and A. H. Somjee's stimulus-response model ("Political Dynamics of the Gujarat Villege," *Asian Survey,* 12 (July, 1972) pp. 602-608)—all emphasize at one point or another the local ties of Indian politiciams. Moreover, as W. H. Morris-Jones has pointed out, "Every member represents a constituency and many members have particular 'interests.' " Morris-Jones then goes on to note the importance of political parties in moderating these local loyalties. *Parliament in India* (London: Longmans, Green, 1957), p. 148. Also note note 15 in this present chapter for further references.

11. "State Legislators in Madras," *Journal of Commonwealth Political Studies,* 7 (March, 1969), pp. 36-57.

12. "Changing Patterns of Political Leadership in West Bengal," *Pacific Affairs,* 32 (September, 1959), pp. 277-287.

13. Ibid., p. 283.

14. Ibid.

15. Other sources describing the local links of state party leaders are Howard Erdman, *The Swatantra Party and Indian Conservatism* (Cambridge: Cambridge University Press, 1967), pp. 65 ff., which discusses the use of local ties to build the party in the late 1950s; F. G. Bailey, "Politics and Society in Contemporary Orissa," in C. H. Phillips (ed.), *Politics and Society in India* (New York: Praeger, 1962), pp. 103 ff. for the influence of local influentials in choosing higher leaders; V. M. Sirsikar, "Leadership Patterns in Rural Maharashtra," *Asian Survey,* 4 (July, 1964), p. 931 for an evaluation of the role of wealth in local ties; Richard Sisson, *The Congress Party in Rajasthan* (Berkeley: Uni-

versity of California Press, 1972), pp. 315-316; especially note Angela Burger, *Opposition in a Dominant Party* (Berkeley: University of California Press, 1969), pp. 78-81. Suzanne H. Rudolph, *The Action Arm of the Indian National Congress: The Pradesh Congress Committee* (Cambridge: Center for International Studies, MIT, 1955).

Many more sources could be given, and will presently be given in the following discussions. The reader may also examine the sources cited above for further references. The general pattern that appears is that indicated in the Forester and Weiner articles.

16.   Congress Position in the General Elections, 1952-1962

Lok Sabha

	% Seats Won by Congress	% Votes Polled by Congress
1952	74.4	45.0
1957	75.1	47.8
1962	73.0	44.7

State Assemblies

1952	68.2	42.1
1957	65.7	45.6
1962	58.4	43.4

Source: Kochanek, *Congress Party of India,* p. 408. See also Weiner, "Political Development in the Indian States," Table 1.12, on p. 45.

17. Weiner, "Political Development in the Indian States," p. 40, summarizes the importance of party membership well:

Compared to many other developing nations, India, in virtually all of its states, has a more institutionalized political process. Politicians work through organized political parties and pressure groups, and all but a handful—less than 10 percent— of all persons elected to the state legislative assemblies and less than 5 percent of those elected to Parliament were independents. Party membership has remained high even for candidates to local offices, such as municipal councils and village panchayats. It would be accurate to say that personal leadership in India is being displaced by party leadership.

A work that takes a broader approach than Weiner's in evaluating political institutionalization in India is L. P. Singh, "Political Development or Political Decay in India," *Pacific Affairs,* 44 (Spring, 1971), pp. 65-80. As the title of this work indicates, it takes an explicitly Huntingtonian approach.

18. In Weiner (ed.), *State Politics in India,* pp. 321-396.

19. Previously cited in note 15 above. This work from time to time covers a period up to 1967.

20. Shrader, "Rajasthan," p. 324.

21. Ibid., pp. 331 ff. for a discussion of the institutional history of the Congress Rajasthan.

22. See "The Circulation of Organizational Elites," pp. 187-193, in Sisson, *Congress Party in Rajasthan.*

23. Ibid., p. 188. Sisson indicates that the election to the first PCC was the occasion for bringing some people into conflict who had previously cooperated.

24. Ibid., p. 190.

25. Ibid., pp. 193-194.

26. It should be pointed out that such integration is only possible as a product of time. That is, in the early days of the Congress in Rajasthan the PCCs could not have enjoyed a very high level of sequential integration with the DCCs simply because there had not been time for the DCC members to have moved into higher positions. But whereas time made such an integration possible, it did not make it inevitable.

27. Weiner notes that, in this period, "There was an enormous scramble for office that has made all elections in India, especially for local offices and for state assembly seats (interestingly enough, less so for parliamentary seats), highly competitive. It was not simply that men ran for office to gain power, but often that men who held personal power at the local level recognized that unless they now won office they would lose their power," "Political Development in the Indian States," p. 40.

28. Parallel data were not available for the remaining two years of the period. There was, however, no major change in this period.

29. Note that we are discussing all members of the Council of Ministers, not only those in the cabinet.

30. The following material is from Robins, "Institutional Linkages with an Elite Body."

31. See Robins, "The Indian Upper House and Elite Integration"; Norman Nichol- son, "The Indian Council of Ministers: An Analysis of Legislative and Organizational Careers." Paper presented to the Twenty-Fifth Annual Meeting of the Association for Asian Studies, Chicago, April 1, 1973.

32. (Princeton: Princeton University Press, 1968).

33. Ibid., "The Period of Centralization and Convergence," pp. 54-74, offers an historical summary which argues for this period being considered a distinct era.

34. Ibid., pp. 111 ff.

35. This summary taken from ibid., pp. 115 ff. Three other sources which are useful for a history not only of the working committee, but of the Congress in the independence period are M. V. Ramana Rao, *Development of the Congress Constitution* (New Delhi: All India Congress Committee, 1958); H. Kabir, "Reorganization of the Congress," *Hindustan Times* (New Delhi), May 29, 1960; U. N. Ehebar et al., *Report of the Reorganization Committee* (New Delhi: All India Congress Committee, 1960).

36. Kochanek, *Congress Party of India,* pp. 121, 122.

37. Ibid., pp. 123 ff.

38. Ibid., p. 126.

39. Ibid.

40. See Robins, "Political Elite Formation in Rural India," for a discussion of the role of the village as a political unit, which draws on the work of Henry Orenstein, *Gaon* (Princeton: Princeton University Press, 1965) among others. Also see Harry Izmirlian, Jr., "Dynamics of Political Support in a Punjab Village," *Asian Survey,* 6 (March, 1966), pp. 125-133. The principal full-length work on the system of sub-district government is Henry Maddick, *Panchayati Raj* (London: Longmans, 1970). Even before the Mehta Report, the term *Panchayati raj* was not used with much precision. Concerning the origins of the members of village government, see pp. 86-100, 195, and all Chapter 14, "Politics and Panchayati Raj," pp. 205-216. An excellent analytic work is A. H. Somjee, *Democracy and Political Change in Village India* (New Delhi: Orient Longmans, 1971).

For a different sort of analysis, one that follows the works of S. N. Eisenstadt, see Jerry M. Silverman's work on South Vietnam: "Political Elites in South Vietnam: A National and Provincial Comparison," *Asian Survey,* 10 (April, 1970), pp. 290-307.

41. Weiner, *Party Building in a New Nation.* This localism is noted in Donald Rosenthal, *The Limited Elite: Politics and Government in Two Indian Cities* (Chicago: University of Chicago Press, 1970), where the author's study of politics in Poona and Agra, especially in the 1950s, demonstrated the importance of local patterns of recruitment. Other sources which deal with urban patterns of recruitment are the papers published in the urban seminar issue of the *Journal of Asian Studies,* 20 (February, 1961): Henry

C. Hart, "Bombay Politics," Myron Weiner, "Violence and Politics in Calcutta," and, most relevant for our purposes, Lloyd Rudolph, "Urban Life and Populist Radicalism."

An extensive study of politics and political recruitment at the district level is Weiner, *Party Building in a New Nation.* Weiner at points (e.g., p. 3) relies on Huntington's concept of political institutionalization. Aside from the village studies we have already cited, the reader is especially referred to A. H. Somjee, *Democracy and Political Change in Village India* (New Delhi: Orient, Longmans, 1971). Somjee here notes the occasional divorce between political success and social and economic advantage (p. 174). Also see the same author's *Voting Behavior in an Indian Village* (Baroda: M.S. University of Baroda, 1959).

42. Frey argues that local ties, though important, rank third (after the possession of intellectual and official statuses). *Turkish Political Elite,* p. 97. In England, there is a strong Burkean attitude toward representation.

43. See Chapter 4, especially that section which dealt with the papacy before the division of the Eastern and Western churches. See the section, "The Division of the Eastern and Western Churches."

44. Rudolph and Rudolph argue that private commitment to caste/community is at a minimum compatible with political modernization and that there is good reason to believe that it may even facilitate it. *The Modernity of Tradition,* see especially p. 130, in the section on "The Future of Equality" pp. 103-131; the Rudolphs cite Harold Gould, "The Adaptive Functions of Caste in Contemporary Indian Society," *Asian Survey,* 3 (September, 1963). Also see Harry W. Blair, "Ethnicity and Democratic Politics in India," *Comparative Politics,* 5 (October, 1972), pp. 107-128, for the utility of caste in certain circumstances for political mobilization. A very good study for a comparative perspective is Humber S. Nelli, *The Italians in Chicago 1880-1930: A Study in Ethnic Mobility* (New York: Oxford University Press, 1970).

45. See Myron Weiner, *The Politics of Scarcity* (Chicago: University of Chicago Press, 1962), which deals with the topic of associational pressure groups in the 1952-1962 period.

46. *Modernity of Tradition:* also see their "The Political Modernization of an Indian Feudal Order: An Analysis of Rajput Adaptation in Rajasthan," *Journal of Social Issues,* 24 (October, 1968), pp. 93-128; "The Political Role of India's Caste Associations," *Pacific Affairs,* 33 (March, 1960), pp. 5-22; Lloyd I. Rudolph, "The Modernity of Tradition: The Democratic Incarnation of Caste in India," *American Political Science Review,* 59 (December, 1965), pp. 975-989.

47. Weiner (ed.), *State Politics in India,* especially the author's own "Political Development in the Indian States," pp. 3-58. See this chapter for additional sources in this regard. See the section, "Summary of Level and Form of Institutional Political Elite Integration in India, 1952-1962," in the present chapter.

48. This is a very difficult matter on which to get precise information, but see Burger, *Opposition in a Dominant Party System,* pp. 66-73, for a discussion of the income among opposition MLAs in Uttar Pradesh; and Sisson, *Congress Party of Rajasthan,* pp. 130-147; it is interesting to note that Mahajan representation decreased fairly soon after independence, p. 134; for source of income among Congress MPs, see Kochanek, *Congress Party of India,* pp. 383-385, also see his section on occupations of fathers, pp. 336-338. Erdman, *The Swatantra Party and Indian Conservatism,* p. 140; Sirsikar, "Leadership Patterns in Rural Maharashtra," gives special attention to this topic. Morris-Jones' discussion of corruption is also informative in this regard: *Government and Politics of India,* pp. 61-64. A theoretical perspective is found in Coleman, "Political Money," especially the section, "The Negotiability of Money and Political Power," p. 1078. Also

see Talcott Parsons, "On the Concept of Influence," *Public Opinion Quarterly,* 27 (Spring, 1963), pp. 37-62, which Coleman relies upon.

49. Donald Rosenthal, *The Limited Elite,* pp. 44 ff. A useful bibliographic supplement to Rosenthal is Ashish Bose, *Urbanization in India: An Inventory of Source Materials* (New Delhi: Academic Books, 1970).

50. Rosenthal, *The Limited Elite,* pp. 44 ff.

51. It is worth noting that Gadgil's source of influence was institutionally in the party at the local level and in the government at the national level, a pattern that could be expected from what we stated about effective institutional patterns in the section, "Summary and Form of Institutional Political Elite Integration in India, 1952-1962."

52. Robert Hardgrave, "The Nadars: The Political Culture of a Community in Change." Ph.D. Dissertation, University of Chicago, 1966; also *The Nadars of Tamilnad* (Berkeley: University of California Press, 1969), and "Varieties of Political Behavior Among Nadars of Tamilnad," *Asian Survey,* 6 (November, 1966), pp. 1-27; Rudolph and Rudolph, *Modernity of Tradition.* Also on caste associations, see R. S. Khare, *The Changing Brahmans: Associations and Elites among the Kanya-Kubias of North India* (Chicago: University of Chicago Press, 1970).

53. Rudolph and Rudolph, *Modernity of Tradition,* pp. 49-64.

54. Conflict between new and old elites was further moderated by the fact that higher-level elites were seldom faced by political pressure from a group, some leaders of which were not a party of or had some connection with one or another key government or party elite.

55. Such was the case in Tokugawa Japan. Here, the shogunate set up a parallel, Tokyo-oriented, administrative structure within the villages, staffing the new service with prestigious villagers of the shogunate's choosing. Harumi Befu, "Village Autonomy and Articulation with the State," *Journal of Asian Studies,* 25 (November, 1965), pp. 19-32.

56. Taub, *Bureaucrats Under Stress.*

57. See notes 42 and 50 in this chapter, and associated text.

58. The two most appropriate analyses on this topic are Rajni Kothari, "The Congress 'System' in India," *Asian Survey,* 4 (December, 1964), especially pp. 1161 ff.; and Huntington, *Political Order in Changing Societies,* pp. 420-433.

59. Huntington, *Political Order in Changing Societies,* p. 408. The following evaluation of Congress Party effectiveness is derived from Huntington's section, "Strong Parties and Political Stability," pp. 408-412. Also see W. H. Morris-Jones, "The Indian Congress Party: Dilemmas of Dominance," *Modern Asian Studies,* (April, 1967).

60. Kochanek, *Congress Party of India,* p. 353.

61. For this analysis and the statistics, see Robins, "Political Development and Party Disintegration"; also see note 8 above.

62. Huntington, *Political Order in Changing Societies,* p. 410.

63. See note 91 and accompanying text below.

64. Brass, *Factional Politics in an Indian State,* pp. 237-240.

65. Huntington, *Political Order in Changing Societies,* p. 410.

66. For a discussion of appeals of the right in India, see Erdman's chapter, "Dimensions of Indian Right-Wing Politics: Social and Doctrinal Aspects," in his *Swatantra Party and Indian Conservatism,* pp. 10-45.

On the akali (Sikh) appeal, see "Punjabi Suba: The Akali Demand," pp. 32-42 in Baldev Raj Naya," *Minority Politics in the Punjab* (Princeton: Princeton University Press, 1966), and also "Sikh Separatism in the Punjab," in Donald E. Smith (ed.), *South Asian Politics and Religion* (Princeton: Princeton University Press, 1966), pp. 150-175.

For the transcendent appeal of Communism in this period, see Gene Overstreet and Marshall Windmiller, *Communism in India* (Berkeley: University of California Press,

1959). This book is historically and organizationally oriented. Sections that deal with the appeal of the CPI may be found in Chapter I, "The Dual Environment of the CPI," pp. 7-18, and also in pp. 487-527. A more analytic work with an earlier focus is John Haithcox, *Communism and Nationalism in India* (Princeton: Princeton University Press, 1971). A more recent study is Ralph Retzloff, "Revision and Dogmatism in the CPI," in R. Scalapino (ed.), *The Communist Revolution in Asia.*

An article that argues that the transcendent appeal of the Congress continued through the 1950s and into the 1970s is B. D. Graham, "Congress as a Rally," *South Asian Review,* 6 (January, 1973), pp. 111-123.

67. Other works of Erdman have also been drawn upon: "Chakravarty Rajagopala-chari and Indian Conservatism" *Journal of Developing Areas,* 1 (October, 1966); "Conservative Politics in India," *Asian Survey,* 6 (June, 1966); "The Swatantra Party and Indian Conservatism," Ph.D. Dissertation, Department of Political Science, Harvard University, 1964. Also note his brief *Political Attitudes of Indian Industry: A Case Study of the Baroda Business Elite* (London: Athlon, 1971), which is a carefully documented work.

68. Erdman, *The Swatantra Party and Indian Conservatism,* pp. 10-64.

69. Ibid., p. 65.

70. Ibid., p. 66.

71. Ibid., pp. 109-146.

72. Ibid., pp. 109-120 for Swatantra's rationalization of substantial anti-Congress conservative opposition. It is especially noteworthy that there were many not only experienced, but veteran politicians among the new elite recruits—men such as J. Mohammed Imam of Mysore. More "modern men," as Erdman characterized them, from the administrative and professional classes, also joined. See ibid., pp. 134-140.

73. A useful study which seeks to relate the Indian political culture to a broader social and historical framework is found in Ashis Nandy, "The Culture of Indian Politics," *Journal of Asian Studies,* 30 (November, 1970), pp. 57-80.

74. Pp. 17-29, and 29-36, respectively.

75. This work first appeared in the *Economic and Political Weekly,* in five parts: December 31, 1966, I: pp. 833-840; January 7, 1967, II: pp. 17-24; January 14, 1967, II: pp. 61-76; February 11, 1967, II: pp. 371-376; February 18, 1967, II: pp. 407-416.

76. The article of February 11, 1967, indicates that after agriculturalist, professional politician was the most common occupation claimed. Of the applicants for nomination, 28% were so characterized, and 35% of the candidates.

77. See note 51 above, and the associated text. See Roy, "Selection of Congress Candidates," for a study of Congress response to such pressures.

78. Morris-Jones, *Government and Politics of India,* section on "Economic Development," pp. 106-112, indicates this modest movement.

79. Rosenthal, *Limited Elite,* pp. 44 ff.; Ray, *Economic and Political Weekly.*

80. (London: Oxford University Press, 1966).

81. The dates of the events to be analyzed fall at the near margins of the period being dealt with. It would, ideally, be preferable if a similar event had been found earlier, but none is available.

82. Pp. 70-91.

83. There was, of course, the countervailing influences of the parliamentary nature of the Indian system, and the more federal nature of the Congress Party.

84. Brecher, *Succession in India,* p. 72.

85. See ibid., pp. 72-73 for the marginal influence of occupational, ascriptive, and associative interest groups on the selection. See p. 90 for the lack of ideological influence.

86. Brecher, *Political Leadership in India.*

87. Ibid., p. 20

88. Ibid., p. 13

89. See Kochanek, *Congress Party of India,* pp. 352 ff. for a discussion of the caste, regional, etc., composition and variation of the figures presented in Table 4. Dagmar Bernstorff, "Candidates for the 1967 General Election in Hyderabad, A.P.," in Edmund Leach and S. N. Mukherjee (eds.), *Elites in South Asia* (London: Cambridge University Press, 1970), pp. 136-151 comments, "A look at the length and nature of the candidates' association with politics shows that most of them have been active in politics for a long time starting early in their lives," p. 150.

90. Ibid., p. 361.

91. Ibid., pp. 362-363.

92. Paul Brass, "Coalition Politics in North India," *American Political Science Review,* 62 (December, 1968), pp. 1174-1191 stresses the importance of generational conflict in the 1964-1967 period, especially see p. 1174.

93. Brass' work on factionalism has already been cited. A highly analytic work on factionalism in India is Mary Carras, *The Dynamics of Indian Political Factions: A Study of District Councils in the State of Maharashtra* (London: Cambridge University Press, 1972); also see her "Congress Factionalism in Maharashtra," *Asian Survey,* 10 (May, 1970), pp. 410-426. An anthropological account of political factions is Oscar Lewis, *Group Dynamics in a North Indian Village—A Study of Factions* (Delhi: Planning Commission, 1954). A recent intensive study is M. K. Saini and W. Anderson, "The Congress Split in Delhi," *Asian Survey,* 11 (November, 1971), pp. 1084-1100. Normal Nicholson, "The Factional Model and the Study of Politics," *Comparative Politics,* 5 (October, 1972), pp. 291-314 is useful for a theoretical perspective; his "Factionalism and the Indian Council of Ministers," *Journal of Commonwealth Political Studies,* 10 (November, 1972), pp. 179-197, is also useful. For comparative purposes, see Chae-Jin Lee, "Factional Politics in the Japanese Socialist Party," *Asian Survey,* 10 (March, 1970), pp. 230-243; and Andrew Nathan, "A Factional Model for CCP Politics," *China Quarterly,* (January/March, 1973), pp. 34-66.

94. Congress politics was very much factional politics. As Brass comments in his study of Uttar Pradesh in the 1950s and early 1960s, "Organizationally, the Congress is a collection of local, district, and state factions forming alliances and developing hostilities in a constant struggle for positions of power in Congress-controlled institutions of state and local government," Brass, *Factional Politics in an Indian State,* p. 232.

95. Ibid., p. 237. Also see pp. 239-240 for damaging aspects of factions.

96. Ibid., p. 240. Brass notes a direct relationship between the intensity of factionalism and the size of the Congress in specific areas, and suggests that factionalism is an aid in recruitment. This idea is a parallel one to Huntington's comment on the utility of the two-party system, *Political Order in Changing Societies,* p. 430. Huntington's factional model on pp. 412-415, and his party hierarchy vs. state-bureaucratic hierarchy conflict model, pp. 426-427, are not applicable in the Indian circumstance due to the Congress Party being only marginally dominant.

97. Brass, *Factional Politics in an Indian State,* p. 241. Peter McDonough, "Electoral Competition and Participation in India: A Test of Huntington's Hypothesis," *Comparative Politics,* 4 (October, 1971), pp. 77-78, supports Huntington's argument on the positive relationship between by-partyism and mobilization.

98. Morris-Jones notes that the principal contribution of the panchayati raj system in this period was that "the foundations of a new and lively system of local government

have been laid," *Government and Politics of India* (London: Hutchinson, 1971 edition), p. 158.

99. See Taub, *Bureaucrats Under Stress;* Braibanti and Spengler (eds.), *Administration and Economic Development in India;* D. N. Rao, "Disparities of Representation Among the Direct Recruits to the I.A.S.," *Indian Journal of Public Administration,* 9 (1963), pp. 33-94; Jay B. Wescott, "Government Organization and Methods in Developing Countries," in Irving Swerdlow (ed.), *Development Administration* (Syracuse, N.Y.: Syracuse University Press, 1963).

100. This is a general point also made in Rudolph and Rudolph, *Modernity of Tradition,* and Robins, "Political Elite Formation in Rural India."

Chapter 7

SUMMARY AND CONCLUSIONS

The theme that pervades this work is that the nature of the political system—especially its predictability and effectiveness—is vitally affected by the form and degree of elite movement among its institutions. Such elite movement (which is briefly characterized as elite integration) and the type of institutional context in which it takes place affects the nature of both the elite and the institutions. This interaction has a great variety of consequences. The ones examined in the previous chapters principally fall under the general analytic heading of institutionalization.

The conceptual framework used for the study of institutionalization was that proposed by Samuel Huntington (institutionalization as described in the dimensions of complexity, coherence, autonomy, and adaptability). Huntington has not been accepted uncritically—several modifications have been made —but the framework used is very largely his, especially in terms of the major evaluatory criteria.

Elite integration and institutionalization are related, the form of their relation is systematic and regular, and this relationship is conditioned by several definable sets of conditions. These conditions were systematically laid out and their effects evaluated. The *conditional* factors were stressed because no simple, unidimensional relation between elite integration and institutionalization exists.

The conditional categories were generated in the following way. First, there is the *form* of elite integration—whether vertical (elites moving up within the same general organization context) or horizontal (elites moving laterally or obliquely between organizational contexts). Then there was the general nature of the organizational context to be considered—whether bureaucratic or political. These two terms were defined in such a way as to distinguish the technically skilled, seniority- or hierarchically oriented organizations from the more open entrepreneurial organizations. Elite movement, horizontal or vertical, may be within either, or between both (political to bureaucratic, and bureaucratic to political) types of organizations. This movement was then evaluated in terms of its effects, using the Huntingtonian criteria of complexity, coherence, autonomy, and adaptability.

Political vertical elite integration, bureaucratic vertical elite integration, political horizontal elite integration, bureaucratic horizontal elite integration, political/bureaucratic horizontal elite integration, and political/bureaucratic vertical elite integration were thus related to the four criteria of complexity, coherence, autonomy, and adaptability just mentioned, providing a basic group of twenty-four elite-institutional contextual dimensions. In almost all cases, moreover, there were subcategories. For example, in the evaluation of autonomy, the nature of recruitment was discussed in terms of two recruitment models developed for this purpose: the mentor-protege and the key institution. Another example of the use of subcategories would be the fact that the concept of adaptation is divided by Huntington into three aspects: chronological, functional, and generational age. Thus, these subdivisions redivided the conditional subdivisions described above.

Summary

Anyone who develops such an elaborate scheme should feel at least a little embarrassed and defensive. There is the best defense that can be made, however. This organizational scheme is the briefest that is possible if one wants to be both comprehensive and systematic. The scheme is also clear and readily comprehensible.

The following comments and generalizations are derived from the categories laid out in the previous chapters. At each point in the theoretical exposition, concrete historical cases were used, and also two long case studies were applied. The chapters were organized by form of elite integration. In summarizing the findings, it would seem to be better to follow the institutionalization evaluating criteria.

COMPLEXITY AND ELITE INTEGRATION

There is a clear and regular positive relationship between the amount of elite integration within an organization and the severity and differentiation of its sub-units. Obviously, there must be some multiplicity and differentiation if there is to be even a possibility of elite movement. However, the analysis of several polities suggests that it is more elite integration that permits the existence of complexity than the reverse. Any complex organization requires substantial levels of the skills peculiar to that area of endeavor, but of equal or greater importance are the varieties of social knowledge that are unique to particular organizations: Who can be counted on to do what kind of job, how reforms can be implemented, and all the other forms of social knowledge that are essential to the operation of any large, subdivided, and differentiated organization. Technical skills are often (though not always) best learned internally, but social knowledge is only so acquired. The principal mechanism for assuring that the leaders at each level have this social knowledge is their recruitment from below.

This generalization applies to both bureaucratic and political systems. The case is more obvious in the bureaucratic, but is in fact no less real in the political. The social knowledge politicians acquire at lower levels is invaluable to the system's effectiveness at higher levels. One of the reasons that Communist parties are so effective in giving stability and direction to socially disrupted countries is due to the fact that the internal recruitment of their leadership provides the leadership with structured and useful information within a broader social context in which such knowledge is hard to come by.

Elite movement from outside the organizational system (horizontal elite integration) is generally harmful, because social and technical knowledge are not likely to have been acquired. It is common, however, for stable and complex organizations to experience a certain amount of exotic horizontal elite movement at their highest levels. A *limited* degree of elite movement from one organization to another at the *higher* levels is sometimes functional. New ideas and new ways of doing things are so introduced, but probably more important is the fact that the top elite of an organization often spend nearly as much time dealing with parallel organizations as with their own. To some extent, consequently, horizontal elite integration at the highest levels has some of the characteristics of elite integration within an organization.

Thus, movement of elites from one organization to another is generally harmful to complexity, except where the movement is small in number and where it occurs at the top level.

COHERENCE AND ELITE INTEGRATION

The form of elite integration—whether horizontal or vertical—is a major variable in the strength of intra-institutional agreement of functional boundaries and procedures for resolving intra-organizational conflicts. It is also a major variable in producing esprit, morale, self-confidence.

In fact, there are probably few things that promote coherence more than the fact that members of an elite share not only a background, but a future as well. The shared background assures a high level of similar socialization and also produces the personal ties and knowledge that a well-integrated organization encourages a positive attitude as well. The Roman Catholic Church and any successful professional military organization will illustrate this principle.

On the other hand, there is nothing that damages the morale and harmony of an organization more than a substantial number of outside leaders being brought in—except perhaps when they are very few in number and brought in at the very highest level. Where the new entrants are antagonistic—as with the State Department reorganization in the early days of the Eisenhower Administration—coherence clearly lessens. The same phenomenon can be seen when an established company is newly purchased and reorganized by outsiders. Similarly, coherence would be severely damaged in an academic department forced to change its leadership and forced to acquire a new student clientele.

Of course, vertical elite integration is not the only way that coherence is established and maintained, and its violation is not the only way coherence is diminished. Some organizations, however, rely on it more than others. It is worthwhile noting that left organizations are more dependent on elite integration for the maintenance of coherence than are right organizations. The reason for this is that right organizations are for a variety of reasons generally firmly integrated to outside groups such as extended families, religious organizations, ethnic associations, and they are also frequently well socialized into a broad set of expectations as to the way disputes should be settled and the proper role of institutions.

Left organizations (and here the assumption is that the left is generally innovative) lack many of these extra-organizational structuring factors. Left organizations consequently must rely a great deal on their own artifice—the political organization and the mechanisms of integration associated with it.

AUTONOMY AND ELITE INTEGRATION

The two bases of an institution's autonomy concern the security of its income and its freedom in choosing its own leaders and members. If one or the other of these bases must be compromised, most organizations prefer to accept limitations on income than on self-selection. It should be noted that some autonomous and powerful organizations have no power of self-selection of members, only of leaders. Membership self-selection is thus not always present, but the basis of elite integration, leadership self-selection, is. The U.S. Senate is an organization that is not self-selecting of its members, but is of its leaders.

Vertical elite integration means that the organization enjoys this vital aspect of maintaining its ability to resist outside pressures. It is theoretically possible to have a formal vertical elite integration, wherein all significant promotions are made with little or no regard to internal organizational wishes. I know of no such organization, however.

Autonomy requires that the boundary of an organization be clear. Vertical elite integration is, of course, such a defining process. The organization's actions and the consequences of these actions are often difficult to define, but if the principle is established that recruitment is from within, at least the source of the authority will be clear.

Where a new elite moves into a position of dominance over another, autonomy clearly is lessened. Members of the new elite will likely have different attitudes and not feel a personal obligation to defend the organization. Organizations that get their elite from outside and especially where this elite changes frequently are not likely to enjoy autonomy.

On the other hand, this defect may sometimes be a virtue, just as the virtue of autonomy may under certain circumstances be a defect. Some organizations become so autonomous that they function badly—they are out of contact with the larger society. If the organization is marginal to the society as a whole and has its own sources of income—e.g., a well-endowed small private college—it can remain irrelevantly autonomous almost indefinitely. But where the institution is essential to the larger society (such as the armed forces or a single pre-eminent university in a small country), then that institution must have its autonomy broken and its internal organization and elite reconstituted.

There is a variety of ways in which such a reconstitution may occur. The old institution may be completely eliminated and a new one substituted, or large numbers of new entrants may be forced or let into the organization. Revolutionary destructiveness or mass influx of the unsocialized and untrained are likely, however, to be the two least effective ways of constituting a new and effective institution. Coherence, autonomy, adaptation, and complexity all require time to develop. A new institution with new elites may do well initially because of enthusiasm and the opportunity of filling a long-neglected need, but it is likely to become less effective when it faces a more nearly normal environment, and the initial esprit is gone.

The most effective way of reforming an overly autonomous institution is by the application of horizontal elite integration. Elites from similar or parallel organizations are placed in positions of authority within the formerly ineffective organization. Such a technique is probably the most commonly used because it preserves the continuity of the non-elite members of the affected institutions and assures the new elites having at least general (and often specific) training as leaders, and provides for extra-organizational continuity. Such an event may happen not only to one institution, but indeed it may occur to nearly the entire governmental elite structure. A military take-over, such as occurred in Pakistan in 1958, is such an example.

A final comment is that left (innovative) organizations are more dependent on elite integration than are right ones for the maintenance of their autonomy, as well as for the previously mentioned maintenance of coherence. Right organizations are shielded and supported by the various ascriptive, fiscal, and religious groupings to which they are related. Again, factors such as the church, the extended family structure, the independent access to wealth protect and help integrate these organizations. For reasons discussed earlier, innovative organizations are more open-ended in their programs and in their access to previously excluded groups, and thus less structurally defined in these regards than are those on the right. Consequently, they are forced to rely—where they are to be successful—on internal means of maintaining autonomy. An emphasis on selection of leadership already serving in an organizational capacity is consequently most commonly encountered among left organizations.

ADAPTABILITY AND ELITE INTEGRATION

Adaptability is more a measure of performance than it is a factor that goes into creating effectiveness. That is, autonomy is very much a derivative of the previous three factors. Adaptation is demonstrated by the capacity of the organization to weather the crises of generational renewal, functional change, and the passage of time itself.

The only evidently independent, elite-related factor in adaptation that has a general relation to effectiveness may be that of the age of the members. Elite integration, especially vertical elite integration, requires individuals to pass through at least one and often several offices before reaching higher status. Such a process inevitably takes time, and so higher organizational levels will tend to be occupied by incumbents in their middle and late years.

It is possible to have older elites without vertical elite integration, but where vertical elite integration exists, the elites will tend to be older. It was indicated that older institutions are more adaptable than newer ones, and older institutions tend to be governed by older elites.

It cannot be demonstrated conclusively that older elites are more effective than younger ones, but the correlation is there, and observation has suggested to many that caution, tact, and patience—virtues of the more mature—may be more effective in systems maintenance than energy and a sense of immediacy.

Conclusion

Elite integration and institutionalization are related, and this relationship is regular, substantial, and systematically variable. A valid theory is worthwhile for its own sake, but it is also worthwhile to know where and how it fits in, illuminates, and modifies the body of knowledge that precedes it. The subject is as broad as all social science, but it is appropriate that some of the relationships should be outlined here.

Two areas are seen as most appropriate for discussion: (1) The relation of this work to that of the body of institutional theorists—not only Huntington but also, especially, Braibanti, Riggs, Esman, and Eisenstadt—should be dealt with explicitly and systematically, although the work of these scholars has already been alluded to at various places in this study. A more general statement is called for. (2) Because this book speaks so much of stability, it also deals with change. Change and stability are two ends of a necessarily single continuum, and the emphasis a writer gives to one or the other is more a consequence of personal temperament and analytic convenience than it is a choice of one subject matter over another. Consequently, a discussion is called for relating what was said in this monograph to some of the major themes—general and technical—relating to rapid political change.

(1) CONTEMPORARY INSTITUTIONAL THEORIES AND ELITE INTEGRATION

Looking at several of the major writers in institutional development— Esman, Eisenstadt, Riggs, Braibanti, and Huntington, among others—one notices certain pervading themes as well as differences.[1] Probably the basic perception that they all share is that the writing on institutions since World War II has suffered from a serious conceptual distortion. The dominant themes and concerns in political change have been those dealing with the participatory processes to the neglect of the administrative and distributive ones.

More broadly, social science—principally in America, which has been the dominant force in this area—has suffered from "inputism," the over-concern with participatory factors affecting the formal governmental structures to the neglect of the independent role that governmental "outputs" may play. This criticism is especially leveled at those who have devoted themselves to the study of the newer polities. Although the participatory aspects of the political system (mass movements, new groups in politics, etc.) are important and quite evident in the newer states, the governments and closely allied institutions of these states actually play a larger independent role than in more socially differentiated and developed polities.

The post-World War II rise in the concern for the participatory functions of the political system was itself a reaction against the earlier tendency to emphasize the institutional component of government. As James W. Fesler[2] observes, one can note a natural history of revolts against conventional wisdom wherein a variable that had been seen as a dependent variable is re-discovered as an independent variable, the previously perceived independent variable now becoming the dependent. Such shifts in emphasis are especially characteristic of the social sciences, where most variables have reciprocal causality.

Elite integration and political institutionalization fall more in the output tradition than in the input. They do not, however, fall completely within that context. Indeed, elite integration is very much a link between the two. Elite integration concerns participation, not so much *into* the administrative and governmental system but *within* it. Furthermore, elite integration is related to participation in that it is one of the principal means by which organiza-tions moderate and control the level and form of participation on them.

The classic input elements of socialization, recruitment, aggregation, and articulation are all mediated by the form and degree of elite integration within and between institutions. For example, in a dominant party state a high level of vertical elite integration in the dominant party will be a means of recruiting elites from a variety of groups. Where the party is integrated exclusively by consultation or patronage, with low levels of vertical elite integration, new groups entering at the bottom will not be recruited into higher positions. Thus the practice (as well as the concept) of elite integration is an important nexus between institutionalization and participation.

This is not to say that elites have been neglected by earlier writers. They have not. Nor do I suggest that replacement of existing elites has not received substantial attention. The point is that, both in policy and in theory, the consequences of the internal movement of elites has been little considered. A major concrete instance of such lack of consideration was the United States-directed reforms in Japan between 1945 and 1950 and the subsequent scholarly literature on that policy.[3] Very little *administrative* reform was instituted in Japan in that period. Elites were dealt with by excluding (and later re-including) certain members closely associated with Axis aggression. Social change was encouraged by means of creating a more participatory party environment. Changes in the level or form of elite integration in the Japanese context may not have been necessary, but there is little reason to think it was considered.

Probably the most important element that this study of elite integration and political institutionalization brings to the broader institutional theories is the emphasis on time. Not that an emphasis on time is distinctive to this study—all the major theorists acknowledge the importance of time in institutional development. Braibanti and Huntington are both very sensitive to the time dimension.

In a way not done by others, however, this work points up the constraint that time sets on institutional development. The time dimension is not only related to the chronological period that institutions take to become established, but rather it is the actual human lifespan that is involved. Years as such are not adequate as a basic measure. The process of individuals moving from one position to another, acquiring the general organizational and technical skills, and especially the necessary social knowledge of the organization must take at least the larger part of a lifetime. Indeed, in the nature of things —providing for generational overlap—for an institution to be developed in terms of the distribution of social knowledge, development must take several lifetimes. There are principles that may be applied to permit this process to begin, to move smoothly, and to bear fruit, but there is no way to avoid it.

It is true that there are forms other than elite integration by which an elite can be tied together. Common background characteristics such as schooling, strongly felt ethnic ties, or membership in extrapolitical organizations such as a church may serve to integrate an elite.[4] These extramural and ascriptive factors may be valuable for many organizations, and indeed are generally adequate for a simple organization or even a more developed one not under great stress. Where the organization is complex, or where it must fact a severe challenge from outside, extramural and ascriptive integrative supports—which are not under its own control—will likely prove inadequate.

Thus, man may manipulate his political environment—within limits and probably at a certain price—but the process requires more than application and ingenuity; it requires an amount of time well beyond the life span of any person.

(2) CERTAIN DOMINANT THEMES CONCERNING RAPID POLITICAL CHANGE AND ELITE INTEGRATION

How is rapid political change evaluated? There are four dimensions of change that all writers concerned with the topic—from Plato to Karl Marx to Crane Brinton—use, although to varying degrees and in different ways. These varieties of change are breaks in the continuity of institutions, in the continuity of values, and in the continuity of elites and policies.[5] Some writers stress one or another of these discontinuities, but all make use of at least one.

Major social upheavals may be viewed as consisting of various mixes of these discontinuities. For example, the American Revolution had a high level of institutional and value discontinuity, a low level of elite discontinuity, and a moderate level of policy discontinuity. The Russian Revolution had high levels of all four types of discontinuity. When social theorists and major social events are referred to, these four dimensions will be used for purposes of categorization and analysis. Of course, other categorizations are possible, but the fourfold one just described appears to be the most useful for the present purposes.

Two characteristics of contemporary writers on rapid and major political change are (a) a tendency to move away from conceptually integrative concepts of rapid social change—such as revolutionary theory—and to stress events *associated* with such change. There has, for example, been a great emphasis on group violence and various forms of internal war; similarly, there has also developed an extensive literature on such matters as informational availability and manipulation as means of coercion.[6] (b) In contrast to this interest in the concomitants and technical aspects of social change, there has been a revival, and especially a reappraisal, of general theories of social change in the Marxist tradition. This neo-Marxism, as it is often called, is well outside the official Marxism of the established Leninist nations. It is, in fact, very much a reaction against the bulk of the official doctrines.[7]

The neo-Marxists are very much concerned with the great variety of social and political development in the twentieth century. In this sense, neo-Marxism may be seen as Marxism applied to political development. In another context, such theories are applied as a critique of contemporary industrially advanced or postindustrial societies. In this sense, neo-Marxism is a specific form of social criticism.

(a) Elite integration and the concomitants of rapid social change. Interest in what may be called the technical aspects and internal structure of rapid political change has rapidly grown in the past quarter-century. This growth has been in large part because social science has demanded increasingly higher levels of conceptual clarity and operationalization in its theory-building. There has consequently been an increasing dissatisfaction with broad, incorporative concepts such as that of revolution that are not evidently operationalizable.

In general terms, most writers in the area of rapid social change appear to believe that revolution is an intuitively clear and even a necessary concept for differentiating among various historical events. But like most major concepts—virtue, justice, freedom—revolution is often more easily perceived than defined. Because it is difficult to define—and also because of the emotional affect associated with it by many—it is difficult to deal with analytically. It should be noted, however, that the technical measures of the concomitants of rapid social change, although an apparent movement away from the broad analytic concept of revolution are in fact, by their continual ad hoc integration, resulting in a clarification of the concept of revolution.

Looking at work such as that by Midlarski and Tanter[8] on causal path analysis and Gurr's more general work on rebellion,[9] one can see the utility of the technically oriented approach for dealing with a wide variety of questions. The concept of elite integration is readily suited to technical analysis complementary to systemic questions, and indeed has been so used in the present volume.

Elite movement within institutions and the exclusion of extra-institutional elites and non-elites is one measure (one aspect) of stability. Such movement is also an indicator of the flow of stable sets of information, if one makes the assumption that individuals acquire such information sets at one level and take the sets with them to the next.

Such movement may be evaluated not only abstractly, but also in practice —data on career paths are among the most reliable and accessible on elites. Absolute and relative percentages, rates of recruitment, areas of recruitment, etc., all may be determined. Such a study was made in Chapter 6, using techniques derived from causal path analysis, and applied to the Indian Council of Ministers. The purpose was to help determine the extent to which the political elite recruitment system was integrated from village to Council of Ministers. This brief study could only answer a part of the more general question, but it did do that, and it also pointed up several areas of discontinuity.

(b) Elite integration as a clarifier of more general concepts of rapid political change. As indicated earlier, it is possible to deal with the concept of rapid political change in several ways: break it down into several discrete dimensions (elites, policies, etc.); identify one determining variable that underlies all others; construct a structured model such as Nadel does,[10] taking Brinton's "classic" revolutions and abstracting their essential characteristics into a model of *revolution.* In all these approaches, however, the role of elites figures prominently.

Although the concept of elite integration is related to all but the most idiosyncratic theory of revolution, it is not a measure of elite system change per se. Rather, it deals with changes within elite subsystems such as the replacement of part of one elite system by other elites. Complete replacement of an elite would not involve elite integration, nor would an absolutely stable elite system.

As indicated earlier, absolute discontinuity is as rare as absolute stability. Elite integration among institutions is common for more mature polities and serves as an indicator of the form and the intensity of the political change under way. Vertical elite integration—where the new elite passes up through the established system—is apt to result in greater continuity than any other form of elite movement. Even horizontal elite integration—which is disruptive —will moderate an otherwise sharp discontinuity, as, for example, in the American Revolution and in the British transfer of power in India. In both these cases, a potentially profoundly disruptive change was undertaken, not without disruption and suffering, but without the series of catastrophes that occurred after such broad-spectrum events as the Russian and Chinese revolutions. The inclusion of the concept of elite integration in the evaluation of these events aids in understanding why the transition in each case resulted in the type and degree of policy, value, and institutional discontinuity that later occurred. It is not sufficient to note the intensity of change among the ruling elites; it is also important to evaluate the form of change. The way the elites changed internally and the institutional sources of the change are essential factors in the understanding of any major historical event.

(3) ELITE INTEGRATION AND NEO-MARXISM

The so-called neo-Marxism referred to a few pages earlier is characterized by certain beliefs and perspectives:

(a) economic factors, especially the institutionalized relation between the owners of property and those who work for them, are the crucial determinants of political history;

(b) these factors are much more useful in accounting for the behavior of the ruling classes, as contrasted with their lesser utility in explaining the behavior of the lower classes;

(c) the neo-Marxists generally reject doctrines of historical inevitability.

This is not the place, nor is there the space available, to review the literature.[11] But it is evident that the role of elites (as distinguished from those of the masses) figures larger in neo-Marxist analysis than in most others with a Marxist origin. The literature—and particularly the criticism of it—indicates, however, that, although the neo-Marxists have avoided the rigidity of the traditional Marxists, they still are subject to some of the old criticism. Prominent among this criticism is the assertion that the neo-Marxists largely ignore the part that cultural and geographic factors apparently play in historical development.

To some extent, this criticism is misplaced. Writers such as Marcuse, Moore, and Wolf essentially argue that, whereas economic factors determine the *nature* of the relationship among groups and institutions, the cultural, historical, and geographical conditions generally affect the *form* and *intensity* of these relations. The solidifying effect of caste in India and the aid to class movement that primogeniture gave in early modern England are clear examples of how idiosyncratic social arrangements vitally structure and condition relations between social classes. The neo-Marxists—much more than their traditional counterparts—do note the conditioning effect of culture and geography, but unfortunately they do not put these variables in any systematic framework.

Can the concept of elite integration do anything to clarify the cultural dimension of neo-Marxism? More specifically, will an examination of elite integration enlighten us as to the form and degree to which the basic economic conditions of society are mediated by cultural factors? Put this way, the answer is clearly yes. This book does not have a neo-Marxist—or any Marxist—orientation, but much of it does concern the way in which economic forces are mediated through the process of intra-institutional elite distribution. Indeed, such an analysis was made at substantial length in the case of the Medieval Catholic Church.

The Church played its mediating role in a variety of ways—by being a tax collector, a gatherer of information, an administrative aid, etc. It was, perhaps most important, a means of recruiting and distributing elites through vertical and horizontal elite integration. Although the Church was for the most part under the domination of the landed authority, to say it was controlled by the secular power would, by itself, be quite incomplete and likely deceptive. The Church also became rich in land and other property, staffed—at certain times —certain governmental institutions, vitally affected the making of policy, and actually challenged the supremacy of the civil power.

Cultural factors—celibacy, supernatural sanctions concerning tax obligations—interacted institutionally with economically dominant forces. In the establishment of the great developmental orders—such as the Cistercians—the economically dominant power was moderated; in the development of avuncular patterns of recruitment, the power was probably sharpened. Thus a study of political-bureaucratic elite integration in the Medieval period points up, and systematically defines in terms of its own dynamics, the interaction of dominant economic influences with conditional cultural factors.

Final Remarks

This chapter has tended to stress the utility of the concept of elite integration. A few additional words should be made concerning its limitations and also on what had to be left undone in this volume.

This theory, like any other, should be developed in a great variety of contextual frameworks. Many cases were drawn on for this volume, and two substantial and integrated studies were offered. More studies of elite integration in additional frameworks will be necessary to fill in the lacunae remaining. Such studies will not only refine the theory, they will also probably change it in certain respects. No worthwhile theory is ever completed.

One area, mentioned by Professor Braibanti in the introduction, that would especially benefit by further study concerns the role values and psychological factors play in the process of elite integration. This book deals with some of these areas—such as socialization—but not to a great extent. In part, this was because the Huntingtonian paradigm was used for the analytic framework rather than a paradigm such as Braibanti's RABCIRR formulation, more sensitive to the role of values and personality in institutional dynamics. Further work in elite integration in this area and by this approach would be of considerable utility.

It is hoped that what has been done is of use on its own terms, and that this volume will enhance the work of others in the fields of elites and institutions.

NOTES

1. Among the major works that are relevant, see: Milton J. Esman, *Administration and Development in Malaysia* (Ithaca: Cornell University Press, 1972); "Ecological Style in Comparative Administration," *Public Administration Review,* 27, (September, 1967), pp. 271-278; "The Elements of Institution Building," in Joseph W. Eaton (ed.), *Institution Building and Development: From Concepts to Application* (Beverly Hills: Sage Publications, 1972); "Some Issues in Institution Building Theory," in Woods et al. (eds.), *Institution Building: A Model for Applied Social Change* (Cambridge, Mass.: Schenkman, 1972); "The Institution Building Concepts—An Interim Appraisal," (Pittsburgh: Graduate School of International Affairs of the University of Pittsburgh, 1967); Esman and J. D. Montgomery, "Systems Approaches to Technical Cooperation: The Role of Development Administration," *Public Administration Review,* 29, (September, 1969), pp. 507-539. Also see S. N. Eisenstadt, "Breakdown of Modernization," in Eisenstadt (ed.), *Readings in Social Evolution and Development* (London: Pergamon Press, 1970); "Bureaucracy and Political Development," in Joseph LaPalombara (ed.), *Bureaucracy and Political Development* (Princeton: Princeton University Press, 1967); "Institutionalization and Change," *American Sociological Review,* 29, (April, 1964), pp. 235-247; "Modernization and Conditions of Sustained Growth," *World Politics,* 16, (July, 1964), pp. 376-394; *Modernization: Protest and Change* (Englewood Cliffs, N.J.: Prentice-Hall, 1966); "Post-Traditional Societies and the Continuity and Reconstruction of Tradition," *Daedalus,* 102, (Winter, 1973), pp. 1-27; "Some New Looks at the Problems of Relations Between Traditional Societies and Modernization," *Economic Development and Social Change,* 3, (April, 1968), pp. 436-449; "Transformation of Social, Political, and Cultural Orders in Modernization," *American Sociological Review,* 30, (October, 1965), pp. 659-673. See also note 3 in Chapter 1, and, for Braibanti and Riggs, note 2 in Chapter 2. A fairly recent article by Huntington that makes a few modifications (though not in his evaluatory criteria) that are of special interest is "The Change to Change: Modernization, Development, and Politics," *Comparative Politics,* 3, (April, 1971), pp. 283-322. See Mark Kesselman, "Order or Movement? The Literature of Political Development as Ideology," *World Politics,* 26, (October, 1973), pp. 139-154 for an evaluation of this article and others. I would like to thank two graduate students of the Department of Political Science of Tulane University, James Meader and Richard Schuldt, for bibliographical aid on this section.

2. James W. Fesler, "Field Administration," in Ferrel Heady and Sybil L. Stokes (eds.), *Papers in Comparative Public Administration* (Ann Arbor: Institute of Public Administration of the University of Michigan, 1962), p. 138.

3. Braibanti, "Transnational Inducement of Administrative Reform," p. 135. Braibanti puts the process of administrative reform in historical context, noting that the Japanese, since the T'ang mandarinate in China, have been notably willing to accept exotic reforms.

4. For a fuller discussion of the varieties of elite integration, see Robins, "The Indian Upper House and Elite Integration."

5. Ibid.

6. A good example of such a study is Nathan Leites and Charles Wolf, Jr., *Rebellion and Authority* (Chicago: Markham, 1970). The government-related RAND Corporation, which has supported a number of such studies, was associated with this one as well. Much of the stimulus for a variety of institutional theories has come out of the involvement of the developed nations, especially the United States, in the process of cultivating and encouraging stability and administrative effectiveness among the less stable and, it was perceived, Communist-prone states. There was, in fact, something of a division of effort between the United States and the Communist countries in stimulating political development in the Third World: the United States was principally active in developing the output functions of these nations and the Communist countries encouraged input organizations which they believed would serve their interests and be consistent with their values.

7. The term "neo-Marxist" does not refer to an organized, self-conscious movement. It refers at a minimum to the revival, in a liberal, open forum, of looking at social change from a perspective of the relation between those who own the means of production and those who do not.

8. Manus Midlarsky and Raymond Tanter, "Toward a Theory of Political Instability in Latin America," *Journal of Peace Research*, No. 3, (1967), pp. 209-227.

9. Tedd Robert Gurr, *Why Men Rebel* (Princeton: Princeton University Press, 1970). A good example of the blending of technical approaches with broad theoretical concepts is found in Gurr's discussion of relative deprivation, pp. 83-91.

10. George Nadel, "The Logic of the *Anatomy of Revolution*, with Reference to the Netherlands Revolt," *Comparative Studies in Society and History*, 2, (July, 1960), pp. 475-476.

11. The neo-Marxists do not form a school as such, and the literature is rarely exclusively neo-Marxist in its point of view. Certain writers and works are generally considered more characteristic than others, however. Barrington Moore, Jr., *Social Origins of Dictatorship and Democracy: Lord and Peasant in the Making of the Modern World* (Boston: Beacon Press, 1966) is generally considered the leading work in the area. A critique of this book (and a response by Moore) may be found in Stanley Rothman, "Barrington Moore and the Dialectics of Revolution," *American Political Science Review*, 64, (March, 1970), pp. 61-85. Another principal writer and work is Eric R. Wolf, *Peasant Wars of the Twentieth Century* (New York: Harper and Row, 1969). Also see, for several related articles (including a useful Introduction and article by Wolf) Norman Miller and Roderick Aya (eds.), *National Liberation* (New York: Free Press, 1971). Two earlier works that the interested reader may wish to consult are Godfrey and Monica Wilson, *The Analysis of Social Change* (Cambridge: Cambridge University Press, 1945), and Karl Polanyi, *The Great Transformation: The Political and Economic Origins of Our Time* (Boston: Beacon Press, 1957). A very good book that is useful for the evaluation of neo-Marxism as social criticism is Kurt H. Wolff and Barrington Moore, Jr. (eds.), *The Critical Spirit: Essays in Honor of Herbert Marcuse* (Boston: Beacon Press, 1967). The articles by Carr, Stein, Mattick, and Moore are especially noteworthy.

SELECTED BIBLIOGRAPHY OF WORKS
CITED AND CONSULTED

Books

Agger, Robert E., et al. *The Rulers and the Ruled: Political Power and Impotence in American Communities.* New York: John Wiley, 1964.

Alford, Robert R. *Party and Society.* Chicago: Rand McNally, 1963.

Apter, David. *The Politics of Modernization.* Chicago: University of Chicago Press, 1965.

Arendt, Hannah. *Origins of Totalitarianism.* London: Allen & Unwin, 1967.

Armstrong, John. *The Soviet Bureaucratic Elite: A Case Study of the Ukrainian Apparatur.* New York: Praeger, 1959.

Balazs, Etienne. *Chinese Civilization and Bureaucracy.* New Haven: Yale University Press, 1964.

Banfield, Edward. *Moral Basis of a Backward Society.* New York: Free Press, 1958.

––– *The Unheavenly City.* Boston: Little, Brown, 1970.

Barghoorn, Frederick. *Politics in the USSR.* Boston: Little, Brown, 1966.

Barnett, A. Doak. *Cadres, Bureaucracy and Political Power in Communist China.* New York: Columbia University Press, 1967.

Beck, Carl and McKechnie, J. Thomas. *Political Elites: A Select Computerized Bibliography.* Cambridge, Mass.: MIT Press, 1968.

Beloff, Max. *The Age of Absolutism.* London: Hutchinson, 1954.

Bendix, Reinhard. *Max Weber: An Intellectual Portrait.* Garden City, N.Y.: Doubleday, 1962.

Benson, Lee. *The Concept of Jacksonian Democracy: New York as a Test Case.* Princeton: Princeton University Press, 1961.

Berger, Morroe. *Bureaucracy and Society in Modern Egypt.* Princeton: Princeton University Press, 1957.

Berger, Peter L. *The Sacred Canopy: Elements of a Sociological Theory of Religion.* Garden City, N.Y.: Doubleday, 1967.

Beshers, J. M. *Urban Social Structure.* New York: Free Press, 1962.

Bethell, L. *The Abolition of the Brazil Slave Trade.* Cambridge: Cambridge University Press, 1970.

Bill, E.G.W. *University Reform in Nineteenth-Century Oxford: A Study of Henry Halford Vaughan.* London: Oxford University Press, 1973.

Blau, Peter M. *The Dynamics of Bureaucracy: A Study of Interpersonal Relations in Two Government Agencies.* Chicago: University of Chicago Press, 1955.

Blum, Jerome. *Lord and Peasant in Russia.* Princeton: Princeton University Press, 1961.

Bone, Hugh. *Party Committees and National Politics.* Seattle: University of Washington Press, 1958.

Bontecou, Eleanor. *The Federal Loyalty-Security Program.* Ithaca: Cornell Press, 1953.

Bose, Ashiah. *Urbanization in India: An Inventory of Source Materials.* New Delhi: Academic Books, 1970.

Bottomore, T. B. *Elites and Society.* New York: Basic Books, 1964.

Boualam, Said Benaissa. *L'Algerie sans la France.* Paris: Editions France Empire, 1963.

Braibanti, Ralph. *Research on the Bureaucracy of Pakistan.* Durham, N.C.: Duke University Press, 1966.

——— and Spengler, Joseph J. (eds.) *Tradition, Values and Socio-Economic Development.* Durham, N.C.: Duke University Press, 1961.

Brass, Paul R. *Factional Politics in an Indian State.* Berkeley: University of California Press, 1965.

Braunthal, Gerard. *The Federation of German Industry in Politics.* Ithaca: Cornell University Press, 1965.

Brecher, Michael. *Political Leadership in India.* New York: Praeger, 1969.

——— *Succession in India: A Study in Decision Making.* London: Oxford University Press, 1966.

Brecht, Arnold and Glaser, Comstock. *The Art and Technique of Administration in German Ministries.* Cambridge: Harvard University Press, 1940.

Breen, T. H. *The Character of the Good Ruler: A Study of Puritan Political Ideas in New England 1630-1730.* New Haven: Yale University Press, 1970.

Briggs, Asa. *The Age of Improvement.* London: Longmans, 1959.

Brinton, Crane. *Anatomy of Revolution.* London: Cape, 1953.

Brogan, D. W. *The Price of Revolution.* London: Hamish, 1951.

Buck, Philip W. *Amateurs and Professionals in British Politics, 1918-1959.* Chicago: University of Chicago Press, 1963.

Burger, Angela. *Opposition in a Dominant Party System.* Berkeley: University of California Press, 1969.

Caplan, Gerald. *The Elites of Barotseland 1878-1969.* Berkeley: University of California Press, 1970.

Carras, Mary. *The Dynamics of Indian Political Factions: A Study of District Councils in the State of Maharashtra.* London: Cambridge University Press, 1972.

Chow, Yung-Teh. *Social Mobility in China.* New York: Atherton Press, 1966.

Dahl, Robert. *Who Governs?* New Haven: Yale University Press, 1961.

Deutsch, Karl W. *Nationalism and Social Communication.* New York: John Wiley, 1953.

——— *The Nerves of Government.* New York: Free Press, 1966.

Dhebar, U. N. et al. *Report of the Reorganization Committee.* New Delhi: All India Congress Committee, 1960.

Downs, Anthony. *An Economic Theory of Democracy.* New York: Harper, 1957.

Downton, James. *Rebel Leadership.* New York: Free Press, 1973.

Dye, Thomas R. *Politics, Economics, and the Public.* Chicago: Rand McNally, 1966.

Eaton, John W. (ed.) *Institution Building and Development.* Beverly Hills: Sage Publications, 1972.

Eberhard, Wolfram. *Social Mobility in Traditional China.* Leiden: E. J. Brill, 1962.

Eisenstadt, S. N. *Modernization: Protest and Change.* Englewood Cliffs, N.J.: Prentice-Hall, 1966.

Emerson, Rupert. *Representative Government in Southeast Asia.* Cambridge: Harvard University Press, 1955.

Epstein, Leon D. *Political Parties in Western Democracies.* London: Pall Mall Press, 1967.

Erdman, Howard. *Political Attitudes of Indian Industry: A Case Study of the Baroda Elite.* London: Athlone, 1971.

――― *The Swatantra Party and Indian Conservatism.* Cambridge: Cambridge University Press, 1967.

Erikson, Erik. *Gandhi's Truth.* New York: Norton, 1969.

――― *Young Man Luther.* New York: Norton, 1958.

Esman, Milton J. *Administration and Development in Malaysia.* Ithaca: Cornell University Press, 1972.

――― and Bruhns, Fred C. (eds.) *Institution-Building in National Development.* Pittsburgh: University of Pittsburgh Press, 1965.

Form, William H. and Sauer, Warren L. *Community Influentials in a Middle-Sized City.* East Lansing: Michigan State University, Institute for Community Development, 1960.

Frey, Frederick. *The Turkish Political Elite.* Cambridge: MIT Press, 1965.

Gimbel, John. *A German Community Under American Occupation: Marburg 1945-52.* Stanford: Stanford University Press, 1961.

Grunsky, O. and Miller, George (eds.) *The Sociology of Organization.* New York: Free Press, 1970.

Gurr, Tedd Robert. *Why Men Rebel.* Princeton: Princeton University Press, 1970.

Guttsman, W. L. *The British Political Elite.* New York: Basic Books, 1963.

Gwyn, William. *Democracy and the Cost of Politics in Britain.* London: Athlone Press, 1962.

Haithcox, John. *Communism and Nationalism in India.* Princeton: Princeton University Press, 1971.

Hardgrave, Robert. *The Nadars of Tamilnad.* Berkeley: University of California Press, 1969.

Hartz, Louis. *The Founding of New Societies.* New York: Harcourt, Brace & World, 1964.

――― *The Liberal Tradition in America.* New York: Harcourt, Brace & World, 1955.

Heath, Peter. *The English Parish Clergy on the Eve of the Reformation.* Toronto: University of Toronto Press, 1969.

Holt, P. *The Mahdist State in the Sudan, 1881-1898.* Oxford: Oxford University Press, 1958.

Hunter, Floyd. *Community Power Structure.* Chapel Hill: University of North Carolina Press, 1953.

――― *Top Leadership, U. S. A.* Chapel Hill: University of North Carolina Press, 1959.

Huntington, Samuel. *Political Order in Changing Societies.* New Haven: Yale University Press, 1968. The edition used in this work was the fourth printing, 1970 edition.

Irschick, E. *Politics and Social Conflict in South India: The Non-Brahman Movement and Tamil Separation, 1916-1929.* Berkeley: University of California Press, 1969.

Jacob, E. F. *The Fifteenth Century: 1399-1485.* London: Oxford University Press, 1961.

Jacob, Herbert, and Vines, Kenneth (eds.) *Politics in the American States: A Comparative Analysis.* New York: Little, Brown, 1965.

Janowitz, Morris. *The Military in the Political Development of New Nations.* Chicago: University of Chicago Press, 1964.

——— *The Professional Soldier: A Social and Political Portrait.* New York: Free Press, 1960.

Jintaro, Fujii (compiler and ed.) *Outline of Japanese History in the Meiji Era.* (translated and adapted by H. K. Colton and K. E. Colton.) Tokyo: Obunsha, 1958.

Johnson, John J. (ed.) *The Role of the Military in Underdeveloped Countries.* Princeton: Princeton University Press, 1962.

Joshi, B. L. and Rose, Leo E. *Democratic Innovation in Nepal.* Berkeley: University of California Press, 1966.

Khare, R. S. *The Changing Brahmans: Associations and Elites among the Kanya-Kubias of North India.* Chicago: University of Chicago Press, 1970.

Kochanek, Stanley. *The Congress Party of India.* Princeton: Princeton University Press, 1968.

Kogedar, S. V. and Park, Richard L. (eds.) *Reports on the Indian General Elections 1951-52.* Bombay: Book Depot, 1956.

Kumar, R. (ed.) *Essays on Gandhian Politics: The Rowlett Satyagraha of 1919.* London: Oxford University Press, 1971.

Lane, Robert E. *Political Life. Why People Get Involved in Politics.* New York: Free Press, 1959.

LaPalombara, Joseph. *Interest Groups in Italian Politics.* Princeton: Princeton University Press, 1964.

Lasswell, Harold, et al. *Comparative Study of Elites.* Stanford: Stanford University Press, 1952.

Lefever, Ernest. *Crisis in the Congo.* Washington, D.C.: Brookings Institution, 1965.

Leites, N. C. and Wolf, C., Jr. *Rebellion and Authority.* Chicago: Markham, 1970.

Lewis, Bernard. *The Emergence of Modern Turkey.* London: Oxford University Press, 1961.

Lewis, Oscar. *Group Dynamics in a North Indian Village—A Study of Factions.* Delhi: Planning Commission, 1954.

Lippman, Heinz. *The Changing Party Elite in East Germany.* Cambridge, Mass.: MIT Press, 1973.

Lipset, S. M. (ed.) *Students and Politics.* New York: Basic Books, 1967.

Litchfield, Edward and associates. *Governing Post-War Germany.* Ithaca: Cornell University Press, 1953.

McConnell, Grant. *Private Power and American Democracy.* New York: Knopf, 1967.

MacIver, R. M. *The Modern State.* London: Oxford University Press, 1964.

McVicker, Charles. *Titoism.* New York: St. Martins Press, 1957.

Maddick, Henry. *Panchayati Raj.* London: Longman, 1970.

Mason, Philip. *The Men Who Ruled India.* Two volumes. London: Jonathan Cape, 1953.

Matthews, Donald R. *U.S. Senators and Their World.* Chapel Hill: University of North Carolina Press, 1960.

Maxwell, Neville. *India's China War.* London: Jonathan Cape, 1970.

Mechan, Lloyd J. *Church and State in Latin America: A History of Politics-Ecclesiastic Relations.* Revised edition. Chapel Hill: University of North Carolina Press, 1966.

Miller, Norman and Aya, Roderick (eds.) *National Liberation.* New York: Free Press, 1971.

Mills, C. Wright. *The Power Elite.* New York: Oxford University Press, 1959.

Moore, Barrington, Jr. *Social Origins of Dictatorship and Democracy: Lord and Peasant in the Making of the Modern World.* Boston: Beacon, 1966.

Moore, Wilbert E. *The Professions: Roles and Rules.* New York: Russell Sage Foundation, 1970.

Morris-Jones, W. H. *Government and Politics of India.* London: Hutchinson, 1971 edition.

——— *Parliament in India.* London: Longmans, Green, 1957.

Mosca, Gaetano. *The Ruling Class.* New York: McGraw-Hill, 1939.

Myrdal, Gunnar. *Asian Dream.* New York: Twentieth Century Fund, 1968, Pantheon edition.

Nayar, Baldev Raj. *Minority Politics in the Punjab.* Princeton: Princeton University Press, 1966.

Neal, Fred W. *Titoism in Practice.* Berkeley: University of California Press, 1958.

Nelli, Humber S. *The Italians in Chicago 1880-1930: A Study in Ethnic Mobility.* New York: Oxford University Press, 1970.

O'Malley, L.S.S. *The Indian Civil Service.* London: Murray, 1931.

Orenstein, Henry. *Gaon.* Princeton: Princeton University Press, 1965.

Organski, A.F.K. *The Stages of Political Development.* New York: Knopf, 1965.

Ostrogorski, M. Y. *Democracy and the Organization of Political Parties.* London: Macmillan, 1902.

Overstreet, Gene and Windmiller, Marshall. *Communism in India.* Berkeley: University of California Press, 1959.

Pantin, W. A. *The English Church in the Fourteenth Century.* Cambridge: Cambridge University Press, 1955.

Parete, Vilfredo. *The Mind and Society.* 4 volumes, Arthur Livingstone (ed.), translated by A. Livingstone and Andrew Bongiorne. New York: Harcourt Brace, 1935.

Parry, Geraint. *Political Elites.* New York: Praeger, 1969.

Parson, Talcott. *Essays in Sociological Theory,* revised edition. New York: Free Press, 1954.

——— *The Social System.* New York: Free Press, 1951.

Pike, Douglas. *Viet Cong.* Cambridge: MIT Press, 1966.

Ping-Ti, Ho. *The Ladder of Success in Imperial China: Aspects of Social Mobility, 1368-1911.* New York: Columbia University Press, 1962.

Polanyi, Karl. *The Great Transformation: The Political and Economic Origins of Our Time.* Boston: Beacon, 1957.

Pollard, A. F. *Factors in American History.* New York: Macmillan, 1925.

Presthus, Robert. *Men at the Top.* New York: Oxford University Press, 1964.

Prewitt, Kenneth. *The Recruitment of Political Leaders: A Study of Citizen-Politicians.* Indianapolis: Bobbs-Merrill, 1970.

Ranney, Austin. *Pathways to Parliament: Candidate Selection in Britain.* Madison: University of Wisconsin Press, 1965.

Rao, M.V. Famana. *Development of the Congress Constitution.* New Delhi: All India Congress Committee, 1958.

Rappaport, David C. "Praetorianism: Government Without Consensus." Ph.D. Dissertation, University of California, Berkeley, 1960.

Reischauer, Edwin O. *Japan: Past and Present.* New York: Knopf, 1946.

Riggs, Fred. *Administration in Developing Countries: The Theory of Prismatic Society.* Boston: Houghton Mifflin, 1964.

——— *Administration and Development.* Bloomington, Ind.: Comparative Administrative Group, American Society for Public Administration, 1963.

——— *The Ecology of Public Administration.* Bombay: East Asia Publishing, 1962.

——— *Thailand: The Modernization of a Bureaucratic Polity.* Honolulu: East-West Center Press, 1966.

Robinson, Richard D. *The First Turkish Republic.* Cambridge: Harvard University Press, 1963.

Rose, Lee E. and Fisher, Margaret. *The Politics of Nepal.* Ithaca: Cornell University Press, 1970.

Rosenberg, Hans. *Bureaucracy, Aristocracy, and Autocracy: The Prussian Experience, 1660-1815.* Cambridge: Harvard University Press, 1958.

Rosenthal, Donald. *The Limited Elite: Politics and Government in Two Indian Cities.* Chicago: University of Chicago Press, 1970.

Ruchelman, Leonard. *Political Careers: Recruitment Through the Legislature.* Cranbury, N.J.: Fairleigh Dickenson Press, 1970.

Rudolph, Lloyd I. and Susanne H. *The Modernity of Tradition.* Chicago: University of Chicago Press, 1967.

Rudolph, Susanne H. *The Action Arm of the Indian National Congress: The Pradesh Congress Committee.* Cambridge: Center for International Studies, MIT Press, 1955.

Sansom, George. *History of Japan, 1615-1867.* Stanford: Stanford University Press, 1963.

——— *The Western World and Japan.* London: Crescent Press, 1950.

Schapiro, Leonard. *The Communist Party of the Soviet Union.* New York: Random House, 1960.

Schlesinger, Joseph. *Ambition and Politics: Political Careers in the United States.* Chicago: Rand McNally, 1966.

Seligman, Lester G. *Leadership in a New Nation: Political Development in Israel.* New York: Atherton, 1964.

Siffin, William J. *The Thai Bureaucracy.* Honolulu: East-West Center Press, 1966.

Sills, David L. *The Volunteers.* New York: Free Press, 1957.

Simon, Herbert. *Administrative Behavior: A Study of Decision-Making Processes in Administrative Organization.* 2nd edition. New York: Macmillan, 1957.

Singer, J. Milton. *The Scientific Study of Religion.* New York: Macmillan, 1970.

Singh, Baljit and Misra, Shridhar. *A Study of Land Reform in Uttar Pradesh.* Honolulu: East-West Center Press, 1965.

Sisson, Richard. *The Congress Party in Rajasthan.* Berkeley: University of California Press, 1972, pp. 315-316.

Smith, Donald Eugene. *India as a Secular State.* Princeton: Princeton University Press, 1963.

——— *Religion and Politics in Burma.* Princeton: Princeton University Press, 1965.

——— *Religion and Political Development.* Boston: Little, Brown, 1970.

Somjee, A. H. *Democracy and Political Change in Village India.* New Delhi: Orient Longmans, 1971.

——— *Voting Behavior in an Indian Village.* Baroda: M.S. University of Baroda, 1959.

Southern, Richard William. *Western Society and the Church in the Middle Ages.* Harmondsworth, England: Penguin Books, 1970.

Stafford, David. *From Anarchism to Reformism.* London: Weidenfield and Nicholson, 1971.

Stein, George H. *The Waffen S. S.* Ithaca: Cornell University Press, 1966.

Streyer, Joseph R. *On the Medieval Origins of the Modern State.* Princeton: Princeton University Press, 1970.

Taub, Richard P. *Bureaucrats Under Stress.* Berkeley: University of California Press, 1969.

Theobald, Alan B. *The Mahdiya.* London: Longmans, 1951.

Tinker, Hugh. *The Foundations of Local Self-Government in India, Pakistan, and Burma.* London: Athlone Press, 1954.

Tocqueville, Alexis de. *The Old Regime and the French Revolution.* Garden City, N.Y.: Doubleday, 1955.

Toynbee, Arnold J. *A Study of History.* Abridgement of Vols. I-VI by D. C. Somerville, New York: Oxford University Press, 1947.

Turner, Frederick C. *Catholicism and Political Development in Latin America.* Chapel Hill: University of North Carolina Press, 1971.

van Leauwan, Arendt. *Christianity in World History.* London: Edinburgh House Press, 1965.

Vatikiotis, P. J. *The Egyptian Army in Politics.* Bloomington, Ind.: Indiana University Press, 1961.

von der Mehden, Fred R. *Politics of the Developing Nations.* Englewood Cliffs, N.J.: Prentice-Hall, 1964.

von Vorys, Karl. *Political Development in Pakistan.* Princeton: Princeton University Press, 1965.

Walton, Hanes, Jr. *The Political Philosophy of Martin Luther King, Jr.* Westport, Conn.: Negro Universities Press, 1971.

Ward, W. R. *Georgian Oxford.* London: Oxford University Press, 1958.

––– *Victorian Oxford.* London: Cass, 1965.

Weiner, Myron. *The Politics of Scarcity.* Chicago: University of Chicago Press, 1962.

––– (ed.) *State Politics in India.* Princeton: Princeton University Press, 1968.

Wheeler, Richard. *The Politics of Pakistan.* Ithaca: Cornell University Press, 1970.

White, Leonard D. *The Republican Era.* New York: Macmillan, 1958.

Wilcox, Wayne. *Pakistan: The Consolidation of a Nation.* New York: Columbia University Press, 1960.

Wildavsky, Aaron. *Leadership in a Small Town.* Totewa, N.J.: Bedminster Press, 1964.

Wilson, Godfrey and Wilson, Monica. *The Analysis of Social Change.* Cambridge: Cambridge University Press, 1945.

Wolf, Eric. R. *Peasant Wars of the Twentieth Century.* New York: Harper and Row, 1969.

Wolff, Kurt H. and Moore, Barrington, Jr. (eds.) *The Critical Spirit: Essays in Honor of Herbert Marcuse.* Boston: Beacon, 1967.

Shorter Works

Abernathy, David and Coombe, Trevor. "Education and Politics in Developing Countries," *Harvard Education Review,* 35 (Summer, 1965), pp. 287-302.

Alker, Hayward, Jr. "Regionalism vs. Universalism in Comparing Nations" in Bruce Russett et al., *World Handbook of Political and Social Indicators.* New Haven: Yale University Press, 1964.

Allardt, E. "Implications of Within-Nation Variations for Cross-National Research" in S. Rokkan and R. Merritt (eds.), *Comparing Nations.* New Haven: Yale University Press, 1966, pp. 337-372.

Ames, Barry. "Bases of Support for Mexico's Dominant Party," *American Political Science Review,* 64 (March, 1970), pp. 153-167.

Aron, Raymond. "Social Structure and the Ruling Class," *British Journal of Sociology,* 1950. Volume I, number 1, pp. 1-16. Volume I, number 2, pp. 126-143.

Azrael, Jeremy. "The Managers" in R. Barry Farrell (ed.), *Political Leadership in Eastern Europe and the Soviet Union.* New York: Aldine, 1970, pp. 224-248.

Bailey, F. G. "Politics and Society in Contemporary Orissa" in C. H. Phillips (ed.), *Politics and Society in India.* New York: Praeger, 1962.

Beck, Carl. "Bureaucracy and Political Development in Eastern Europe" in Joseph LaPalombara (ed.), *Bureaucracy and Political Development.* Princeton: Princeton University Press, 1963, pp. 268-300.

Befu, Harumi. "Village Autonomy and Articulation with the State," *Journal of Asian Studies,* 26 (November, 1965), pp. 19-32.

Bernstorff, Dagmar. "Candidates for the 1967 General Election in Hyderabad, A.P." in Edmund Leach and S. M. Mukherjee (eds.), *Elites in South Asia.* London: Cambridge University Press, 1970, pp. 136-151.

Binder, Leonard. "National Integration and Political Development," *American Political Science Review,* 58 (September, 1964), pp. 630-631.

Blair, Harry W. "Ethnicity and Democratic Politics in India," *Comparative Politics,* 5 (October, 1972), pp. 107-128.

Bolton, Seymour. "Military Government and the German Political Parties," *The Annals,* 267 (January, 1950), pp. 55-67.

Bottomore, T. B. "Cohesion and Division in Indian Elites" in Philip Mason (ed.), *India and Ceylon: Unity and Diversity.* New York: Oxford University Press, 1976, pp. 244-259.

Bowman, Lewis and Boynton, G. R. "Recruitment Patterns Among Local Party Officials: A Model and Some Preliminary Findings in Selected Locales," *American Political Science Review,* 60 (September, 1966), pp. 667-676.

Braibanti, Ralph. "Administrative Reform in the Context of Political Growth" in Fred W. Riggs (ed.), *Frontiers of Development Administration.* Durham, N.C.: Duke University Press, 1970, pp. 227-246.

——— "Comparative Political Analytics Reconsidered," *Journal of Politics.* 30 (February, 1968), pp. 25-65.

——— "External Inducement of Political-Administrative Development: An Institutional Strategy" in Ralph Braibanti (ed.), *Political and Administrative Development.* Durham, N.C.: Duke University Press, 1969, pp. 3-106.

——— "Introduction" to *Asian Bureaucratic Systems Emergent from the British Imperial Tradition.* Ralph Braibanti (ed.), Durham, N.C.: Duke University Press, 1969, pp. 3-22.

——— "Public Bureaucracy and Judiciary in Pakistan" in Joseph LaPalombara (ed.), *Bureaucracy and Political Development.* Princeton: Princeton University Press, 1963, pp. 390-395.

Braibanti, Ralph. "Reflections on Bureaucratic Reform in India" in Ralph Braibanti and J. Spengler (eds.), *Administration and Economic Development in India*. Durham, N.C.: Duke University Press, 1969, pp. 3-68.

––– "The Relevance of Political Science to the Study of Underdeveloped Areas" in Ralph Braibanti and J. Spengler (eds.), *Tradition, Values and Socio-economic Development*. Durham, N.C.: Duke University Press, 1961, pp. 139-180.

Brass, Paul. "Coalition Politics in North India," *American Political Science Review*, 68 (December, 1968), pp. 1174-1191.

––– "Political Participation, Institutionalization and Stability in India," *Government and Opposition*, 4 (Winter, 1969), pp. 23-53.

Carras, Mary. "Congress Factionalism in Maharashtra," *Asian Survey*, 10 (May, 1970), pp. 110-126.

Cnudde, Charles F. and McCrane, Donald J. "The Linkage between Constituency Attitudes and Congressional Voting Behavior: A Causal Model," *American Political Science Review*, 55 (March, 1966), pp. 66-72.

Cohn, Bernard S. "Recruitment and Training of British Civil Servants in India, 1600-1860" in Ralph Braibanti (ed.), *Asian Bureaucratic Systems Emergent from the British Imperial Tradition*. Durham, N.C.: Duke University Press, 1969, pp. 87-140.

Coleman, James S. "Political Money," *American Political Science Review*, 64 (December, 1970), pp. 1074-1087.

deSchweinitz, K. "Growth, Development, and Political Modernization," *World Politics*, 22 (July, 1970), pp. 518-540.

Diamant, Alfred. "The Bureaucratic Model: Max Weber Rejected, Rediscovered, Reformed" in Ferrell Heady and Sybil L. Stokes (eds.), *Papers in Comparative Public Administration*. Ann Arbor: Institute of Public Administration, 1962, pp. 59-96.

Dogan, Mattei. "Political Ascent in a Class Society: French Deputies, 1870-1958" in Dwaine Marvick (ed.), *Political Decision Makers*. New York: Free Press, 1961, pp. 57-90.

Dorsey, John. "The Bureaucracy and Political Development in Viet Nam" in Joseph LaPalombara (ed.), *Bureaucracy and Political Development*. Princeton: Princeton University Press, 1963, pp. 318-359.

Edinger, Lewis J. and Searing, Donald D. "Leadership: An Interdisciplinary Bibliography" in Lewis J. Edinger (ed.), *Political Leadership in Industrialized Societies: Studies in Comparative Analysis*. New York: Wiley, 1967, pp. 348-366.

Eisenstadt, S. N. "Breakdowns of Modernization" in S. N. Eisenstadt (ed.), *Readings in Social Evolution and Development*. London: Pergamon Press, 1970.

––– "Bureaucracy and Political Development" in Joseph LaPalombara (ed.), *Bureaucracy and Political Development*. Princeton: Princeton University Press, 1963, pp. 96-119.

––– "Institutionalization and Change," *American Sociological Review*, 29 (April, 1964), pp. 235-247.

––– "Modernization and Conditions of Sustained Growth," *World Politics*, 16 (July, 1964), pp. 376-394.

––– "Political Struggle in Bureaucratic Societies," *World Politics*, (October, 1956), pp. 15-36.

––– "Post-Traditional Societies and the Continuity and Reconstruction of Tradition," *Daedalus*, 102 (Winter, 1973), pp. 1-27.

Eisenstadt, S. N. "Religious Organizations and Political Process in Centralized Empires," *Journal of Asian Studies,* 21 (May, 1962), pp. 271-294.

––– "Some New Looks at the Problems of Relations Between Traditional Societies and Modernization," *Economic Development and Social Change,* 3 (April, 1968), pp. 436-449.

––– "Transformation of Social, Political, and Cultural Orders in Modernization," *American Sociological Review.* 30 (October, 1965), pp. 659-673.

Erdman, Howard. "Chakravarty Rajagopalachari and Indian Conservatism," *Journal of Developing Areas,* 1 (October, 1966).

––– "Conservative Politics in India," *Asian Survey.* 6 (June, 1966), pp. 338-347.

––– "India's Swatantra Party," *Pacific Affairs,* 36 (Winter, 1963-1964), pp. 394-410.

Erikson, Erik. "Hitler's Imagery and German Youth," *Psychiatry,* 5 (1942), pp. 475-493.

Esman, Milton J. "Ecological Style in Comparative Administration," *Public Administration Review,* 27 (September, 1967), pp. 271-278.

––– "The Elements of Institution Building" in Joseph W. Eaton (ed.), *Institution Building and Development: From Concepts to Application.* Beverly Hills: Sage Publications, 1972.

––– "The Institution Building Concepts—An Interim Appraisal." Pittsburgh: Graduate School of International Affairs of the University of Pittsburgh, 1967.

––– "Some Issues in Institution Building Theory" in D. Woods Thomas et al. (eds.), *Institution Building: A Model for Applied Social Change.* Cambridge, Mass.: Schenkman Publishing Co., 1972, pp. 65-90.

––– and Montgomery, J. S. "Systems Approaches to Technical Cooperation: The Role of Development Administration," *Public Administration Review,* 29 (September, 1969), pp. 507-539.

Fainsod, Merle. "Bureaucracy and Modernization: The Russian and Soviet Case" in Joseph LaPalombara (ed.), *Bureaucracy and Political Development.* Princeton: Princeton University Press, 1963, pp. 233-267.

Feit, Edward. "Pen, Sword, and People," *World Politics,* 25 (January, 1973), pp. 251-273.

Fesler, James W. "Field Administration" in Ferrell Heady and Sybil L. Stokes (eds.), *Papers in Comparative Public Administration.* Ann Arbor: Institute of Public Administration of the University of Michigan, 1962.

Fleron, Frederic. "Representation of Career Types in the Soviet Political Leadership" in R. Barry Farrell (ed.), *Political Leadership in Eastern Europe and the Soviet Union.* New York: Aldine, 1970.

Forester, Duncan. "State Legislators in Madras," *Journal of Commonwealth Political Studies,* 7 (March, 1969), pp. 36-57.

Fox, T. and Miller, S. M. "Occupational Stratification and Mobility" in S. Rokkan and R. Merritt (eds.), *Comparing Nations.* New Haven: Yale University Press, 1966, pp. 217-237.

Frey, Frederick. "Arms and the Man in Turkish Politics," *Land Reborn,* 11 (August, 1960), pp. 3-14.

Friedland, William H. "Some Sources of Traditionalism Among Modern African Elites" in William J. Hanna (ed.), *Independent Black Africa.* Chicago: Rand McNally, 1964, pp. 363-369.

Friedman, Robert S. "State Politics and Highways" in Herbert Jacob and Kenneth Vines (eds.), *Politics in the American States: A Comparative Analysis.* New York: Little, Brown, 1965.

Friedrich, Carl J. "The Theory of Political Leadership and the Issue of Totalitarianism" in R. Barry Farrell (ed.), *Political Leadership in Eastern Europe and the Soviet Union.* New York: Aldine, 1970, pp. 17-27.

Gehlen, Michael P. "The Soviet Apparatchiki" in R. Barry Farrell (ed.), *Political Leadership in Eastern Europe and the Soviet Union.* New York: Aldine, 1970, pp. 140-156.
––– and McBride, Michael, "The Soviet Central Committee: An Elite Analysis," *American Political Science Review,* 62 (December, 1968), pp. 1232-1241.

Gerth, Hans. "The Nazi Party: Its Leadership and Composition," *American Journal of Sociology,* 45 (1940), pp. 530-531.

Gittings, John. "Army-Party Relations in the light of the Cultural Revolution" in John W. Lewis (ed.), *Party Leadership and Revolutionary Power in China.* London: Cambridge University Press, 1970, pp. 373-403.

Gould, Harold. "The Adaptive Functions of Caste in Contemporary Indian Society," *Asian Survey,* 3 (September, 1963), pp. 427-432.

Graham, B. D. "Congress as a Rally," *South Asian Review,* 6 (January, 1973), pp. 111-123.

Gusfield, Joseph R. "Social Structure and Moral Reform: A Study of the Woman's Christian Temperance Union," *American Journal of Sociology,* 61 (November, 1955), pp. 221-232.

Hardgrave, Robert. "Varieties of Political Behavior Among Nadars of Tamilnad," *Asian Survey,* 6 (November, 1966), pp. 1-27.

Hart, Henry C. "Bombay Politics," *Journal of Asian Studies,* 20 (February, 1961), pp. 267-274.

Hawley, A. H. "Community Power and Urban Renewal Success," *American Journal of Sociology,* 68 (January, 1963), pp. 422-431.

Heady, Bruce. "The Civil Service as an Elite in Britain and Germany," *International Review of Administrative Science,* 38 (1972), pp. 41-48.

Hegedus, Andras. "Marxist Theories of Leadership: A Marxist Approach" in R. Barry Farrell (ed.), *Political Leadership in Eastern Europe and the Soviet Union.* New York: Aldine, 1970, pp. 28-58.

Hill, Larry, "The International Transfer of Political Institutions: A Behavioral Analysis of the New Zealand Ombudsman," Ph.D. Dissertation, Tulane University, 1970.

Hoselitz, Bert. "Levels of Economic Performance and Bureaucratic Structures" in Joseph LaPalombara (ed.), *Bureaucracy and Political Development.* Princeton: Princeton University Press, 1963, pp. 96-119.

Huntington, Samuel P. "The Change to Change: Modernization, Development, and Politics," *Comparative Politics,* 3 (April, 1971), pp. 283-322.
––– "Patterns of Violence in World Politics" in Samuel P. Huntington (ed.), *Changing Patterns of Military Politics.* New York: Free Press, 1962, pp. 44-47.
––– "Political Development and Political Decay," *World Politics,* 17 (April, 1965), pp. 386-430.

Izmirlian, Harry, Jr. "Dynamics of Political Support in a Punjab Village," *Asian Survey,* 6 (March, 1966), pp. 125-133.

Jiang, P. L. "Towards a Theory of Pariah Entrepreneurship" in Gehan Wijayewardene (ed.), *Leadership and Authority.* Singapore: University of Malaya Press, 1968, pp. 147-162.

Kabir, H. "Reorganization of the Congress," *Hindustan Times*. New Delhi, May 29, 1960.

Kesselman, Mark. "Order or Movement?: The Literature of Political Development as Ideology," *World Politics*, 26 (October, 1973), pp. 139-154.

Khanna, B. S. "Bureaucracy and Development in India" in Edward W. Weidner (ed.), *Development Administration in Asia*. Durham, N.C.: Duke University Press, 1970, pp. 236-238.

Kilson, Martin. "Authoritarian and Single-Party Tendencies in African Politics," *World Politics*, 15 (January, 1963), pp. 262-304.

Kothari, Rajni. "The Congress 'System' in India," *Asian Survey*, 4 (December, 1964), pp. 1161-1178.

LaPalombara, Joseph. "An Overview of Bureaucracy and Political Development" in Joseph LaPalombara (ed.), *Bureaucracy and Political Development*. Princeton: Princeton University Press, 1963, pp. 3-33.

––– "Parsimony and Empiricism in Comparative Politics" in Robert Holt and John Turner (eds.), *The Methodology of Comparative Research*. New York: Free Press, 1970, pp. 123-150.

Lee, Chai-Jin. "Factional Politics in the Japanese Socialist Party," *Asian Survey*, 10 (March, 1970), pp. 230-243.

Lemarchand, P. and Legg, K. "Political Clientalism and Development," *Comparative Politics*, 4 (January, 1972), pp. 149-178.

Lerner, Daniel and Robinson, D. "Swords and Ploughshares: The Turkish Army as a Modernizing Force," *World Politics*, 13 (October, 1960), pp. 19-44.

Lewis, Paul H. "The Spanish Ministerial Elite, 1938-1969," *Comparative Politics*, 5 (October, 1972), pp. 83-106.

Lieberson, S. and O'Connor, James F. "Leadership and Organizational Performance," *American Sociological Review*, 37 (April, 1972), pp. 117-130.

Lieuwen, Edwin, "Militarism and Politics in Latin America" in John J. Johnson (ed.), *The Role of the Military in Underdeveloped Countries*. Princeton: Princeton University Press, 1962.

Lipset, S. M. "Political Cleavages in 'Developed' and 'Emerging' Politics" in Erik Allard and Yrjo Littunen (eds.), *Cleavages, Ideologies and Party Systems*. Helsinki: Westermarck Society, 1964.

––– "Some Social Requisites of Democracy: Economic Development and Political Legitimacy," *American Political Science Review*, 53 (March, 1959), pp. 69-105.

McCloskey, Herbert, "Consensus and Ideology in American Politics," *American Political Science Review*, 58 (June, 1964), pp. 361-382.

McConaughy, John B. "Certain Personality Factors of State Legislators in South Carolina," *American Political Science Review*, 44 (December, 1960), pp. 897-903.

McDonough, Peter. "Electoral Competition and Participation in India: A Test of Huntington's Hypothesis," *Comparative Politics*, 4 (October, 1971), pp. 77-88.

Marvick, Dwaine. "Political Recruitment and Careers," *International Encyclopedia of the Social Sciences*, 12 (New York: Macmillan and the Free Press, 1968), pp. 273-282.

Marx, Fritz Morstein. "The Higher Civil Service as an Action Group in Western Political Development" in Joseph LaPalombara (ed.), *Bureaucracy and Political Development*. Princeton: Princeton University Press, 1963, pp. 62-95.

Messinger, Sheldon L. "Organizational Transformation: A Case Study of a Declining Social Movement," *American Sociological Review*, 20 (February, 1955), pp. 3-10.

Meyer, Alfred G. "Historical Development of the Communist Theory of Leadership" in R. Barry Farrell (ed.), *Political Leadership in Eastern Europe and the Soviet Union.* New York: Aldine, 1970, pp. 5-16.

Meynaud, Jean. "Introduction: General Study of Parliamentarians," *International Social Science Journal,* 12 (1961), pp. 513-543.

Midlarsky, Manus and Tanter, Raymond. "Toward a Theory of Political Instability in Latin America," *Journal of Peace Research,* No. 3 (1967), pp. 209-227.

Milder, N. D. "Some Aspects of Crozier's Theory of Bureaucratic Organizations," *Journal of Comparative Administration,* 3 (May, 1971), pp. 61-82.

Miller, I. "Social-Psychological Implications of Weber's Model of Bureaucracy," *Social Forces,* 49 (September, 1970), pp. 91-102.

Montgomery, John D. "Sources of Bureaucratic Reform: A Typology of Purpose and Politics" in Ralph Braibanti (ed.), *Political and Administrative Development.* Durham, N.D.: Duke University Press, 1969, pp. 427-471.

Morris-Jones, W. H. "The Indian Congress Party: Dilemmas of Dominance," *Modern Asian Studies,* (April, 1967).

Nadel, George. "The Logic of the *Anatomy of Revolution,* with Reference to the Netherlands Revolt," *Comparative Studies in Society and History,* 2 (July, 1960), pp. 473-484.

Nandy, Ashis. "The Culture of Indian Politics," *Journal of Asian Studies,* 30 (November, 1970), pp. 57-80.

Nathan, Andrew. "A Factional Model for CCP Politics," *China Quarterly.* (January/March, 1973), pp. 34-66.

Nayar, Baldev Raj. "Sikh Separatism in the Punjab" in Donald E. Smith (ed.), *South Asian Politics and Religion.* Princeton: Princeton University Press, 1966, pp. 150-175.

Needler, Martin C. "Political Development and Military Intervention in Latin America," *American Political Science Review,* 60 (September, 1966), pp. 616-626.

Neumann, Sigmund. "Toward a Comparative Study of Political Parties" in Sigmund Neumann (ed.), *Modern Political Parties.* Chicago: University of Chicago Press, 1956, pp. 403-405.

Nicholson, Norman. "Factionalism and the Indian Council of Ministers," *Journal of Commonwealth Political Studies,* 10 (November, 1972), pp. 179-197.

――― "The Factional Model and the Study of Politics," *Comparative Politics,* 5 (October, 1972), pp. 291-314.

――― "The Indian Council of Ministers: An Analysis of Legislative and Organizational Careers," a Paper presented to the Twenty-fifth Annual Meeting of the Association for Asian Studies, Chicago, April 1, 1973.

Oksenberg, Michel. "Getting Ahead and Along in Communist China: The Ladder of Success on the Eve of the Cultural Revolution" in John W. Lewis (ed.), *Party Leadership and Revolutionary Power in China.* London: Cambridge University Press, 1970, pp. 304-347.

Packenham, Robert A. "Approaches to the Study of Political Development," *World Politics,* 17 (1964), pp. 108-120.

Parsons, Talcott. "On the Concept of Influence," *Public Opinion Quarterly,* 27 (Spring, 1963), pp. 37-62.

Perlmutter, Amos. "The Praetorian State and the Praetorian Army: Towards a Theory of Civil-Military Relations in Developing Polities," (unpublished paper, Institute of International Studies, University of California, Berkeley).

Polsby, Nelson. "The Institutionalization of the U.S. House of Representatives," *American Political Science Review,* 62 (March, 1968), pp. 144-168.

Potter, David C. "Bureaucratic Change in India" in Ralph Braibanti (ed.), *Asian Bureaucratic Systems Emergent from the British Imperial Tradition.* Durham, N.C.: Duke University Press, 1969, pp. 141-208.

Powell, John. "Peasant Society and Clientalist Politics," *American Political Science Review,* 64 (June, 1970), pp. 411-425.

Prewitt, Kenneth and Eulau, Heinz. "Social Bias in Leadership Selection, Political Recruitment, and Electoral Context," *Journal of Politics,* 3 (May, 1971), pp. 293-315.

Putnam, Robert. "Studying Elite Political Culture: The Case of 'Ideology,' " *American Political Science Review,* 65 (September, 1971), pp. 651-681.

Pye, Lucian W. "Armies in the Process of Political Modernization" in John J. Johnson (ed.), *The Role of the Military in Underdeveloped Countries.* Princeton: Princeton University Press, 1962, pp. 76-79.

——— "Bureaucratic Development and the Psychology of Institutionalization" in Ralph Braibanti (ed.), *Political and Administrative Development.* Durham, N.C.: Duke University Press, 1969, pp. 400-426.

——— "The Non-Western Political Process," *Journal of Politics,* 20 (August, 1958), pp. 468-486.

——— "The Political Context of National Development" in Irving Swerdlow (ed.), *Development Administration: Concepts and Problems.* Syracuse: University of Syracuse Press, 1963, pp. 25-44.

Rao, D. N. "Disparities of Representation Among the Direct Recruits to the I. A. S.," *Indian Journal of Public Administration,* 9 (1963), pp. 33-94.

Retzloff, Ralph. "Revision and Dogmatism in the CPI" in R. Scalapino (ed.), *The Communist Revolution in Asia.* Englewood Cliffs, N.J.: Prentice-Hall, 1965, pp. 309-342.

Riggs, Fred W. "Bureaucrats and Political Development: A Paradoxical View" in Joseph LaPalombara (ed.), *Bureaucracy and Political Development.* Princeton: Princeton University Press, 1963, pp. 120-167.

——— "The Idea of Development Administration" in Edward W. Weidner (ed.), *Development Administration in Asia.* Durham, N.C.: Duke University Press, 1970, pp. 25-72.

——— "Modernization and Development Administration," in *CAG Occasional Papers.* Bloomington, Ind.: Indiana University Press, 1966.

——— "Structure and Function: A Dialectical Approach," a paper prepared for delivery at the Annual Meeting of the American Political Science Association, September, 1967.

——— "The Theory of Political Development" in James Charlesworth (ed.), *Contemporary Political Analysis.* New York: Free Press, 1967.

Robins, Robert S. "Elite Career Patterns as a Differential in Regional Analysis: A Use of Correlation Techniques and the Construction of Uniform Strata," *Behavioral Science,* 14 (May, 1969), pp. 232-238.

——— "The Indian Upper House and Elite Integration." Paper delivered at the Sixty-fifth Annual Meeting of the American Political Science Association, New York, 1969.

——— "Institutional Linkages with an Elite Body," *Comparative Politics,* 4 (October, 1971), pp. 109-115.

Robins, Robert S. "Political Development and Party Disintegration: The Old Congress Party, 1952-67," unpublished paper read at the Salt Lake Meeting of the Rocky Mountain Political Science Association, March, 1972.

––– "Political Elite Formation in Rural India: The Uttar Pradesh Panchayat Elections of 1949, 1956, and 1961," *Journal of Politics,* 29 (November, 1967), pp. 838-860.

Rokkan, Stein. "The Comparative Study of Political Participation: Notes Toward a Perspective on Current Research" in Austin Ranney (ed.), *Essays on the Behavioral Study of Politics.* Urbana: University of Illinois Press, 1962, pp. 73-76.

––– "Norway: Numerical Democracy and Corporate Pluralism" in Robert A. Dahl (ed.), *Political Opposition in Western Democracies.* New Haven: Yale University Press, 1966, pp. 70-115.

Rothman, Stanley. "Barrington Moore and the Dialectics of Revolution," *American Political Science Review,* 64 (March, 1970), pp. 61-85.

Roy, Rameshray. "Selection of Congress Candidates." This work first appeared in the *Economic and Political Weekly:* December 31, 1966, I: pp. 833-840; January 7, 1967, II: pp. 61-76; February 11, 1967, II: 371-376; February 18, 1967, II: pp. 407-416.

Rudolph, Lloyd I. "The Modernity of Tradition: The Democratic Incarnation of Caste in India," *American Political Science Review,* 59 (December, 1965), pp. 975-989.

––– "Urban Life and Populist Radicalism," *Journal of Asian Studies,* 20 (February, 1961), pp. 283-297.

––– and Susanne H. Rudolph. "The Political Modernization of an Indian Feudal Order: An Analysis of Rajput Adaptation in Rajasthan," *Journal of Social Issues,* 24 (October, 1968), pp. 93-128.

–––and Susanne H. Rudolph. "The Political Role of India's Caste Association," *Pacific Affairs,* 33 (March, 1960), pp. 5-22.

Rudolph, Susanne Hoeber. "Conflict and Consensus in Indian Politics," *World Politics,* 13 (April, 1961), pp. 385-399.

Rustow, Dankwart A. "The Army and the Founding of the Turkish Republic," *World Politics,* 11 (July, 1959), pp. 513-552.

––– "The Study of Elites: Who's Who, When, and How." *World Politics,* 18 (July, 1966), pp. 690-717.

Saini, M. K. and Anderson, W. "The Congress Split in Delhi," *Asian Survey,* 11 (November, 1971), pp. 1084-1100.

Sandbrook, Richard. "Patrons, Clients, and Unions: The Labour Movement in Kenya," *Journal of Comparative Political Studies,* 10 (March, 1972), pp. 3-27.

Scalapino, Robert A. "Which Route for Korea?" *Asian Survey,* 2 (September, 1962), pp. 1-13.

Schurmann, H. F. "Organizational Principles of the Chinese Communists," *China Quarterly,* 2 (April-June, 1960), pp. 47-58.

Shrader, Lawrence. "Rajasthan," in Myron Weiner (ed.), *State Politics in India.* Princeton: Princeton University Press, 1968, pp. 321-398.

Sigelman, Lee. "Do Modern Bureaucracies Dominate Underdeveloped Politics?" *American Political Science Review,* 66 (June, 1972), pp. 525-528.

Silverman, Jerry H. "Political Elites in South Vietnam: A National and Provincial Comparison," *Asian Survey,* 10 (April, 1970), pp. 290-307.

Singh, L. P. "Political Development or Political Decay in India," *Pacific Affairs,* 44 (Spring, 1971), pp. 65-80.

Sirsikar, V. M. "Leadership Patterns in Rural Maharashtra," *Asian Survey,* 4 (July, 1964), pp. 929-939.

Smith, M. P. "Self-Fulfillment in a Bureaucratic Society: A Commentary on the Thought of Gabriel Marcel," *Public Administrative Review,* 29 (January/February, 1969), pp. 25-32.

Sniderman, P. M. and Citrin, J. "Psychological Sources of Political Belief," *American Political Science Review,* 65 (June, 1971), pp. 401-417.

Somjee, A. H. "Political Dynamics of a Gujarat Village," *Asian Survey,* 12 (July, 1972), pp. 602-608.

Starbuck, William H. "Organization Growth and Development" in James G. March (ed.), *Handbook of Organizations.* Chicago: Rand McNally, 1965.

Stewart, P. D. et al. "Political Mobility and the Soviet Political Process," *American Political Science Review,* 66 (December, 1972), pp. 1269-1290.

Sutton, F. X. "Social Theory and Comparative Politics" in Harry Eckstein and David E. Apter (eds.), *Comparative Politics.* New York: Free Press, 1963, pp. 67-81.

Tichy, Noel M. "An Analysis of Clique Formation and Structive in Organizations," *Administrative Science Quarterly,* 18 (June, 1973), pp. 194-208.

Watanuki, Joji. "White Collar Workers and the Pattern of Politics in Present-Day Japan" in S. M. Lipset and Stein Rokkan (eds.), *Cleavage and Consensus: Cross-National Perspectives.* New York: Free Press, 1965.

Weiner, Myron. "Political Development in the Indian States" in Myron Weiner (ed.), *State Politics in India.* Princeton: Princeton University Press, 1968, pp. 3-60.

––– "Violence and Politics in Calcutta," *Journal of Asian Studies,* 20 (February, 1961), pp. 275-281.

Wescott, Jay B. "Government Organization and Methods in Developing Countries" in Irving Swerdlow (ed.), *Development Administration.* Syracuse, N.Y.: Syracuse University Press, 1963.

Wheeler, D. L. "Thaw in Portugal," *Foreign Affairs,* 48 (July, 1970), pp. 769-781.

Wilson, David A. "Nation-Building and Revolutionary War" in Karl W. Deutsch and William Foltz (eds.), *Nation-Building.* New York: Atherton Press, 1963, pp. 84-94.

Wilson, James Q. "Innovation in Organization: Notes Toward a Theory" in James D. Thompson (ed.), *Approaches to Organizational Design.* Pittsburgh: University of Pittsburgh Press, 1966, pp. 193-218.

Wint, Guy. *The 1958 Revolution in Pakistan,* St. Antony's Papers, No. 8, London: Chatto and Windus, 1960.

Zald, Mayer N. and Denton, Patricia. "From Evangelism to General Service: The Transformation of the YMCA," *Administrative Science Quarterly,* 8 (September, 1963), pp. 214-234.

ABOUT THE AUTHOR

ROBERT S. ROBINS is a member of the faculty of political science at Tulane University, where, since 1965, he has been responsible for graduate and undergraduate studies in the politics of developing areas. A graduate of Duke University, Dr. Robins has served as a visiting researching faculty member of the Institute of Commonwealth Studies (University of London) and was elected and served as Senior Associate Member of St. Antony's College, Oxford University. Professor Robins has travelled throughout the world and has published articles in a variety of scholarly journals.

NOTES

NOTES